The Great Cypress Swamps

Other Books by John V. Dennis

A Complete Guide to Bird Feeding
Beyond the Bird Feeder
The Wildlife Gardener
World Guide to Tropical Drift Seeds and Fruits (with C. R. Gunn)

The Great Cypress Swamps

John V. Dennis

Photographs by Steve Maslowski

Louisiana State University Press / Baton Rouge and London

96 95 94 93 92 91 90 89 88   5 4 3 2 1

Designer: Albert Crochet
Typeface: Linotron Times Roman
Typesetter: The Composing Room of Michigan
Printed and bound in Hong Kong through Four Colour Imports, Ltd.

Library of Congress Cataloging-in-Publication Data

Dennis, John V.
    The great cypress swamps / John V. Dennis; photographs by Steve
Maslowski.
      p.   cm.
    Includes index.
    ISBN 0-8071-1501-0 (alk. paper)
    1. Cypress swamp ecology—United States.   I. Maslowski, Stephen.
  II. Title.
QH104.D46 1988
508.73—dc19   88-19119
                                   CIP

Except where noted otherwise, all photographs
are by Steve Maslowski.

*To all those who enjoy our swamplands and work to protect them,
and especially to Gary M. Williamson, a good friend who has provided me
with invaluable help with the field work*

Contents

Maps

Acknowledgments

TO A LARGE DEGREE this book has been a cooperative venture in which many persons have participated. Without the help and advice of these persons, I could have hardly commenced a work of this scope. First, I wish to express my thanks to those at LSU Press who have borne with me through the years that this book has been in the making. I particularly wish to thank Beverly Jarrett, Catherine F. Barton, Albert Crochet, and John Easterly. No less important to me were those who assisted with photographs and maps. My thanks go to my good friend Steve Maslowski, whose photographs have contributed so much to telling the story of the swamps. Always behind Steve were the talents of his father, Karl Maslowski, whose name for years has been synonymous with perfection in wildlife photography. My thanks go to him as well, and to Sharon Himes, whose maps grace the pages of this book.

Gary M. Williamson, to whom this book is dedicated, has provided help and inspiration ever since the idea of doing a book on the great cypress swamps was conceived. In a very real sense, he has been my eyes and ears in picking up much that I otherwise would have missed in visiting swamps from Maryland and Illinois to Louisiana. My special thanks go also to the following experts: to Daniel McKinley and John W. Hardy for help with extinct bird species, David W. Stahle and James P. Reger for help in the field of paleobotany, D. Gray Bass for help with Florida fishes, Richard Stalter for help with literature on cypress trees, C. R. Gunn for help with plant names, and J. Merrill Lynch and Julie Moore for reading portions of the manuscript and providing information.

Listing by state other persons who have been of assistance, I thank C. Dwight Cooley in Alabama; Rene C. Dennis, Calvin L. Guthrie, and William Shepherd in Arkansas; Mr. and Mrs. Joseph W. Fehrer, Holger H. Harvey, and Richard L. Stanton in Delaware; Rick Bantz, Mr. and Mrs. James L. Brann, and Henry M. Stevenson in Florida; John D. Schroer and C. T. Trowell in Georgia; Max D. Hutchison in Illinois; Michael A. Homoya and W. William Weeks in Indiana; Dr. and Mrs. Herbert L. Clay, Mark Evans, and Carolyn Lynn in Kentucky; Louis A. Bannon, Melanie J. Blanchard, Desmond Clapp, Hiram F. Gregory, Stephen K. Joyner, John Marony, David M. Soileau, and Dr. and Mrs. Paul R. Wagner in Louisiana; Mr. and Mrs. Joseph W. Fehrer, Katherine Fisher, and Wayne Klockner in Maryland; Gerald L. Clawson in Missouri; David L. Jennette and Eloise F. Potter in North Carolina; Norman L. Brunswig, John E. Cely, Evelyn Dabbs, L. L. Gaddy, and Robert S. McDaniel, Jr., in South Carolina; Wendell E. Crews, Anne P. Fairless, and Marvin L. Nichols in Tennessee; Elizabeth Cornelius, David D. Diamond, and David H. Riskind in Texas; and John F. Byrne, Mary Keith Garrett, and Gerald F. Levy in Virginia.

Photographer's Note

MY INTRODUCTION to swamps came indirectly. At home in Ohio in the early 1950s my father built a swimming pier for a little pond we owned. The pier was quite sturdy, but over time the elements took their toll, and in the early 1980s the pier had to be rebuilt. Cinder blocks had disintegrated, steel had rusted through, and wooden beams the size of telephone poles were thoroughly rotted. The only part of the pier that was salvageable was the top decking. It was cypress.

This cypress seemed as solid as the day it had been put on. There was no sign of rot, and it held nails beautifully. In addition, it had been used before it was put on the pier. My father salvaged the wood from a water tank in the township that was dismantled to make room for a larger facility. Nobody knows how old that cypress planking might be. Certainly we mortals sunbathing on that pier will never enjoy the longevity of those pieces of wood.

It was not long after rebuilding the pier that I began discussing this book with John Dennis. Photographing the world of cypress swamps seemed like a wonderful assignment.

But I must admit that sitting on a cypress-topped pier as a teenager listening to the radio while covered with sun lotion had done little to prepare me for what I found. In the cypress's native range, from Maryland to southern Florida and from Illinois to Texas, there is, above all, staggering variety.

For example, consider the types of swamps. There are brownwater swamps, blackwater swamps, lake swamps, river swamps, Carolina bay swamps, and swamps on hillsides as well as in lowlands. Some swamps are almost eternally wet, others are often dry, and still others are unpredictable. I learned about this last type the hard way when waters of the Congaree rose so quickly that they marooned my car, which I had parked so I could do a bit of hiking. It was only by dumb luck that I had parked the car on a high point on the road; otherwise, with its horrible indifference, the water would have submerged the vehicle along with everything else.

Then, too, there is the variety of vegetation within these swamps. A comprehensive list of the different shrubs and vines would probably fill up the New Orleans telephone book. The Yellow Pages might be comprised of the wildflowers. But my favorite plant of the swamps is the cypress itself. It is always visually interesting, with its distinctive knees and lacy foliage. Sometimes cypress trees are heavily ornamented, too, with bromeliads or Spanish moss. Where old behemoth cypress trees covered with Spanish moss dominate, the scenery seems out of a picture book of elves and gnomes. The fact that the cypress is often in water adds to its visual appeal. It can create mirror-perfect reflections, silhouettes against sunset-colored waters, and ghostlike fog-bound apparitions.

As with vegetation, lists of wildlife in cypress swamps would be lengthy. I especially enjoyed the birds. Some of the south Florida swamps offer nearly the best birding and bird photography on the continent. And nowhere are reptiles and amphibians—from little salamanders and stinkpot turtles to alligators—more abundant than in the swamps. However, since wildlife activity is irregular, visitors will not always encounter a veritable zoo of wildlife in the swamp, but the potential for it is certainly there.

Along with the natural history of the swamps goes the human history. Swamps have often been regarded as forbidding lands, and indeed there are a number of tales of woe in swamp history. On the other hand, nearly everybody I personally met in the course of my work loved the swamp. My friends the Branns and the Wagners, and the many park and refuge officials who guided me, always wanted to show me far more than I could ever dream of photographing. Yet, it is obvious that swamps can be dangerous and can easily swallow those with a careless attitude or with bad luck.

For the swamps themselves, human enterprises of the past two centuries have on the whole been devastating. Swamps often have tremendous agricultural potential if drained, and drained they have been. And of course there is the immense value of the timber, especially the cypress. One of the great disappointments of the assignment for me was the scarcity of stands of truly large cypress. My experience with the wood of the pier, however, explains why so few of the venerable and mighty ones remain. Fortunately, there is probably no better guide to the locations and lore of these untouched remnants than John Dennis. I will always be indebted to John for showing me the best of our nation's swamps.

Nearly 90 percent of the photography for this book was done with 35mm equipment and Kodachrome 64 film. Lenses employed ranged from an f/2.2 35mm to an f/5.6 600mm. Accessories included extension tubes and proxar lenses for close-up work, four flash units, tripods, and a blind.

A few of the photos were taken with a larger-format camera that provides transparencies about two inches square. To some degree this camera was used simply to give me a bit of variety in the course of taking hundreds and hundreds (if not thousands and thousands—I'm afraid to count!) of exposures. The equipment is somewhat cumbersome, however, and most often was used where portability was not important, such as in a blind. Blinds were used mainly to photograph nesting birds.

The curse of swamp photography is lighting. Swamps are usually very dark because of the overhead forest canopy. And where the sun does shine through, such as in a break in the canopy created by a fallen tree, the light is harsh. If exposure is set for the sunlit areas, anything shaded goes black on the film.

Because of the darkness of the swamp, tripods are indispensable. Time and time again, the photographer will use shutter speeds of $\frac{1}{30}$ of a second or slower. When animals are involved, such slow shutter speeds may be useless, and flashes must be used.

There was not a single day on which I entered a swamp and found nothing photogenic. In every case the scenery offered countless possibilities. In season, there were wildflowers, turtles sunning on logs, prothonotary warblers visiting nests, flocks of herons gathered at little pools to feed. The photographs in this book just touch the surface of swamps. One needs only to read the text to get a better idea of all the subjects awaiting the photographer.

S. M.

The Great Cypress Swamps

1 / The Cypress Swamp

Found widely in lowlands of the Atlantic Coast from Delaware southward and along the Gulf Coast and up the Mississippi Valley are wetlands that are loosely called cypress swamps. No two of these swamps are quite the same, but the presence of cypress trees gives them a special identity. Like the redwoods and sequoias, to which they are related, cypress trees are noted for their size and longevity. Although the cypress has always been regarded as a noble tree, the swamps where cypresses grow have not always enjoyed the goodwill of the public. They were once regarded as treacherous sinkholes—dangerous, unhealthy, and, if at all possible, to be avoided. The one notion uppermost in the minds of the white settlers was to drain the swamps and convert them into land suitable for homes and agriculture. Draining swamps was not easy in the early days of American history. Even with an abundance of slave labor, it was a difficult and often impossible feat. Not until around the end of the nineteenth century was there machinery and equipment available to drain the swamps successfully. In the 1890s, lumber barons from the North moved into the South to begin wholesale exploitation of its timber resources. The cypress, with its rot-resistant wood, was one of the trees in greatest demand. Lumbering was often followed by drainage and land clearing; in other cases the swamp was left to recuperate and grow back.

But as settlement spread and ever fewer places were left to hunt, fish, and otherwise enjoy nature, the swamps came to be viewed in a different light. They were no longer regarded as something to be banished from the landscape. They came to be seen by many people as a retreat for wildlife and a place where man could find solitude and enjoy a variety of recreational activities. The earliest efforts to save swamps were made by people living near them. For example, in the "Night Riders' War"—a conflict that occurred in western Tennessee during the first decade of this century—local residents banded together to prevent a group of entrepreneurs from draining Reelfoot Lake. After several years of bitterness, the disturbance came to an end in 1908 with a complete victory for the residents. Not far away in Arkansas, settlers were able to save Big Lake and what little was left of a once huge cypress swamp. Their efforts led to the creation of the Big Lake National Wildlife Refuge in 1915. Thanks to victories like these, some of the best and largest of the cypress swamps have been saved. Others have been destroyed—flooded by dams, drained, filled in, cut, channelized. A more enlightened attitude toward swamps has prevented the process from going further than it has. But there are still those who are not convinced that swamps are worthwhile. These persons see them in somewhat the same light as did the pioneers.

Not to be lost sight of in the effort to save swamps is the cypress tree itself—the sentinel that stands guard over an empire of trees and water. It is a tree so different from any others that it evokes wonder and awe. Even a few cypress trees lend a certain solemnity to otherwise ordinary-looking woodland. The tree is a centerpiece that holds the interest of those wishing to see something of primitive America. It has an air of timelessness about it that evokes past geological epochs.

But what of the swamps where the tree is found? How are we to distinguish them from other wetlands?

Swamp is a word that resists precise definition. Sometimes defined as a tree-studded wetland and other times as a tract of wet, spongy land saturated and often partially or intermittently covered with water, a swamp is not always easily separated from a marsh. Seasonal flooding and the presence of trees, therefore, are two of the best clues in distinguishing a swamp from a marsh. And during periods of drought or dry times of the year a swamp can become dry ground, so dry that it can be invaded by fire.

The term *swamp* is often broadened to include open land and bodies of water within the borders of the swamp proper. For example, Lake Drummond, in the heart of the Great Dismal, is clearly a part of the swamp, as are also the Dismal's canals and other waterways. Much the same is true of lakes and marshes that make up a sizable share of the Okefenokee Swamp in Georgia. So long as wet, wooded areas exceed the acreage of open areas, the term *swamp* for the whole seems appropriate. But if the open areas are more extensive than the wooded, it may be difficult to apply a fitting term. The Everglades in Florida, for instance, raise this problem.

The cypress, an opportunist, is one of the first trees to invade newly created land. Taking root in mud flats bordering rivers, the cypress gets off to a good start so long as it is not covered by water for any length of time in early stages of growth or shaded out by other plants. Once it reaches a large size and penetrates the canopy, it will hold its own. Other trees around it die, and new ones take their place, but once a cypress tree has become firmly established, it is capable of living for hundreds of years. Generations of other trees come and go, but the cypress stands supremely aloof from them.

Several characteristics are useful in distinguishing the cypress from other trees. In spring the foliage of the cypress is a vivid green, like that of fresh lawn grass. The green contrasts sharply with the majestic trunk and branches, which on a cloudy day seem stark and solemn-looking. In younger trees the bark is a reddish brown; in old trees it is much paler, almost gray. Although the cypress belongs among the conifers, it loses its needles in the fall, unlike most other cone-bearers, and therefore is deciduous. The common name "bald cypress" comes from this attribute. Even the twigs are deciduous. The ones bearing needles fall off with the needles still attached to them.

The swollen or buttressed base found in cypress trees in wet situations is another helpful clue to the tree's identity. But it is not a unique feature. Water tupelo, swamp tupelo, and some other wetland trees also acquire enlarged bases if subjected to periods of inundation. But no other tree possesses anything that looks like the "knees" that surround cypress trees growing in wet situations. Roughly conical in shape and rising to heights of six feet or more, the knees are a part of the tree's root system.

Depending upon whose taxonomy one goes by, there are one to three species in the genus *Taxodium,* to which the bald cypress belongs. The bald cypress (*Taxodium distichum*) was first described in 1753. A second, closely similar tree, the pond cypress, was recognized as a variety in 1818. In 1833 this tree was upgraded to species status. Although the pond cypress (*T. ascendens*) is listed as a species in many botanical works, the present trend is to call it a variety, *i.e.,* not recognize it as a separate entity. M. J. Duever and coauthors, writing in the volume *Cypress Swamps,* state that in the Big Cypress Swamp in Florida they found it impossible to differentiate between the two trees. They suspect that the differences, such as they are, are determined more by age and site conditions than by genetics. Northward, the pond cypress takes on more of an identity of its own and can usually be distinguished from the bald cypress.

For those who recognize the pond cypress as below specific rank, it has the Latin name *Taxodium distichum* var. *nutans* and grows in quiet, shallow waters of streams, ponds, and lakes from southeastern Virginia through the coastal plain to south Florida and westward along the Gulf Coast to southeastern Louisiana. The tree has needles closely appressed against the twigs instead of standing out from the twigs, as in the bald cypress. The pond cypress is a smaller tree and not as long-lived. In nearly all other ways, including having knees that grow from the root system, the two trees are similar.

The bald cypress has a wide range throughout the humid lowlands of the South. It is often present in river valleys, lakes, ponds, and other wetlands. It is absent from salt-marsh communities but often occurs at borders of brackish marshes. It grows well in peat and other acidic soils and, at the opposite extreme, in limestone formations. Even though capable of growing in uplands, the bald cypress does best under flooded conditions, especially where the water level is subject to periodic fluctuation. Drastic flooding, such as happens when water inundates a sizable portion of the lower trunk for extended periods of time, can, however, have a lethal effect.

The bald cypress ranges from southern Delaware and Maryland southward through the coastal plain to extreme south Florida, then westward to south-central Texas, and northward in the Mississippi Valley as far as southeastern Missouri, southern Illinois, and southwestern Indiana. Although for the most part a lowland tree, it reaches an elevation of 1,750 feet in south-central Texas and about 500 feet in the upper Mississippi Valley.

Still another cypress, the Montezuma bald cypress (*Taxodium mucronatum*), barely crosses the border between Mexico and the United States. It is found in the vicinity of Brownsville and southward through Mexico to Guatemala. In the Mexican state of Oaxaca at Santa Maria del Tule is the famous Tule Tree. This Montezuma cypress has a circumference of 112 feet at its base—twice the girth of the largest bald cypress known. But there is speculation that two or more cypress trees during early stages in growth became fused together to form the huge trunk.

Known as "the wood eternal," cypress is used for a wide range of building purposes. The wood's renowned resistance to decay has made it useful for everything from water pipes and gutters to grave markers. Hollow cypress logs installed as water pipes in New Orleans in 1798 were still serviceable and free from decay when removed in 1914. There are accounts of cypress shingles still protecting the exteriors of old homes after 250 years. One cypress grave marker was in use for 160 years. Add to this the fact that the wood is easy to work and resistant to wear, and it is no wonder the tree has been in great demand.

Older trees—and sometimes younger ones as well—are subject to a fungus disease known as "pecky cypress." Once the disease becomes established in the heartwood, it eats away the wood and, in time, leaves nothing but the outer shell of the tree. Although an infected tree may look perfectly sound, a lumberman can tell that it is hollow and not worth cutting. The fact that many old trees have been

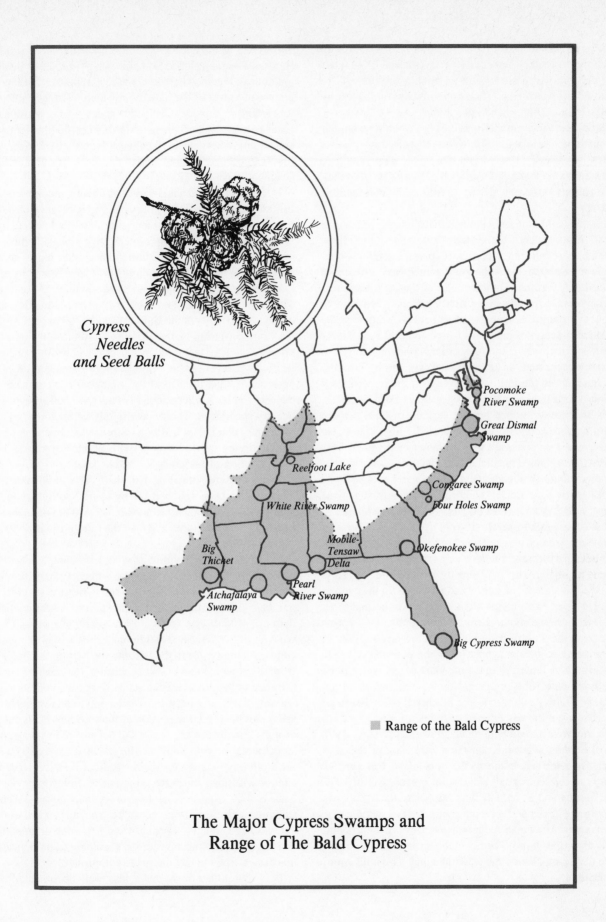

Cypress Needles and Seed Balls

Pocomoke River Swamp

Great Dismal Swamp

Reelfoot Lake

Congaree Swamp

Four Holes Swamp

White River Swamp

Mobile-Tensaw Delta

Okefenokee Swamp

Big Thicket

Pearl River Swamp

Atchafalaya Swamp

Big Cypress Swamp

■ Range of the Bald Cypress

The Major Cypress Swamps and Range of The Bald Cypress

spared is explained partly by presence of heartwood decay and partly by another defect known as "shakes." The latter takes the form of twisted grain, an abnormality thought to be caused by wind stress. Trees having wood impaired by "shakes" are worthless and left standing.

Interior paneling is sometimes made of wood with numerous small holes visible. The wood happens to be pecky cypress in which the decay has not progressed far enough to impair the wood's strength seriously. Pecky cypress paneling is highly ornamental and therefore in considerable demand.

Although it is commonly thought that all cypress knees are hollow, most of them are actually solid. The only hollow knees are those infected with pecky cypress. But hollow ones are often exhibited, and many are turned into artifacts of various kinds. William Bartram reported that hollow cypress knees were used as beehives. Early accounts tell also of hollow cypress knees being used as buckets. Although the biological function of the knees is in dispute, they probably act to some degree as respiratory organs, bringing oxygen to the root system and, in turn, discharging carbon dioxide. This function of the knees is not vital to the tree, since it continues to live even after the knees have been removed. Knees are best developed on root systems of trees that are subject to permanent flooding or periodic high water. On higher ground the knees are small or lacking altogether. This is true of trees planted in upland sites and the occasional trees that grow naturally outside the normal swamp wetlands.

In 1890, N. S. Shaler, an authority on swamps, suggested that not only cypress knees but also the buttressed bases of cypress trees serve to aerate the root systems. He also suggested that the bases of water tupelo and swamp tupelo (black gum) trees perform the function of aeration. Moreover, according to Shaler, the two tupelos have another aeration method equivalent to the one he had proposed for the cypress knee. He noted that tupelos established in wet ground often show aboveground root systems. These, unlike the cypress knee, are in the form of coils or arches. On many occasions I have tripped or nearly tripped over these exposed tupelo roots, which lie like traps in the mud and murky water at the base of the tree. Shaler thought that the arched roots are pneumatophores bringing oxygen to starved root systems of trees growing in poorly drained or flooded soil.

Not everyone agreed with Shaler. For example, in a 1952 issue of *Ecology,* Paul J. Kramer and coauthors, on the basis of extensive testing, came to the conclusion that cypress knees scarcely serve at all as aeration organs. But in 1977 R. O. Teskey and T. M. Hinckley supported the hypothesis that both the knees and the buttressing help supply the tree with oxygen. They also thought that knees and buttressing help anchor trees more securely in the unstable environment where they grow. Thus, the structures play a dual function, they thought.

Looking at the cypress knee from a different viewpoint, Herman Kurz and Delzie Demaree in a 1934 issue of *Ecology* maintained that the knees tend to grow as high as the average high-water level of the locality in which the tree is situated. According to this idea, very tall knees would be found in river bottoms subject to periods of high floodwaters, and conversely, short knees would be found where very little flooding occurs. I have noted this correlation in all the swamps I have visited.

Heights up to seven and eight feet are not uncommon. In a few swamps I have found knees ranging in height from ten to twelve feet. This does not mean that all of the knees in these swamps are this tall. Shorter knees grow alongside the taller ones. But some of these shorter knees can reach heights approaching those of their neighbors. I have found my taller knees in big river swamps from South Carolina to Louisiana. The very tallest knees I have ever seen were along the banks of the Santee River in the Guillard's Lake Recreation Area of the Francis Marion National Forest in South Carolina. One knee was twelve feet three inches tall, and another one next to it was twelve feet tall. Oddly, these knees and other tall ones nearby had been dead for a number of years. Yet the cypress trees on whose root systems they had grown were healthy specimens. The answer to this riddle apparently lay in the fact that a dam had been constructed upstream on the Santee during the 1930s and 1940s and had eliminated the high flooding of previous years. The knees, no longer performing a useful function, had died. That this sometimes happens has been vouched for by G. H. Collingwood and Warren D. Brush in *Knowing Your Trees.* They state that the knees die when the area in which the trees grow is no longer subject to flooding.

No discussion of cypresses would be complete without mentioning the role that water and birds play in disseminating the seeds. Cypress seeds—some twenty to thirty in number—are contained in a globular cone slightly smaller than a golf ball. The seeds are irregularly shaped and have what might be described as semblances of wings along their edges. As they ripen in the fall, the seeds either are released from the cone while it is still attached to the tree or fall with the cone to the ground. Both seeds and cones float in water. As water levels rise in swamps and along watercourses in late fall and winter, a large portion of the seed harvest is carried away. Those that strand in wet soil not covered by water may sprout and grow into small seedlings. But if covered by water for prolonged periods, the seedlings die. Likewise, seedlings cannot withstand intensive competition from other plants. This is why little regeneration of cypress trees is seen in swamps with closed canopies. To become established, a cypress needs relative openness and not much competition. But once the seedling has reached a fair height, its chances of reaching a ripe old age are greatly improved.

Bird dissemination is much less well documented than

transport by water. It is believed that the now extinct Carolina parakeet was an important agent in transporting the seeds. The parakeet both ate the seeds and used cypress trees as places to roost and nest. As flocks moved from one swampy area to another, seeds passing through the digestive tract would be voided and therefore scattered far and wide.

Another likely distributor of cypress seeds is still with us—the wood duck, a bird that also spends much of its time in cypress swamps. John K. Terres and others have reported that cypress seeds are an important item in the diet of this beautiful duck. Like the Carolina parakeet, wood ducks travel from one feeding ground to another. Their travels, taking them to lakes, ponds, rivers, and streams, could well be an important factor in the distribution of cypress trees. The presence of cypresses on man-made impoundments, such as farm ponds, may, in many instances, be due to the presence of wood ducks.

Wood ducks seem responsible for some of the isolated stands of bald cypresses found to the north of the tree's natural range. Examples of bald cypresses in habitats utilized by wood ducks in the North are given by Richard Stalter in an article in *Castanea*. He tells of a stand near the Bear Mountain Bridge, thirty-five miles north of New York City, another at a pond in eastern Long Island, and still another in a swampy area near Newark, New Jersey. The inference is that the seeds were eaten by wood ducks in ornamental plantings not far away and carried by the birds in their crops or stomachs to the sites in question. Specimens of cypresses planted by man can be found in a number of areas farther north, including New York State, Massachusetts, and Michigan.

Taking root is only the first step in the cypress tree's long and hazardous journey to maturity. If the seedling has become established at a favorable site with adequate sunlight and moisture, it may add about a foot in height yearly. But gnawing by rodents and grazing by herbivores are hazards faced by young saplings. Still another hazard is fire. Given the thin bark of the cypress, young trees are often damaged or killed when fire invades a wetland during a dry year. However, older trees seem relatively resistant to fire. J. Merrill Lynch of the Nature Conservancy told me that he has seen many cypress stands that have withstood severe ground fires without apparent ill effect. On the other hand, cypresses, like most trees, cannot withstand the flames and intense heat of a crown fire. But fire in another form—lightning—has destroyed many cypress trees that have survived all the other hazards. Older trees, particularly those tall enough to reach above the canopy, are the most vulnerable. It may take several lightning strikes before one of these giants is severely damaged or killed. Like immense torches, trees already hollow because of pecky cypress may burn for days after being hit by lightning.

One reason that cypress rules supreme in the swamps where it is found is its resistance to strong wind. Firmly anchored by a deep taproot and horizontal roots pinned down by the knees, cypress trees can withstand hurricane-force winds that topple other trees growing around them. Veterans of numerous storms and hurricanes may lose branches and have their tops blown off, but the trunk nearly always remains upright. Not only does cypress possess a wood regarded as eternal, but the tree itself has qualities of eternity. Hollow, battered, and shorn of most of its limbs, it goes on living in seeming defiance of the laws of nature.

References

Collingwood, G. H., and Warren D. Brush. *Knowing Your Trees.* Washington, D.C., 1964.

Ewel, Katherine C., and Howard T. Odum, eds. *Cypress Swamps.* Gainesville, Fla., 1985.

Kramer, Paul J., Walter S. Riley, and Thomas T. Bannister. "Gas Exchange of Cypress Knees." *Ecology,* XXXIII (1952), 117–21.

Kurz, Herman, and Delzie Demaree. "Cypress Buttresses and Knees in Relation to Water and Air." *Ecology,* XV (1934), 36–41.

Shaler, Nathaniel S. "Fresh-Water Morasses of the United States." *U.S. Geological Survey Annual Report,* X (1890), 313–39.

Stalter, Richard. "Some Ecological Observations of *Taxodium distichum* (L.) Richard, in Delaware." *Castanea,* XLVI (1981), 154–61.

Terres, John K. *The Audubon Society Encyclopedia of North American Birds.* New York, 1980.

Teskey, R. O., and T. M. Hinckley. *The Southern Forest Region.* Washington, D.C., 1977. Vol. II of U.S. Fish and Wildlife Service Biological Service Program, *Impact of Water Level Changes on Woody Riparian and Wetland Communities.* FWS/OBS-77/59.

Cypress is not only old in the sense that the wood is long lasting, but it has a fossil history dating back thousands of years. Moreover, certain living specimens surpass all but a few western trees for the honor of having attained the greatest longevity. Much the same can be said of the size of the cypress. Only a few western trees, including the redwood and the giant sequoia, attain a greater size.

At one time, ancestors of today's cypresses had a very wide range, being present in Europe and much of North America. Pushed back by the Ice Age, the cypress survived in warmer parts of our South but died out completely in Europe. Evidence of its wider range on this continent is seen, according to Charlotte Gantz, in buried remains of bald cypresses discovered in peat bogs in Maine and New Hampshire. Other finds support the fact that cypress once grew much farther north than it does now. A petrified log at the Cape Cod Museum of Natural History at Brewster, Massachusetts, has been labeled *Taxodiaceae* and assigned an age of about 80,000 years. The specimen washed up on the beach from the nearby ocean bottom, where it may have been deposited by the glaciers some 10,000 years ago. Still another specimen, this one described by Edward E. Wildman, was found during excavations for a subway in Philadelphia in 1931. It was a cypress stump, seventeen feet in circumference, at a depth of thirty-eight feet below the surface and ten feet below sea level. The age of this relic was estimated to be 100,000 years.

Closer to or within the present range of the bald cypress are fossil or semifossil deposits of logs, knees, and other parts of cypress in the Chesapeake Bay region. In 1905 Arthur Bibbins reported ancient cypress logs on the bottom of Baltimore Harbor in the Patapsco River and extensive deposits nearby along the western shore of the Chesapeake Bay. According to Bibbins, peat deposits, one to six feet thick or more, containing stumps, limbs, and knees of cypress, as well as wood of other trees, occur widely in this area. These deposits are either underwater or partially submerged at the edges of shorelines. He reported finding the most extensive deposits opposite a place called Bodkin Heights in maps of his time. This may have been near present-day Bodkin Point at the mouth of the Patapsco River, where cypress knees were discovered along with stumps resembling "huge partly submerged rocks." One measured ten feet in diameter, and a knee measured two feet around. Residents of Pinehurst, on the Chesapeake Bay near Bodkin Point, say that stumps are sometimes seen when a combination of low tides and strong northwest winds exposes the bottom. They also report that the area has been vastly altered by shore erosion.

Bibbins, who did not think the deposits were particularly old, pointed out that the wood was remarkably well preserved and was "undergoing the very first stages of carbonization." He noted that, with few exceptions, the deposits were at an elevation close to the present sea level. On the other hand, David W. Stahle, a paleobotanist at the University of Arkansas, who has looked at rings in cypress (present and ancient) throughout the tree's range in a study of past climate, thinks the Baltimore deposits are ancient, perhaps up to 100,000 years old.

Horace G. Richards, who, like Wildman, described the ancient stump found in Philadelphia, reported fossil cypress logs about 100,000 years old in Washington, D.C., buried thirty-five to forty feet below ground level and uncovered during excavations for the Mayflower Hotel in 1922. Also, "cypresslike conifers" seem to have left carbonized logs in the stream bed at Northwest Branch Park on the outskirts of the city. These logs, according to Bill and Phyllis Thomas, date back more than 120 million years.

The oldest known log of a bald cypress to date is one uncovered at a gravel pit near Brandywine, Maryland, late in 1986. The location, only twelve miles southeast of the nation's capital, is in the same general area as the Mayflower Hotel logs and the cypresslike logs at Northwest River Park. The discovery was made during the normal course of operations at the gravel pit. A foreman, seeing the log and deciding that it was something unusual, notified the Maryland Geological Survey. This set off a flurry of activity. The log, fifteen feet in length, with a diameter of three and a half feet, and buried at a depth of twenty-five feet, was only one of many priceless finds. Sifting through a blue-gray clay, which had preserved portions of plants that grew millions of years ago, paleontologists found hundreds of leaves, catkins, and seeds, and large quantities of pollen. This material has re-

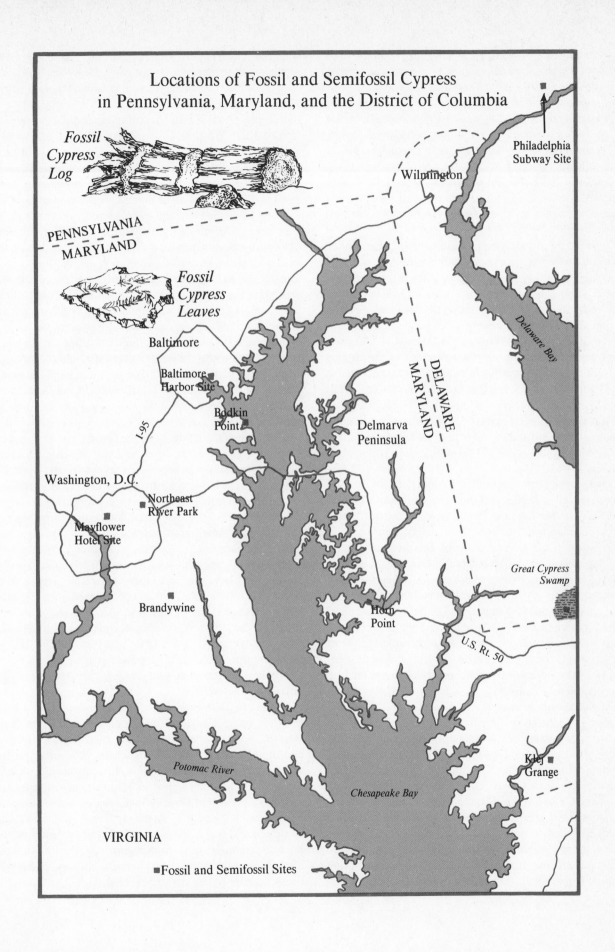

Locations of Fossil and Semifossil Cypress
in Pennsylvania, Maryland, and the District of Columbia

Fossil
Cypress
Log

Fossil
Cypress
Leaves

PENNSYLVANIA
MARYLAND

Wilmington

Philadelphia
Subway Site

Delaware Bay

DELAWARE
MARYLAND

Baltimore

Baltimore
Harbor Site

Bodkin
Point

I-95

Delmarva
Peninsula

Washington, D.C.

Northeast
River Park

Mayflower
Hotel Site

Great Cypress
Swamp

Brandywine

Horn
Point

U.S. Rt. 50

Klej
Grange

Potomac River

Chesapeake Bay

VIRGINIA

■Fossil and Semifossil Sites

vealed the presence of an ancient swamp forest that may have once existed in an oxbow lake and become covered over with sediment. Many of the plants, including bald cypress, sycamore, sweet gum, hickory, elm, tupelo, oak, and alder, are ones found in present-day swamps; many others have not yet been identified or are plants no longer found in the region. For example, one of the plants is a water chestnut no longer native to North America. As yet, the age of this prehistoric swamp forest has not been established. Researchers judge the deposits to be in a range from the late Miocene to early Pliocene—roughly somewhere between four to seven million years ago.

Across the bay on Maryland's Eastern Shore, other buried logs testify to the presence of vast cypress and Atlantic white cedar swamps throughout the region when the climate was warmer. Among the recent finds are buried bald cypress or white cedar stumps at Horn Point on the Choptank River, a location about five miles west of Cambridge. These stumps have been estimated to be between 34,000 and 35,000 years old. A second find—this one discovered during the digging of a flushing system for a hog house at a hog farm located at Klej Grange between Snow Hill and Pocomoke City—contained cypress stumps believed to be 30,000 to 40,000 years old. But state geologist James P. Reger writes me that the stumps could be much older—somewhere between 100,000 and 200,000 years—too old to date using radiocarbon methods.

At the northernmost part of the present range of the bald cypress, which is in Sussex County in southern Delaware, there were at one time the most extensive beds of buried cypress logs known. The logs lay in peat beds in what was known as the Great Cypress Swamp. This swamp (which I am going to describe in more detail in Chapter 3) also contained large stands of living cypress trees. The trees, many of them very large, provided material for a thriving shingle-making industry that had its beginnings during the early part of the nineteenth century. At first the shingles were used locally only on the largest and most costly buildings. Most were exported, some overseas. By 1850, according to Delaware historian Anthony Higgins, cypress shingles were in such demand that hardly a decent-sized cypress tree was left standing in the whole swamp. The Great Cypress Swamp at this time covered about fifty thousand acres. Lumbermen then turned to Atlantic white cedar trees, also plentiful in the swamp, for shingles until the supply of them also dwindled.

Shortly before the Civil War the industry was revitalized by an astonishing discovery. Only a few feet below the surface of the Great Cypress Swamp, huge cypress logs were found embedded in peat and as sound as when the trees had first toppled over. A new era of cypress shingle making was at hand. Higgins vividly described the nineteenth-century process for mining the logs: "Tons of soggy peat were scooped from above tree-trunks. Oxen foundered and wheezed, chains pulled taut, men cursed, and the logs were dragged out to where crosscut saws could be used." The crosscut log sections were then cut with hand tools into shingles thirty inches long.

Because of the introduction of cheaper redwood shingles from the Far West, however, cypress log shingle making declined in the early twentieth century and was defunct by 1920. Much of the swamp's great deposit of buried cypress logs might still exist if it were not for a devastating fire in 1930 that burned for eight months, destroying most of the peat and embedded logs and leaving a watery waste of blackened snags. Unfortunately, the buried logs had disappeared before anyone got around to determining the age of this buried forest by means of radiocarbon dating.

After the fire, renewed efforts were made to drain what was left of the swamp and turn its black soil into agricultural land. Some of the water was siphoned off by ditches leading to the Pocomoke River, the swamp's natural outlet. The Pocomoke and its tributaries offer some of the best stands of cypress left today at the northeasternmost limits of the tree's range. After fifty miles of blackwater swamp, the Pocomoke discharges its acid-stained waters into the Chesapeake Bay. Still other ditches diverted the swamp's water eastward toward the Atlantic coast.

Local inhabitants now gave the Great Cypress Swamp a more appropriate name. They called it the Burnt Swamp. Slowly the swamp was becoming only a memory. Little was left of it in 1961, when a native son, Ted Harvey, returned after a long absence and saw what was happening. A staunch conservationist, he was shocked and dismayed by what he saw. He immediately set about raising money in order to save what he could. After an initial purchase of 1,200 acres, he went on to acquire additional acreage of remaining swampland in both Delaware and nearby Maryland. That was the beginning of Delaware Wild Lands, a conservation organization dedicated to saving swamps, marshes, and other wild lands. Today, the organization founded by Harvey owns over 11,000 acres in the Great Cypress Swamp (now a swamp once again) and approximately 1,000 acres in swampland to the west containing both bald cypress and Atlantic white cedar.

Thanks to Delaware Wild Lands, thousands of cypress trees are being planted in the once-blackened ruins of the Great Cypress Swamp. Some have been planted by hand, and other thousands have been seeded from small planes. Those that have been planted in open fields have done best. Competition from red maple, sweet gum, and Virginia chain fern have prevented good growth by cypress seedlings in many parts of the swamp. At the same time, water levels are being restored and wildlife protected. The swamp is returning to a semblance of its former grandeur. But bringing one all the way back after near destruction is not easy. It may take many decades before that is achieved.

Other deposits of buried cypresses, apparently not as large as those found in the Great Cypress Swamp, have been discovered in other parts of the tree's range. The earliest reference to semifossil deposits seems to have been made by the intrepid naturalist-explorer William Bartram. In 1778, in poor health and suffering from an eye affliction, he was botanizing along the lower Mississippi. As the small boat that he and his party were traveling in passed a high bluff on the east bank of the river, he saw something that excited his curiosity. Logs, stumps, and other woody debris at the base of the bluff gave the appearance of having been eroded out of the bluff and not deposited by high water. In spite of his indisposition, Bartram must have insisted upon making a landing so that he could view the objects more closely. In his *Travels* he tells of seeing "vast stumps of cypress and other trees, which at this day grow in these low, wet swamps." Describing the stumps, he said they were sound, stood upright, and seemed "rotted off about two or three feet above the spread of their roots."

The deposits viewed by Bartram were at the present-day community of Port Hudson, above Baton Rouge. Apparently, little or nothing is left of them. The site where they were found is now occupied by a large industrial plant. However, a few samples of the wood have been found, and they were determined to be around ten thousand years old.

Still other buried cypresses can be found at the bottom of Lake Drummond in Virginia's Great Dismal Swamp and reportedly in the watersheds of the Tombigbee and Alabama rivers in Alabama. Long-submerged logs have also been found at Allred Lake in southeastern Missouri. The work of analyzing these and other finds has barely begun. When such deposits are aged and the tree rings counted, we will have better information on past climate and on such events as huge forest fires.

The upright stumps and broken-off trunks described by Bartram can probably be explained by the natural tendency of old or dead cypress trees to break off at ground level rather than uproot. It is at ground level that the wood is most vulnerable to decay. In addition, the tree, with its deep taproot and spreading roots, anchored with knees, is almost invulnerable to being uprooted—even during hurricanes. But a tree breaking off near ground level would leave its trunk, branches, stump, roots, and knees to sink gradually into the mud and eventually become covered over with peat. The same process, taking place generation after generation, would lead to deposits many feet in thickness. The wood, highly resistant to decay, would be further protected under layers of peat.

During earlier days of timber cutting, cypress logs were floated in large numbers to sawmills. If the wood had not been sufficiently cured by first girdling the tree and letting it stand for a period of six months to a year prior to cutting, the logs were likely to sink. Judging from the number of cypress logs still lying on river and creek bottoms today, the lumbermen of around a century ago must have been careless about proper curing. Presently there is a thriving business in dredging the logs from swamp bottoms, where they have typically remained in a perfect state of preservation.

David Stahle and other researchers are gathering ring data from long-buried or -submerged trunks of cypress, as well as living trees, to establish chronologies concerning past climate over a period of as much as five thousand years. One of the few North American trees capable of producing a longer record is the bristlecone pine (*Pinus aristata*) of high mountain regions of the West. Samples of ancient wood of this pine, together with ring counts from living trees, have provided chronologies going back as far as 6700 B.C. Living trees have reached the exceptional age of approximately four thousand years.

Although not able to compete with the bristlecone pine in regard to longevity, the bald cypress furnishes the longest age records of any tree east of the Rockies. O. Gordon Langdon, writing in 1958, stated that trees in virgin stands are often from 400 to 600 years old and that individual trees are known to reach approximately 1,200 years. But pinpointing the ages of very old cypress trees is usually difficult. Often some sections containing the annual rings are missing. Also, under some circumstances a cypress tree will lay down more than one ring during the course of a year's growth. False rings, as they are called, can be detected by persons skilled in determining the ages of trees by counting rings in cross-sections and by taking borings. But it is safe to say that many reputed ages of cypress trees are too high because of failure to make due allowance for false rings.

Stahle has added valuable new information regarding the true ages sometimes reached by the bald cypress. Using growth rings of living cypresses in his reconstruction of past climate, he has discovered trees with ages that exceed 1,200 years, for example, in the Black River Swamp in southeastern North Carolina. Two trees there were dated at ages of between 1,220 and 1,250 years. Stahle calls the trees the two oldest absolutely dated cypress trees known. But his hypothetically oldest tree is much older. It is a giant in the Beidler Forest in Four Holes Swamp in South Carolina, which he estimates to be at least 1,500 and possibly as much as 2,000 years old. Since the interior of this tree contains heart rot, it is impossible to establish a more precise age.

Other swamps where Stahle has obtained records of very old trees include those in the areas of the lower Altamaha River and Ebenezer Creek in Georgia, the Cache River and Bayou DeView in Arkansas, and the Kirk tract on the Blackwater River in Virginia. Stahle was particularly excited about the ages of trees he discovered in the Kirk tract—a small stand of ancient cypresses and water tupelos. But he had not finished analyzing his data when I last communicated with him.

A rule of thumb for determining the ages of cypress trees is to allow one hundred years for each foot of the tree's diameter. This is reasonably accurate for trees subject to good growing conditions and young enough to add substantially to their growth each year. But this method cannot be applied to very old trees whose growth has slowed.

One must be wary about accepting ages supplied by tourist bureaus and other agencies interested in promoting cypress trees as tourist attractions. For example, a very large, well-known cypress tree at Sanford, Florida, has been reported to be 3,000 years old. Although undoubtedly a quite venerable tree, the age given is far in excess of that for trees aged by precise scientific methods. But credence should be given to a report of a 1,600-year-old tree cut for lumber early in this century in the Santee River Swamp in South Carolina. The age of that tree was measured by a highly qualified forester.

The American Forestry Association, as well as state forestry agencies, has for many years been collecting data on sizes reached by North American trees. Size is determined by measurements taken of the tree's girth, height, and amount of spread in the crown. Each measurement is added up, and based on a standard formula, the tree is awarded a number of points. Trees with a sizable number of points sometimes qualify as state or national champions. According to the point system, the bald cypress is the largest tree in North America east of the Rockies. In the Far West, champion western redcedars, redwoods, sequoias, and Sitka spruces have more points than the largest bald cypresses.

Presently the national champion bald cypress is a tree in the Cat Island Swamp in north-central Louisiana that has a score of 748 points. (I describe this tree in Chapter 16). Florida is the home of a number of very large cypress trees. The state champion is a tree in the Suwannee River drainage area in northern Florida that has a score of 644 points. The venerable tree at Sanford, whose reputed age I mistrust, is only slightly behind this tree in terms of number of points. The state champion in North Carolina is a tree near Windsor in the Cashie River watershed that has 605 points. Yet, on viewing this tree, I discovered that it is only a hollow shell. The outside four or five inches is living woody tissue supporting a trunk 138 feet tall and its branches. That such a decay-ridden tree is still alive and may go on living for many more years is another mystery that surrounds the bald cypress.

It is sad to observe the destruction or decline of a cypress tree whose age may predate Columbus' discovery of America. Having withstood the hazards of centuries, a tree may be the victim of one too many lightning strikes or become nothing but a shell because of the inroads of pecky cypress. Several of the very large specimens that I have seen were dead, blackened hulks, burned and ravaged through the years, but still standing thanks to the tree's remarkably resistant wood.

In 1976 the end finally came for a former national champion located in a remote cypress slough near Greenfield in northwestern Tennessee. Overlooked for years, the tree began to receive public attention in 1949. A giant among pygmies, it had a circumference of 39 feet 8 inches, a height of 122 feet 5 inches, and a spread of 47 feet. Given the name Tennessee Titan, the tree proved to be such an attraction that the land around it was turned into a state park. Fate, however, was unkind to this ancient tree that had looked down upon the Indians and later the white settlers. The renowned Davy Crockett built a cabin only ten miles away. A hint of the trouble that lay ahead was seen in the pronouncement by foresters that the tree was hollow and weakened from pecky cypress, though that did not necessarily mean that it was doomed to early destruction. However, after a violent windstorm blew off the top of the trunk and many of the branches, the tree was little more than a battered hulk with a wide opening at its base. Visitors could now enter the inside hollow and gaze about them in awe. As many as thirty-six persons were said to have gathered at one time in this interior chamber. A second calamity, in the form of a lightning strike, overtook the tree in July of 1976. Setting the tree on fire, the lightning started a blazing inferno fanned by air entering the opening at the tree's base. Flames shot upward for a hundred feet or more from the chimneylike hollow at the top of the tree. The fire burned for two weeks, leaving only a blackened hulk.

When I visited the tree in April, 1984, all that was left was a splintered trunk some forty feet in height with a gaping hole at its base. Reaching the tree was no easy task. The water of the slough, which for years had acted as a moat protecting the tree from fire, was over waist-deep. Partly by wading and partly by climbing on slippery logs, I made my way to the tree. Slowly I worked my way around its perimeter, stretching my tape to get a reading of the circumference at breast height. As a result of fire and decay, the tree's circumference had shrunk from over thirty-nine feet to little more than thirty-seven feet.

But even in this state, the tree was an awe-inspiring sight. I was glad that I had taken the trouble to visit it. More than any of our other trees, the bald cypress seems capable of enduring calamities. Even when dead, it is a monument worth preserving.

References

Bibbins, Arthur. "The Buried Cypress Forest of the Upper Chesapeake." *Records of the Past,* IV, No. 2 (1905), 47–53.

Collingwood, G. H., and Warren D. Brush. *Knowing Your Trees.* Washington, D.C., 1964.

Gantz, Charlotte O. *A Naturalist in Southern Florida.* Coral Gables, 1971.

Harper, Francis, ed. *The Travels of William Bartram*. New Haven, 1958.

Higgins, Anthony. *Delaware: A Guide to the First State*. New York, 1938.

Jones, F. M., ed. "Answers to Sundry Queries Relative the Indian River, or Cypress Swamps, in the Delaware State, in a Letter to Thomas McKean, Esq. from a Citizen of the Said State." *Delaware History,* III (March, 1949), 123–37.

Langdon, O. Gordon. *Silvical Characteristics of Baldcypress*. U.S. Forest Service Southeast Forest Experiment Station Papers, No. 94. Washington, D.C., 1958.

Richards, Horace G. "The Subway Tree: A Record of a Pleistocene Cypress Stump in Philadelphia." *Bartonia,* XIII (1931), 1–6.

Stahle, David W., E. R. Cook, and J. W. C. White. "Tree-ring Dating of Baldcypress and the Potential for Millennia-long Chronologies in the Southeast." *American Antiquity,* L (1985), 796–802.

Thomas, Bill, and Phyllis Thomas. *Natural Washington*. New York, 1980.

Wildman, Edward E. *Penn's Woods, 1682–1932*. Philadelphia, 1944.

Even for those who love the out-of-doors, there is a certain melancholy about a cypress swamp that is hard to shake off. It can be attributed partly to the cypress trees, with their flaring buttresses and strangely grotesque knees. If the trees, as in more southern portions of the range, are draped with Spanish moss, this adds a ghostly effect that is most pronounced toward dusk. In keeping with these trappings is the dark water that surrounds the trees. Often an inky black, the water reinforces the feeling of gloom that so easily settles upon those who first visit a cypress swamp. The swamp seems timeless, menacing, and an entirely different world from the one we are used to. But as we become better acquainted with the swamp, we lose our early misgivings. On a bright sunny day, when birds are singing, the swamp takes on a brighter and more cheerful aspect.

It must be admitted, however, that part of the swamp's reputation as a place of grief and danger is well deserved. Owing to its inaccessibility, the swamp was once a haven for runaway slaves. Others, such as escaped convicts, draft dodgers, bootleggers, and smugglers, have used the swamps as convenient retreats or places to set up stills and other illegal operations.

It would be difficult to find a sizable swamp from Delaware and Maryland southward that did not have a shadowy history. Events in the environs of the town where I was born and now live, for example, have contributed to the rich folklore and history of swamps. My birthplace, the small town of Princess Anne, is not far from the watery domain of the cypress tree. It has been the home of Dennises for many generations. My grandparents on my mother's side had a farm not far from town on a winding tidal creek. I spent much of my early boyhood on that farm. It was a life close to nature but also often a lonely life, as I had few playmates and my brother was away much of the time. My indulgent grandparents did not dream of putting me to work. I read boys' books and spent long hours climbing trees, fishing, hiking, and, when my brother was with me, building towns for imaginary animals. The homes we constructed of bricks and shingles were for imaginary foxes, rabbits, squirrels, and other small mammals. But there were so many real insects—both crawling and flying—that we called our largest town Bug-

ville. Other real animals were all around us as we labored on our villages. In the nearby marshes muskrats built their domed homes in the cattails. Nesting ospreys occupied a dead pine tree not far away, and kingfishers plunged into the murky waters of the creek. Snapping turtles came out onto dry land to lay their eggs. Black rat snakes glided by, seeking out bird nests to rob. In early fall blackbirds passed over in seemingly endless flocks. Later the Canada geese came.

Thanks to my grandfather, who had once been an ardent sportsman, I learned a fair amount about plants, animals, and the ways of the weather. It was mainly through his influence that I avoided the traditional family law degree and became a naturalist.

One day while exploring a swamp at the edge of the farm, I came to an overgrown place with uneven ground in the form of small mounds rising above the wet woodland soil. I had taken only a few steps when the ground gave way. I found myself in a hole two to three feet deep. Badly shaken, I discovered that I had fallen through a rotten coffin that held the bones of someone who had died probably a hundred or more years before. The Eastern Shore is dotted with small family burial grounds, most of them abandoned and forgotten.

The cypress swamps, for the most part, occupy midportions of the long, narrow Delmarva Peninsula, which lies between the Chesapeake Bay and the Atlantic Ocean. In a senseless fashion, boundary lines divide the peninsula into parts of three states—Delaware taking up a sizable chunk in the northeastern corner; Maryland's Eastern Shore hugging the Chesapeake Bay on the west, its lower counties fronting both the ocean and the bay; and Virginia's Eastern Shore occupying what little there is left at the southern tip of the peninsula.

The Pocomoke River, from its headwaters in the Great Cypress Swamp in Delaware to where it flows into the Chesapeake Bay, is the key to most, but not quite all, of the peninsula's cypress swamps. Poor drainage and a mild climate help explain the presence of cypress here at its northernmost outpost on the Atlantic Coast. Amid a complex network of creeks and peat bogs, cypress grows side by side with sweet bay, red maple, water oak, and an accompanying retine of shrubs and vines that are predominantly southern in origin. Along the Pocomoke is a swamp that has the appearance of having been transported bodily from somewhere farther south.

The name *Pocomoke* comes from the Algonquin Indians and means "black water." Like the Indians, the early white settlers were impressed by the inky blackness of the water in this river and other rivers like it. From Virginia southward, one cannot travel far along the coastal plain without coming to a Black River, Blackwater River, or Black Creek. To the geographer, a blackwater river is a southern river that has black water, a relatively narrow floodplain, and a drainage system lying entirely within the coastal plain. In contrast, there is a second kind of river called a brownwater river. Having its source in the Piedmont or higher, the brownwater river is much more subject to flooding, and the silt carried by its floodwaters stains the water a muddy brown. Brownwater rivers have a wide floodplain and are much given to meandering.

The term *blackwater* is somewhat misleading. If some "black water" is scooped up in a glass, it is seen to be amber in color. It would be equally accurate to call it tea- or winecolored. The same light coloring shows through in shallow shoals or where the water spills over a dam. Dyes from the roots and decaying leaves of plants provide the coloring. Unless there is a source of lime in the floodplain, the water is likely to be highly acidic.

The Great Cypress Swamp, which in former times flourished at the headwaters of the Pocomoke, has a written history going back to the eighteenth century. An anonymous author who was a keen observer well versed in natural history wrote an account of the swamp that appeared in 1797. His account, spanning approximately the years from 1765 until almost the end of the century, contains both folklore and surprisingly accurate descriptions of the flora and fauna. He told of green cypress (Atlantic white cedar) reaching majestic heights and "casting such a venerable shade that it kept every other tree of the forest at an awful distance." Bald cypress, he said, covered a vast tract but was somewhat less numerous than the green cypress. By *green* cypress, he meant evergreen, in contrast to the deciduous foliage found in the bald cypress. In many other ways, including their foliage, their bark, the long-lasting nature of their wood, and their habitat, the two trees are quite similar.

Describing the bald cypress, he called it a beautiful tree rising to a height of 140 feet and "having but few branches till near the top, and these spread like an umbrella." He told of trees with trunks four to eight feet in diameter and knees reaching heights of eight to ten feet. He probably exaggerated the knee heights, but his description of the tree—its bark, leaves, flowers, and cones—is faultless. He said that hollow tops of the knees were used by the local people for making buckets and other objects.

Black bears, plentiful in the swamp during his day, were, he said, noted for their ability to find honey in hollow trees. He told of honeycombs as long as eighteen feet. But he had much more to say about the rabbits. They were so plentiful that as many as thirty could be killed in a day with little trouble. He ridiculed the prevalent folklore that claimed rabbits changed their sex with the seasons—no females being found in winter and no males in summer. He was less discriminating concerning folklore about snakes. He did not question the statement by a neighbor who said a rattlesnake had swallowed a young fawn. He wondered about the oft-repeated statement that snakes mesmerize their victims and thought perhaps rays of light reflected from the snake's eyes might have such an effect. He stated that snakes were never found in the cypress swamp until after it was burned or logged, which is fairly accurate.

Several species mentioned by the anonymous writer have since disappeared from the swamp and the entire peninsula. The black bear was last seen in the Great Cypress Swamp in 1906, and the timber rattlesnake may have disappeared even earlier. Among poisonous snakes, only the copperhead is left for peninsula inhabitants to worry about.

Even before timbering and the other woes that overtook the Great Cypress Swamp, the swamp had an implacable enemy—fire. In dry years, according to the anonymous writer, frequent fires invaded the swamp, "very much lessening the number of green, as well as of bald cypresses."

He described a "terrible conflagration" that began in June, 1782, and burned for many weeks. Three thousand acres of woodland were destroyed, the flames rising to a hundred feet, trees falling, and "the atmosphere full of live coals rising to amazing heights and appearing like flaming meteors." At one point he and his family were in peril because of the smoke. By lying down and breathing as close to the ground as possible, they were able to survive until a change in wind direction gave relief. Flames from the fire, he said, could be seen seventy miles away.

In considerable detail he described what he called a "raining tree." His son, emerging from the swamp one day in September, 1778, discovered a tree that seemed to produce a continuous "shower of fine rain." They watched the tree, an old black gum, for a period of years. Spells of "rain" were observed in late summer in some years and not in others. What he and his son may have been witnessing was occasional late-summer infestations of the tree by cicadas. Ejecting juice sucked from the foliage of the tree, swarms of these insects are capable of producing a rainlike mist. Trees subject to such infestations are sometimes called rain trees. It is worth noting that in 1985 a rain tree was discovered in the Nassawango Creek Swamp, in the same watershed as the Great Cypress Swamp. That tree was a sweet gum.

Thomas Nuttall, a botanist and ornithologist who paid a two-day visit to the swamp in 1809, took a different view of it

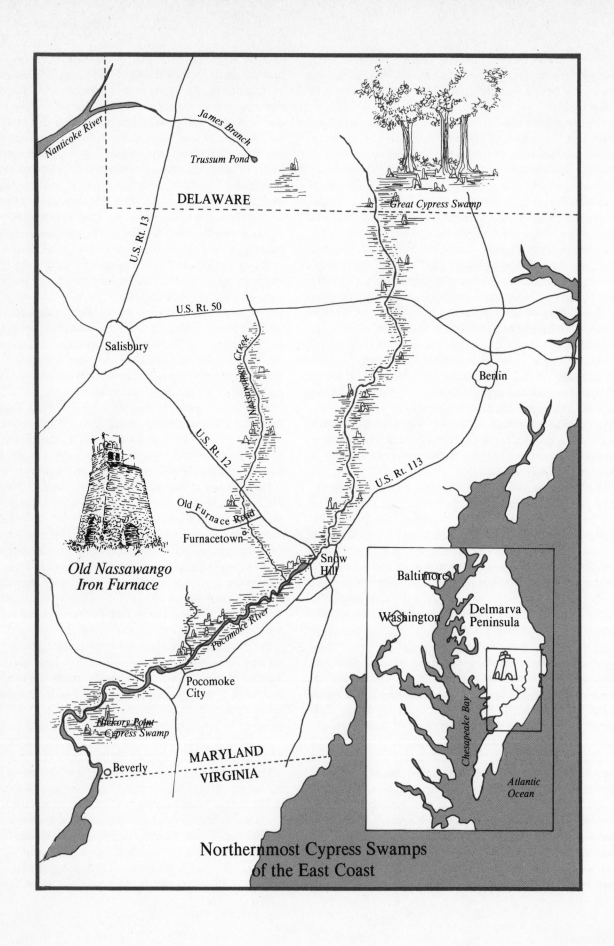

Nanticoke River

James Branch

Trussum Pond

DELAWARE

Great Cypress Swamp

U.S. Rt. 13

U.S. Rt. 50

Salisbury

Berlin

Nassawango Creek

U.S. Rt. 12

U.S. Rt. 113

Old Furnace Road

Furnacetown

Snow Hill

Old Nassawango Iron Furnace

Pocomoke River

Pocomoke City

Hickory Point Cypress Swamp

MARYLAND

Beverly

VIRGINIA

Baltimore

Washington

Delmarva Peninsula

Chesapeake Bay

Atlantic Ocean

Northernmost Cypress Swamps of the East Coast

from the anonymous writer of a few years before. Only twenty-three years old at the time of his visit and mainly interested in discovering new plants, Nuttall found the swamp to be "one of the most frightful labyrinths you can imagine." With a local guide, he entered the swamp by way of a causeway constructed of logs—probably a logging road. If one stepped off the causeway, he said, one would be knee-deep in ponds filled with sphagnum moss. Two species of water-lilies grew in the ponds, and cypress trees stood at their edges. Open areas, called savannahs, were dry in summer and wet through much of the rest of the year. Nuttall collected forty-three kinds of plants on his trip. Besides the expected ones, he found red bay, a wetland tree not previously known that far north. The plant has disappeared and been found again in the swamp since Nuttall's visit. Currently, it is once again missing. He had little to say about the fauna except that bears were frequently to be met with. As many as seven had recently been caught.

Nuttall, happiest when exploring little-known territory, conducted his most successful expeditions in newly opening frontier lands in the Mississippi and Missouri valleys. Like John James Audubon, who was visiting that part of America at about the same time, he was in the habit of floating down rivers on a flatboat. But, according to Virginia S. Eifert, he was oppressed by the silence of the dank, dark bottomland forests along the Mississippi, with their endless stretches of willows and cottonwoods. And he did not find much of botanical interest. Unlike the anonymous writer of the late eighteenth century, Nuttall was not a lover of swamps.

Today the boundary-line region, where the Great Cypress Swamp laps over into Maryland, is more like the swamp of the anonymous writer and Nuttall. The trees are larger, and if one is traveling south, sizable cypress trees make their appearance for the first time. Sweetleaf, a small southern tree that is at its northernmost limits here, is plentiful. The same is true of water oak and muscadine grape, both also at their northern limits. American holly is the common understory species. Within this forest is a dead pine tree that for years has held an active nest of the bald eagle. Bird watchers know the region as the place to go to look for the rare Swainson's warbler. Four or five nesting pairs in the area and another small colony downstream represent the northernmost populations of this swamp-loving warbler.

Southward only a few miles the swamp narrows and the Pocomoke becomes little more than a drainage ditch as its flows in a southwesterly direction toward the Chesapeake Bay. Not until the town of Snow Hill, about halfway between the Big Cypress Swamp and the bay, does the river widen and take on the picturesque beauty for which it is noted. Cypresses follow the river along its course on both banks, and there are few signs of human habitation except at Snow Hill and a few miles downstream at Pocomoke City, a medium-sized town. For much of its length the river is flanked by protected lands in the form of wildlands, recreation areas, and forests owned by the state. Absence of high ground at the river's edge has made it difficult for developers to take advantage of the river's scenic beauty.

Jay Abercrombie, in his guidebook for hikers and naturalists on the Delmarva Peninsula, states that the river and its swamps were an important link in the Underground Railroad. Escaping slaves followed the river north to Delaware and, if they were lucky, found their way to eventual freedom. But not infrequently these fugitives were captured and returned to the South. The notorious Patty Cannon, who lived on the Delaware-Maryland line, was one of the most active of the low characters who made their living by murder and intercepting fugitives seeking their freedom. She had no qualms about murdering slave dealers who stopped at the inn where she conducted her nefarious business. With the help of a gang of desperadoes, she pursued her work of kidnapping and murder until finally brought to justice in 1829. But three weeks before her execution, she took poison and died in agony. For years afterward, black mothers would quiet their young children by telling them, "Hush or Patty Cannon will git you!"

In justice to the Pocomoke River, which witnessed enough dark crimes without help from Patty Cannon, it should be pointed out that the river where she shipped most of her captives south was the Nanticoke. Like the Pocomoke, the Nanticoke has its source in Delaware, but it takes a more northern course to reach the Chesapeake. Both bald cypresses and Atlantic white cedars, sometimes growing side by side, are found in portions of its watershed. The best stands can be found at Trussum Pond and James Branch in the southwestern corner of Delaware. Thanks to Delaware Wild Lands and the Delaware state government, cypress swamps in this area are well protected.

To return to the Pocomoke, two miles below Snow Hill it is joined by a tributary called Nassawango Creek. That stream, flowing in a southeasterly direction, is noted for its iron ore deposits and the old furnace in which the ore was refined. The creek, and the Pocomoke River, were once busy arteries for the transport of iron to northern markets and return cargoes of oyster shell used in the smelting process. Prospectors discovered the iron ore deposits in 1788, but after the building of a smelting furnace, a village for workmen, and a canal for transporting the finished product, and numerous other delays, it was 1830 before the actual production of iron began. The bog iron, dug from the swamp with pickaxes, was hauled by oxcart and barge to the furnace. There it was stacked inside the furnace between layers of oyster shell and charcoal. In order to create draft to heat the interior of the furnace to the required temperature of 2,500° F, a bellows, operated by a water wheel, was installed at the base of the furnace. The entire edifice, built of stones and brick and rising to a height of thirty-five feet, was erected upon a platform of cypress logs. The logs were used as a foundation after it was discovered that the site was soggy ground. Over a century and a half later, excavations revealed that the cypress logs were still intact and supporting an edifice weighing hundreds of tons. Few greater tributes could be paid to the enduring qualities of this wood!

For a while the furnace enterprise, backed by money and skills from states to the north, thrived. A town, appropriately called Furnace Town, was built on high ground nearby. Besides many simple homes for workers, the town had an imposing overseer's residence, a store, a hotel, a church, a tavern, a gristmill, a blacksmith shop, a sawmill, and a warehouse. For about twenty years smoke belched from the furnace's chimney, oxcarts hauled in ore and charcoal, and barges were loaded and unloaded at the edge of the canal. It was a scene of intense activity and evident prosperity. But during the 1840s, better iron ore was discovered and shipped east from the upper Great Lakes region. Nassawango and its furnace could not compete. The enterprise was abandoned. It was not long before the buildings in the empty town began to crumble. The furnace itself, a more solid structure, was soon engulfed in a carpet of vegetation. Like a Mayan ruin, it reached above the trees that surrounded it.

By 1900 the only inhabitant of the deserted town was an elderly black man whom local people called Sampson Hat. He lived alone in a hut with his black cat and foraged for food in the surrounding forest. He was a skilled hunter and therefore needed little from the outside world. His one request was that he and his cat be buried on the grounds of the furnace. But before he died, he was removed to a home for the elderly. His request that he be buried at the furnace was not honored, and according to local tradition, his ghost haunts the old ruins on windy nights. His black cat can also be heard caterwauling somewhere in the darkness. For most people, that was reason to avoid the vicinity of the furnace after darkness fell.

Another legend, this one going back to the time when the furnace was active, purported that entire teams of oxen, and the wagons to which they were hitched, sometimes disappeared in quicksand. That tale appears to be apocryphal in view of the apparent absence of any quicksand in the swamp at the present time. But one always needs to be alert about one's footing in almost any swamp. There are soft, muddy places where a person can sink in to his waist, and there are also stump holes created by rotted-out stumps and roots of trees. Under the present management policies of the Nature Conservancy, the current owner of most of the swamp, sticks are placed in old stump holes so that the unwary hiker will be able to avoid them.

If one knows where to look in the swamp, he can still see signs of the earlier exploitation of its iron ore and also outcrops of bog iron. Slag heaps, charcoal-permeated soil, oyster shells, and piles of unrefined bog iron tell of the activity that once took place in the vicinity of Furnace Town.

The geological process that resulted in the deposition of bog ore in and near the creek took place over thousands of years in an environment in which sand, particles of iron, and water existed in just the right combination. Rainwater, soaking down through fallen cypress needles and other forest litter, takes on enough acid to leach out iron from the sands below; the dissolved iron moves underground into the winding creek, where it oxidizes on contact with the air and forms a patch of scum on the water's surface. The color may be rust brown, iridescent blue, or a combination of the two. Many people today see what to them appears to be an oil slick, and they wonder if the creek has somehow received pollutants. Of course, that is not the case. The oil-like slick eventually permeates the sandy soil at the edge of the creek, leading to the formation of a sandstone composite known as bog iron. In many places along Nassawango Creek, particularly above the old furnace, one can find deposits of bog iron ranging from ten inches to a foot in thickness. In some places the entire bed of the creek is a solid mass of bog iron. The geological process that created these formations is still going on. For proof one needs only to see the slicks and the ore that lines the creek.

Like the Pocomoke River, Nassawango Creek is a cypress swamp in which bald cypress grows alongside red maple, black gum, sweet gum, loblolly pine (in the higher sites), and sweet bay. In contrast to Pocomoke River cypresses, which are mostly 130 years old or younger, many of those on Nassawango Creek are 300 years old or older. Except where the cypress trees are growing in bottoms of old millponds, they are widely scattered and not in solid stands. In areas of dense shade, there is little or no regeneration. But other tree species are not as firmly rooted in the soil as the cypresses. Therefore, windstorms see many of them uprooted. As many as ten or more fallen red maples and sweet gums can sometimes be seen in one small area. Openings left by fallen trees give the bald cypresses a chance to regenerate. The same can be said of Atlantic white cedars, which are much less common here than bald cypresses.

After the iron furnace closed down, quiet settled upon the winding creek and the swamp forest along its banks. It was not long, however, before the area was once again a setting for the time-honored practices of fishing, hunting, logging, and escaping from authority. Deserters used the swamp as a refuge during the Civil War, and bootlegging, an important occupation, thrived under the dense canopy of oaks, maples and bald cypresses. During Prohibition, customers could leave empty jugs at appointed locations and on their return from a trip to town find them filled.

A new era for the creek and the old furnace began in 1966, when the Worcester County Historical Society initiated efforts to restore the furnace property and its ruins. The society's work has progressed ever since under the direction of the Furnace Town Foundation. Presently a large-scale

The roots and buttressed base of a cypress tree
at Wakulla Springs, Florida

*The wood duck, a major disseminator
of cypress seeds*

*The closely appressed needles
of pond cypress*

A cypress seed ball

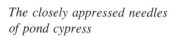

(right) *A giant cypress tree in
the Great Dismal Swamp*

Buttressed or swollen bases are seen in these cypresses and water tupelos. Such swelling is an adaptation to high water levels.

(left) *The circumference of a tree is measured by tape at breast-high level. This one is a record overcup oak.*

Blue-gray gnatcatcher

(right) *Carolina wren in a sycamore*

Fungi on a decaying log

*A forest of cypress knees at the edge
of Reelfoot Lake*

Canoeists on Nassawango Creek

Winterberry holly
(Ilex verticillata)

(right) *Red maple in the fall,*
Nassawango Creek

Rankin's yellow jessamine
(Gelsemium sempervirens)

Cardinal flower
(Lobelia cardinalis)

(left) *Spider lily* (Hymenocallis crassifolia)

Flowering dogwood (Cornus florida)

(right) *A fern-covered forest floor in the Big Thicket*

Blossom of a southern magnolia
(Magnolia grandiflora)

renovation is under way, which includes restoration of the furnace and portions of the old town. Several buildings from the town's historical period have been moved to Furnace Town. The historical society owns a tract of twenty-five acres that includes the heart of the Furnace Town operation and a portion of the swamp.

A second undertaking, aimed at preserving the swamp, with its rich flora and fauna, began in 1979 with a first purchase of land by the Nature Conservancy. Since then, the Conservancy has added to its holdings and now has title to 2,689 acres—most of the Nassawango watershed from the Pocomoke River to the creek's headwaters, a distance of eighteen miles. A stewardship committee, headed by Joseph W. Fehrer of Snow Hill, busies itself with maintenance of trails, posting signs, and all the other work that goes into proper care of a preserve of this size. Hiking and canoeing are now the chief recreational activities in the swamp, though bird watching takes first place in late spring and early summer.

In June, 1981, Chandler S. Robbins, well-known ornithologist and writer of bird guides, conducted a series of twenty-minute counts of birds seen or heard in the swamp. At fourteen listening posts scattered through the swamp, he recorded fifty-two breeding species. At every one of those stopping places he recorded the yellow-billed cuckoo, Acadian flycatcher, tufted titmouse, red-eyed vireo, and prothonotary warbler. At every point but two or three, he recorded the red-bellied woodpecker, downy woodpecker, wood thrush, white-eyed vireo, Louisiana waterthrush, common grackle, cardinal, and scarlet tanager. Red-shouldered hawk and pileated woodpecker were found at more than half the points. Other common breeding species encountered were the great crested flycatcher, blue jay, Carolina chickadee, blue-gray gnatcatcher, yellow-throated vireo, worm-eating warbler, northern parula warbler, yellow-throated warbler, ovenbird, and Kentucky warbler.

Besides these common species, Robbins reported upon the presence of singing male brown creepers in cypress trees at two points. As extraordinary as it may seem to find this small bird so far from its northern breeding range in summer, it now appears that this is not so unusual. The brown creeper seems to have an affinity for cypress swamps. In a 1982 issue of *Maryland Birdlife* there are reports of the bird's presence at the Battle Creek Cypress Swamp in June; in addition, twenty-five or more brown creepers were reported at various stations in the Pocomoke and Nassawango swamps. Battle Creek is a hundred-acre cypress swamp on the western side of the Chesapeake Bay near Prince Frederick, Maryland. It is the only such swamp on Maryland's western shore, and like most of Nassawango Creek, it is owned by the Nature Conservancy.

The birdlife recorded by Robbins along Nassawango Creek is much the same as that of the Pocomoke Swamp and, for that matter, swamps throughout the South. Besides so-called rarities, the swamp offers many of the same birds that are found in the residential areas of towns and cities. As at Nassawango, swamps to the south have their resident downy and red-bellied woodpeckers, chickadees, tufted titmice, Carolina wrens, and cardinals. No matter how large or wild the swamp may be, those familiar birds will be present.

In a footnote to his report, Robbins reported seeing an odd-looking cat that was walking slowly along an old logging road. "It was slim, very long legged," he wrote, "and had a long tail curled up over its back." Reports of odd-looking cats are common in more southern swamps, where there is always a remote chance of spotting a cougar. Large size and a long tail are helpful in identifying this rare species. On the other hand, a short tail is a helpful clue to identifying the bobcat, an inhabitant of many larger swamps. But nothing helps with the animal seen by Robbins, which might have been an aberrant form of the domestic cat.

Cats of various colors, sizes, and shapes have been a part of the swamp's folklore since the days of Sampson Hat's black cat. A woman who lives at the edge of the swamp has owned a dozen or more cats over the years, and she tells me that all her black cats have met untimely ends. White cats, on the other hand, have fared much better. Presently there is a sleek and friendly white cat living at the old furnace. This differentiation based on color may be pure coincidence or imagination, but it is the fabric from which tall tales are woven.

The Pocomoke below Nassawango Creek widens slightly and receives the waters of several other small creeks. The river flows past Pocomoke City and several old plantations and then makes a wide bend just before brackish marshes make their appearance along both banks. Within the bend is an officially designated state wildland of over 1,500 acres containing Pocomoke cypress and Atlantic white cedar of the best quality. Known as the Hickory Point Cypress Swamp, the area is so inaccessible that not many people venture into it. Choosing a day in early May when the swamp was relatively dry, I was able to make my way into a part of the swamp where Atlantic white cedar, true to the anonymous eighteenth-century writer's description, "kept other trees at an awful distance." The cedars, tall and straight, shaded soggy ground covered with soft cushions of sphagnum moss. I spotted a palamedes butterfly as I came out of the swamp. As I learned later, Hickory Point contains the northernmost breeding colony of this typical swamp butterfly.

Red bay, no longer in evidence in more northern portions of the Pocomoke drainage, is present here. A rare orchid, southern twayblade (*Listera australis*), grows within the shadow of the Atlantic white cedars. In recent years bald eagles have taken to roosting in cypress trees in the swamp in winter. As many as fifty have been seen leaving the roost in the morning. The swamp also contains the other of the two colonies of Swainson's warblers known in the Pocomoke drainage.

Playing a role of their own in the history of the Pocomoke and its swamps were the Dennises, whose ancestral home stands on high ground just below the Hickory Point Cypress Swamp. The home, called Beverly, is on the east bank of the river not far from where it empties into the bay. The first of the line to reach our shores was Donnoch Dennis, who, from what little information my wife and I can obtain, arrived from Ireland as an indentured servant. He lived first in the Virginia portion of the peninsula, and there in 1661 he married a widow, also of Irish descent. When Lord Baltimore was offering land on the Maryland side of the state line, Donnoch promptly moved north, taking his family and cattle with him. He soon acquired extensive holdings on both sides of the Pocomoke near its mouth. Energetic, if not rebellious, by nature, he made a name for himself. He prospered and became High Sheriff, in spite of the fact he signed his will with a mark, indicating that he was illiterate. His descendants also prospered. Cattle, tobacco, and trade with the West Indies appear to have been the chief sources of their wealth. Cutting the cypresses that lined the river provided additional income. When Donnoch's grandson Littleton Dennis inherited the family's wealth, there was ample means at hand to build a magnificent Georgian mansion—the present-day Beverly. The house, not completed until after Littleton's death in 1774, was and still is a showplace.

Beverly was inherited by my great-grandfather, John Upshur Dennis, known for his business acumen and succession of wives. He was a large land- and slaveholder, and following family tradition, he shipped cypress to the West Indies and, in the same ships, brought back molasses. In 1838 he married his third wife, the beautiful Louisa Jane Holland, whom he won in a competition for her affections with his oldest son. His previous two wives, we suspect, had died in childbirth. Mortality was great among mothers and children in those days. Of the twenty-one children that he fathered during the course of his three marriages, only ten reached adulthood.

His successful wooing of Louisa Jane is a tale that has been passed down from generation to generation since the event occurred. Disconsolate over the loss of his second wife ten months earlier, he was seen only at mealtimes. A guest at Beverly that summer was the lovely Louisa Jane, whom a daughter by an earlier marriage had brought home from a school vacation. Gay and vivacious, she impressed everyone, including the oldest son. She seems to have kept the truth about her affections to herself, and when the time came for her departure, she gave everyone a fond farewell except the master of the house. He was nowhere in sight. But when she got in the carriage and the coachman started the horses down the lane, the saddened father suddenly appeared, saddled a horse, and disappeared down the lane in pursuit of the

carriage. Soon catching up with it, he slowed down to a trot and conducted a conversation with the startled Louisa Jane. We can only guess at what he said and what her response to him was. But we do know that she consented to marriage. She was eighteen and he was forty-five when the wedding took place.

Another event from about this time may have caused the successful suitor some embarrassment. The tombstone for his late wife arrived on the same schooner that brought a coach for the bride.

After John Upshur Dennis died, Louisa Jane, younger than many of the children by former marriages, was faced with the prospect of managing a huge estate and soothing the feelings of those who felt they had not received a fair share of the property. The year was 1851, and the Eastern Shore, no longer as prosperous as it had been, was soon to be torn over the question of slavery and the great conflict that grew out of it. Louisa Jane's iron will and considerable abilities saw the family through this period and the even more difficult days of Reconstruction. Although impoverished, they carried on in much the same way as before. Sons, for the most part, left home to obtain the best education that they could. Many became successful lawyers or combined law with politics. Daughters generally married.

When Louisa Jane died in 1900 at the age of eighty, the old plantation life was a thing of the past. To live on a large estate, one almost had to have a substantial outside income. Nevertheless, children and grandchildren clung to Beverly as long as they could. They had a strong love for the land. My father, Alfred P. Dennis, was one of those who came back to Beverly after a doctorate at Princeton and a teaching career. Following family tradition, he, too, cut timber and worked in the swamps with crews of men, a life filled with "toil, sweat, and mules," as he put it. He later served with the United States Department of Commerce in Europe and, finally, with the United States Tariff Commission in Washington. Like John Upshur Dennis, he married a girl of eighteen when he himself was forty-five. By this time, the family was much less prolific. Only my brother Alfred and I were left to carry on the family name.

The year 1910 saw a tragic event that cast a spell of gloom over Beverly and the river that flowed close by its portals. The river has long been known for its uncharted depths and unpredictable currents, and there have been many drownings in it. The Dennises knew the river well. They were brought up on the water, learning to fish, swim, and handle a boat at an early age—skills that I, too, learned as a boy in these waters.

On the afternoon of October 15, 1910, my uncle Henry Dennis, at the age of twenty-five and home on vacation from his job with an engineering firm in Massachusetts, decided, apparently on the spur of the moment, to go for a sail. He had returned to Beverly with his fiancée, his best friend, and his best friend's fiancée. It is not clear how it came about, but he embarked, not with his own fiancée, but with his friend's fiancée, the lovely Caryl Eaton, daughter of the president of Beloit College. Had there been a last-minute change in preferences? We do not know. But according to those who saw the departure, the couple left in a cheerful mood, and someone tossed them a bouquet of flowers.

Hours went by, and the couple did not return. Toward evening their sailboat was spotted idly drifting in the river and without human occupants. Two days later the bodies of the couple were found in the river. Obviously they were victims of drowning, but how it happened no one knows.

The next year, my father and his brothers sold Beverly to an aspiring couple who were relatives. But this man's wife could not stand the isolation or the mosquitoes. Soon Beverly was back in the hands of the family that had originally owned it. For some years a younger brother held on to it. Finally, with the financial reverses of the Great Depression, the old mansion had to be sold. Today, completely refurbished and with well-cared-for grounds, it stands as a reminder of a former way of life that once flourished on these shores.

When I visit there, I am as much interested in the old trees on the grounds as I am in the mansion. One of the trees, a bald cypress, is the Maryland state champion. Its height is not remarkable, but its wide trunk and gnarled base, with a network of roots and knees forming a platform at the river's edge, seem out of all proportion to other, smaller trees along the river. It is the first large tree that navigators see upon entering the river. This ancient landmark could well be over five hundred years old. Families have their day. But a cypress tree, given half a chance, seems to live on forever.

References

Abercrombie, Jay. *Walks and Rambles on the Delmarva Peninsula: A Guide for Hikers and Naturalists.* Woodstock, Vt., 1985.

Eifert, Virginia S. *Tall Trees and Far Horizons: Adventures and Discoveries of Early Botanists in America.* New York, 1965.

Ringler, Robert F. "The Season." *Maryland Birdlife,* XXXVIII (December, 1982), 135–43.

Robbins, Chandler S. "Visitation Report to the Nassawango Preserve Committee." Unpublished manuscript 1982. Copy in author's possession.

Traveling from north to south, one begins to find typical southern plants in southern Delaware and along the Pocomoke River and its tributaries. After one crosses the mouth of the Chesapeake Bay, the general aspect of the flora changes even more. Southern magnolia and crepe myrtle, planted by man, are in every town and along almost every street. On dunes close to salt water, sea oats (*Uniola paniculata*) make their appearance. A surprising number of other southern plants reach the northern limits of their ranges in the southeastern corner of Virginia. Several of these southerners, including American wild olive (*Osmanthus americana*), live oak (*Quercus virginiana*), and bluejack oak (*Quercus incana*), can be seen to best advantage at Seashore State Park, a 2,770-acre preserve in Virginia Beach. Woody vines, a part of every southern swamp, are conspicuous along the trails. Climbing hydrangea, at its northern limit, is at home growing on the trunks of many trees, especially cypresses. Muscadine grape, which reaches southern Delaware, is another of the woody climbers in the park, and so are supplejack and yellow jessamine, both at approximately their northern limits.

The park is also the place to find Spanish moss at its northernmost limit. This epiphyte, belonging to the pineapple family, festoons the trunks and branches of cypress trees growing in wet swales between ancient sand dunes now clothed with trees. Spanish moss grows abundantly at these sites and then all but disappears from the landscape until one reaches eastern North Carolina.

Painted turtles are common in the park's wetlands. And for those on this southward journey who have called every watersnake they have seen to the north a moccasin, here at last are water moccasins, or cottonmouths, within their home range.

Should anyone wonder if a bamboolike reed growing in low areas on the southwestern side of the bay is a true bamboo, the answer is yes. Cane or switch cane once covered vast areas throughout much of the South and as far north as the lower valley of the Ohio River. In the Chesapeake Bay region, cane occurs in small patches as far north as near Baltimore. From Virginia Beach and Norfolk southward, it is still a common plant and sometimes covers hundreds of acres of peat-filled boglands.

At Northwest River Park, about twenty miles south of Norfolk, I have found sizable stands of silky camellia (*Stewartia malacodendron*), a rare southern shrub also present in the Great Dismal Swamp. The white camellialike flowers of this shrub appear in April. At about the same time, the white blossoms of the Atamasco lily carpet the ground in parts of Northwest River Park and the Great Dismal Swamp to the west. This lily, as well as water tupelo, water ash, pond cypress, southern magnolia, swamp leucothoe, fetterbush, and titi, are at or close to their northern limits in southeastern Virginia.

Since this book devotes a whole chapter to the Great Dismal Swamp (see Chapter 8), here I will move on to a lesser-known wilderness area in North Carolina about ten miles south of the Virginia line. Merchants Mill Pond State Park, reached by driving west on Highway 158 from Sunbury and marked by an entrance sign on the left, is as good a place as any to obtain an introduction to the flora of the great swamps that lie to the south of Virginia and, in the Mississippi Valley, to the south of Illinois. The 2,500-acre park, with its 600-acre millpond, contains within its borders a surprisingly large sample of plants, both common and rare. No fewer than 165 species of aquatic and wetland plants have been identified within the park. This constitutes one of the most diverse assemblages of wetland plants in the mid-Atlantic region. Two outstanding rarities among them are featherfoil (*Hottonia inflata*) and yellow water crowfoot (*Ranunculus flabellaris*). Logfern (*Dryopteris celsa*), whose other stronghold is the Great Dismal Swamp, grows abundantly in a swampy area of the park.

The best way to explore Merchants Mill Pond is either to rent a canoe at the park headquarters or take one's own. The lake, formerly a beaver pond, was greatly enlarged by a dam built in 1811 to provide an ample source of water to turn the wheels of a gristmill. Bald cypress and water tupelo, growing in the old millpond, seem to have been subjected to stress from rising and falling water levels. The trees have responded to this condition by developing enormously enlarged basal buttresses. From a distance, their trunks, small compared with their swollen bases, look like matchsticks stuck in rounded mounds of putty.

The water tupelos, as well adapted to growing in standing

water as bald cypress, provide still another enormity. High on the trunks of many of them are curious swollen places. I was told by a botanist that these swellings were probably caused by infestations of mistletoe. A parasitic plant that is spread by seeds deposited by birds on branches of trees, mistletoe in the Southeast is most commonly found on red maple, tupelo, and black gum.

The misshapen cypress trees in the millpond are dwarfed by giants that grow upstream in a secluded backwater called Lassiter Swamp. Of a dozen large trees, one had a circumference that exceeded twenty feet and a knee that reached six feet. On higher ground near this grove are silky camellia bushes. The park also contains a rare wildflower—dwarf trillium. Long-leaf pine (*Pinus palustris*) once grew abundantly on high ground in this area. But here, and in southeastern Virginia, at its northern range limit, the tree has been virtually wiped out by overzealous cutting.

While viewing the botanical wonders of the park, one should watch for some of the many forms of wildlife found there. The millpond offers ducks and wading birds. Late spring and summer are best for herons, egrets, and other large wading birds; the winter is best for ducks. Of the more exciting birds seen in recent years, the anhinga, purple gallinule, glossy ibis, and white ibis deserve special mention. The park bird list now runs to about 160 species. A total of 26 species of fish have been recorded, 25 species of mammals, and 47 species of reptiles and amphibians.

As one becomes better acquainted with the flora, as more and more swamps are visited, it becomes apparent that certain plant species will be encountered over and over again. Like the cypress, they belong to the swamp. Some of them also grow in uplands; others are found only in the swamp, having become so adapted to its harsh conditions that they will grow nowhere else. Moreover, the swamp itself is divided into plant communities based upon slight differences in elevation and drainage. Plants adapted to the wettest part of the swamp, for example, are often absent from any other part of the swamp.

The visitor will soon discover that pines, for example, if they are present at all, are nearly always restricted to higher parts of the swamp. The pine most commonly found in swamps everywhere except in parts of the Mississippi Valley is the loblolly. The trees often reach a very large size. Pond pine, a small pine tree found from southern New Jersey to south-central Florida, is common in peat bogs but absent from river swamps. The opposite is true of spruce pine, a tree of slow-moving blackwater streams from south-central South Carolina to eastern Louisiana. This picturesque pine is one of the more common trees in Four Holes Swamp in South Carolina.

But it is in the swamp's wettest parts that one finds the forms of plant life most characteristic of the swamp. Besides the bald cypress and water tupelo, obvious components of flooded portions of the swamp, there is a small tree, usually less than thirty feet tall, that seems equally at home in standing water. This is Carolina ash, a swamp and bottomland tree found from southeastern Virginia to Florida and Texas. Given even the slightest protection from flooding, red maple makes its appearance in the wettest areas of the swamp. Seeds of this maple that lodge on old stumps of cypress and other trees have a way of sprouting and growing into large trees. The stump is utilized as both a perch and source of rich humus. When logging is accompanied by moderate drainage, red maple often becomes the dominant tree.

Not far behind red maple in occupying low ground is swamp tupelo, also known as swamp black gum. Not to be confused with water tupelo, which has much larger leaves and the ability to grow in standing water, swamp tupelo flourishes on ground slightly higher than the wettest part but not as high as where pines, oaks, and hickories make their appearance. In a number of swamps, swamp black gum grows in nearly solid stands covering hundreds of acres. This is true in parts of the Francis Marion National Forest in South Carolina and the Pearl River Swamp in Louisiana. In the Congaree Swamp in South Carolina, swamp black gum, along with sweet gum, red maple, and American holly, grows on boggy ground fed by springs. As already mentioned, slight differences in elevation account for rather abrupt shifts from one plant community to another. The tree that happens to be most common is usually the one that gives its name to the community. Hence, there are cypress swamps, maple swamps, gum swamps, and many other kinds.

Dominant trees reach up above the others and form the canopy. If the trees are growing close together, little sunlight will reach the ground. Under such conditions, few herbaceous plants will be found on the forest floor. Seasonal flooding also inhibits growth below the canopy and makes for parklike conditions. Examples of open parklike growth can be found in many swamps, including the Congaree Swamp, the Pascagoula Swamp in Mississippi, the Pearl River Swamp in Louisiana, and the Lower Cache River Swamp in Illinois. However, no matter how large the trees and how open the ground is beneath them, there will always be breaks in the canopy. Trees, regardless of their age, are subject to destruction from a wide range of agents. Aside from destruction by man, the most common means of losing trees in swamps seems to be windfall. Insecurely anchored by their roots, many trees, including the red maple, sweet gum, and oaks, topple over when the wind reaches a strong enough velocity. The fallen trees leave gaps in the canopy. These openings permit sunlight to get through, with the result that a dense, often luxuriant vegetation develops at ground level. The same thing happens when a swamp forest has been opened up through lumbering.

A second group of trees consists of those not tall enough to reach the canopy. The smaller trees—trees of immature growth and of species that never attain a great height—form the subcanopy. The ironwood is an example of a common swamp tree that never reaches any great height and therefore belongs to the subcanopy. At a still lower level are under-story species. In this group are still younger or dwarfed members of canopy species and also shrubs and small trees.

Finally, the ground floor of the swamp forest is dominated by a number of shrubs able to endure dense shade and highly moist conditions. Among the more common shrubs of the understory are dwarf palmetto, possum haw holly, sweet pepperbush, and spicebush. Cane may also be common in the understory. But it reaches its best growth in open forests and along sunlit borders. Judging from accounts going back to colonial days, vast areas of forests, including swampland, were parklike. An early writer stated that the trees were large and stood so wide apart that deer and buffalo could be seen at a long distance.

Woody vines, making up an important component of the swamp forest, are present in every plant community. In a struggle to reach sunlight, many of them climb to the tops of the tallest trees. Others are a part of the understory and sprawl over tree trunks, shrubs, stumps, and one another. The most insidious of these vines is poison ivy, which not only climbs high up into the trees but, if the forest is suffi-ciently open, forms low shrublike tangles that effectively block passage by foot. The greenbriers, equally insidious because of their thorny, tangled growth, compete with poi-son ivy for human disfavor. Like poison ivy, greenbriers become especially rampant after the forest has been opened up by lumbering.

Another vine looks menacing but harms only the small trees and shrubs that it engulfs in its folds. This is supplejack, or rattan, a smooth-barked vine that wraps itself like a snake around everything with which it comes into contact, includ-ing other supplejack vines. Among the welter of other vines that cling to whatever supports they can find are wild grape, peppervine, climbing hydrangea, Virginia creeper, cross-vine, and trumpet creeper. For those who are used to trumpet creeper stems no more than two or three inches in diameter, those growing in the swamps are giants. Nourished by rich soil and abundant moisture, the vines grow to the tops of the tallest cypress trees and have diameters as large as sizable trees. Vines measured in the Nassawango Creek Preserve in Maryland and Nottoway River Swamp in Virginia have stem or trunk diameters of between ten and eleven inches. Poison ivy and supplejack in these and other swamps had stems as big around as a man's arm. Chinese wisteria (*Wisteria sinen-sis*), which sometimes finds it way into swamps, wraps itself around trees in a deathlike grip.

The swamps are a home for two native wisterias. Far less rampant than the Chinese wisteria (which was introduced by man), the two are small vines that decorate the edges of waterways. Concerning these plants, the eminent botanist John K. Small wrote: "The most attractive spring-flowering plant in all the swamps is the native wisteria. This is a woody vine that climbs into the shrubs and trees and bears numerous drooping clusters of beautiful flowers. This species and an-other, which occurs in the Mississippi Valley, are the only representatives of the genus in the New World." American wisteria (*Wisteria frutescens*) is found in swamps from east-ern Texas to Florida and north to Virginia, whereas Ken-tucky wisteria (*Wisteria macrostachya*) is primarily a species of the Mississippi Valley.

If given slightly improved conditions, the herbaceous flora may become a more important element in the plant life of the swamp. Where flooding is not severe, the entire forest floor may become covered with ferns. Some species escape the hazards of flooding by adapting relatively secure lodging places. The resurrection fern attaches itself to limbs and trunks of trees; others, including the netted chain-fern, sen-sitive fern, and royal fern, escape the worst flooding by lodging on floating logs and the buttressed bases of large trees. Ferns reach their greatest development in southern Florida swamps, where the entire forest floor may become matted with them. The leather fern of Florida swamps has fronds up to twelve or fifteen feet in length.

So long as there is adequate sunlight, sedges and grasses become important components of the herbaceous flora. Many are adapted to open sites at edges of streams or even grow in water. Maidencane (*Panicum hemitomon*) grows not only at the edge of water but also well out into shallow parts of lakes and ponds. Growing in dense shade or in open areas, lizard's-tail (*Saururus cernuus*) is probably one of the most ubiquitous of the herbaceous plants. This water-tolerant wildflower can be recognized by its tiny white blossoms, which are in long spikes with drooping tips. Nettles of sev-eral species thrive in the same low ground where lizard's-tail grows. Two of the most common species, clearweed and false nettle, often take root on floating logs and rotting stumps. Together with ferns, St. John's-worts, and woody shrubs like Virginia willow, the nettles form a part of what is known as the floating log community. Members of this com-munity also find a toehold on cypress knees and tree but-tresses, where they achieve somewhat sunnier and drier sites than they might elsewhere.

The gloomy atmosphere of the swamp, which many early writers emphasized, loses its hold when the wildflowers are in bloom. Beginning in early spring with violets and jack-in-the-pulpit and lasting until the cardinal flower and jewelweed are through blooming in the fall, there is a steady profusion of blossoms that bring brightness and color to the rather somber greens of other plants and the blackness of sloughs and bayous. One of the showiest of the early flowers is the Atamasco, or Easter lily, a species found in low ground in the more eastern swamps. The equally attractive spider lily, also with pure white blossoms, is more widespread and lends its charm to edges of waterways. Swamp lily (*Crinum ameri-*

canum), like the others a member of the amaryllis family, blooms over much of the year in swamps from Florida to Texas.

Flowers with red or red-orange blossoms are not uncommon in the swamps. One of the earliest of the red-flowered plants is red buckeye, a shrub whose range coincides closely with that of the bald cypress. Its tubular red flowers appear in March or April. Crossvine, whose flowers are sometimes mistaken for those of trumpet creeper, begins blooming in April. The tubular flowers are red-orange on the outside and yellow within. The familiar trumpet creeper, as common in the swamps as it is in the uplands, blooms throughout the summer. Two wildflowers of the forest floor add their red blossoms to the gaudy reds that are found at higher levels. Indian pink presents its tubular blossoms, red on the outside and yellow within, as early as March. Much later, cardinal flower, with the brightest reds of all, presents its clusters of blossoms at favored locations along shady stream banks.

In many swamps yellow outdoes red by covering large areas of low, wet ground. Butterweed (*Senecio glabellus*), with yellow blossoms from early spring until mid-June, is responsible for much of the yellow. A member of the composite family, this invasive plant becomes particularly abundant where the swamp forest has been opened through logging. A more delicate wildflower, yellow jessamine is often in bloom before the trees have leafed out. This high-climbing vine presents its trumpet-shaped yellow flowers as early as March. The variety to look for in swamps from North Carolina to Florida is Rankin's yellow jessamine—recognized by its odorless blossoms.

From early spring into late summer, flowering shrubs add their blossoms to those of the plants already mentioned. Among the earliest to bloom and most beautiful are the azaleas. Most have pink or white blossoms. A white-flowered species, swamp azalea (*Rhododendron viscosum*) is noted for its highly fragrant blossoms that appear in summer. I became aware of an orange-blossomed species when, in late March, I was exploring the Escambia River Swamp in western Florida. This beautiful azalea turned out to be *Rhododendron austrinum,* a species with a limited range along the Gulf Coast. Swamp azaleas seem to do best in openings where some sunlight reaches them.

Stream edges are favored by the fringetree (*Chionanthus alba*), a small tree whose filmy white flowers appear in early spring. This tree, and also mountain laurel (*Kalmia latifolia*), share wet ground at edges of swamps in southern Delaware and nearby Maryland. In early summer the showy pinkish white flowers of mountain laurel stand out in contrast to its dark foliage and the equally dark tones of the swamp.

As our list grows, it reads more and more like a nursery catalog offering prized ornamentals for the yard and garden. Some of the plants I mention are strictly swamp species, whereas others are found in both swamps and uplands. Sil-verbell trees are found in both environments. The small white bell-shaped blossoms of these trees brighten the swamp in early spring. Later, white flowers in long, slender racemes appear on a swamp and bog shrub, titi. Its highly fragrant flowers are attractive to bees.

The swamp edge also makes its contributions. One of the most beautiful is flowering dogwood, which is at home in the understory of higher parts of the swamp. Even more common is swamp dogwood, a much less showy species with reddish branches and pale blue fruit. It also does well in wetter sections. The hollies, which grow in our yards and are thought of as upland plants, are better represented in the swamps than are the dogwoods. The largest and most handsome is American holly. It thrives in moist zones, drier than those where bald cypress grows but wetter, as a rule, than elevations where flowering dogwood is found. Other common hollies include dahoon, possum haw, and winterberry. The latter two lose their leaves in winter. Possum haw, common in the big river swamps, is tolerant of seasonal flooding. The viburnums, representing another group of ornamentals, bear clusters of creamy-white flowers and have showy, colorful fruits. The two common swamp species are arrowwood and southern witherod. The hawthorns, not so highly rated as ornamentals, are represented in swampland by two common species—green hawthorn and parsley hawthorn.

Shallow water at edges of ponds and slow-moving rivers will almost certainly be the home of two common aquatic shrubs—buttonbush and waterwillow. Buttonbush produces a succession of globular, buttony white flowers through the summer months. Waterwillow, also known as swamp loosestrife, produces small pink or purple flowers in its leaf axils in late summer.

Orchids, uncommon in many upland habitats, are sometimes abundant in boggy swampland and even common in the shade of the swamp forest. One of the most common and widespread species is ladies' tresses (*Spiranthes* spp.). Rose pogonia (*Pogonia ophioglossoides*), grass pink (*Calopogon pulchellus*), and water-spider orchid (*Habenaria repens*) are common in savannahlike wetlands supporting sphagnum moss. The green-fly orchid (*Epidendrum conopseum*), often half hidden in clumps of resurrection fern, is a tree or epiphytic species and is uncommon in the swamps where it is found.

Trilliums, in contrast to many orchids, do best in upland woodlands. But dwarf trillium is a rare bottomland species found at Merchants Mill Pond, Four Holes Swamp, and the Great Dismal Swamp. In some instances it is debatable whether this tiny wildflower is the variety *Trillium pussillum* var. *virginianum.* The form found in these swamps is smaller than dwarf trilliums elsewhere. Whatever the case, the flowers are snow white when they first appear; then they turn blue and finally violet.

An entirely different group of wildflowers is found in open

bodies of water. Called aquatics, they grow at edges of swamp waterways and ponds or blanket the surface of these waters. Edge species include the irises, pickerelweed, golden club, and arrowheads. The water-lilies, whose broadly heart-shaped leaves cover the surface of the water with a matting of green, provide the swamp with some of its most beautiful flowers. Well named, the fragrant water-lily produces an almost unending sequence of many-petaled fragrant white flowers throughout the summer. The blossoms are open only during the morning. Spatterdock, or yellow pond lily, outdoes its rival by offering a display of small yellow blossoms from April to October. The most striking of the water-lilies is American lotus, little different in appearance from the East Indian sacred lotus. The plant has huge parasol-like leaves and many-petaled yellow flowers on long stalks. In the Mississippi Valley, where the plant reaches its greatest abundance, entire bodies of water become covered with these plants.

Quite apart from the more decorative aquatic plants are submerged ones that clog waterways and deplete the oxygen supply in the water. These plants foul fishing lines and impede boat traffic. But to some extent, the same can be said of the aquatics already mentioned and floating ones such as water lettuce, duckweeds, floating ferns, and water hyacinth. The latter, one of the most troublesome of the aquatic plants, now covers thousands of acres of water surface in the Atchafalaya Swamp in Louisiana and is present in other swamps as well. It must be admitted, however, that its sky blue flowers brighten waters that otherwise might be dark and gloomy.

If anything is more closely associated in the popular mind with swamps than aquatic plants, it is Spanish moss. This bromeliad, draped from branches of cypress trees, gives the swamp its haunted look and makes the perfect background for a scene showing egrets and alligators. No artist would think of omitting Spanish moss from a work showing a truly southern swamp. Although Spanish moss reaches southeastern Virginia on the Atlantic Coast, it penetrates only as far north as southern Arkansas in the Mississippi Valley.

Wherever cypress is found, there are a group of other plants that almost always accompany it. A few of these are waterwillow, muscadine grape, water oak, and resurrection fern. Although cypress has its close associates, changes in the composition of the swamp flora do take place as one travels from north to south or from east to west. Along the way some plants drop out, and new ones take their place. There are also differences in flora seen between one kind of swamp and another. The plant life of big river swamps differs somewhat from that of smaller blackwater streams. Peat bogs have a somewhat different flora from stream and river valley swamps. It is therefore a misconception to regard all swamps as having essentially the same plant life. Swamps differ in topography, scenery, fauna, and flora. This is one reason they are so interesting and why a sizable number need to be visited before one has a clear concept of what they are like.

References

Dennis, W. Michael, and Wade T. Batson. "The Floating Log and Stump Communities in the Santee Swamp of South Carolina." *Castanea,* XXXIX (1974), 166–70.

Small, John K. "Old Trails and New Discoveries." *New York Botanic Gardens Journal,* XXII (1921), 25–40, 49–64.

5 / Hazards of the Swamp
Snakes, Insects, Spiders, and Getting Lost

Snakebite was one of my foremost concerns when I began visiting swamps. But as the years went by and no harm from snakes came to me, I put that fear behind me. I still watch where I step and back away if I see a snake in my path. From my point of view the snake always has the right-of-way—an attitude that I wish was more widespread. Persons who are bitten by snakes have nearly always provoked the snake either by accident or intentionally. Those who handle snakes run the greatest risk.

By keeping to cleared paths, watching where one steps, and wearing sensible footwear and clothing, a person can greatly minimize any chance of being bitten. On the grounds of both sound ecology and proper out-of-doors ethics, do not kill a snake! As an interesting and often useful part of our wildlife heritage, a snake deserves our sympathy.

Many people lump the poisonous cottonmouth with the water snakes. Although commonly seen in the water and easily mistaken for a water snake, the cottonmouth is a pit viper not related to the group to which the water snakes belong. The bite of the cottonmouth is far more serious than that of the copperhead and is potentially fatal. Not at all timid, the cottonmouth will often stand its ground when approached. Coiling and rearing its head back, it will often hold its mouth wide open in an intimidating display. The interior of the mouth is a cottony white; hence the name.

Once, while exploring Merchants Mill Pond State Park in North Carolina with my naturalist friend Gary Williamson, I was startled by an unfamiliar sound two or three feet in front of me. We had already encountered about a dozen cotton-mouths that day and therefore were watching closely where we stepped. It turned out that the noise came from the tat-toolike beating of the water's surface by the tail of a large cottonmouth. The warning came almost too late. Before I could move away, the snake made a lunge in my direction. In a split second I, too, made a lunge, but in the opposite direction and in time to avoid the snake. Although I do not wish to ignore the danger of such encounters, I am nonetheless convinced that the snake was only trying to get out of our way.

The cottonmouth is primarily a snake of backwaters and bayous. One looks for it in the dark, often stagnant waters of isolated ponds and sloughs. There it is often seen stretched out on piles of driftwood and fallen logs. In the water the cottonmouth swims with its head above water and the body close to and sometimes on the surface. Other snakes are much more likely to swim with only the head above water and body submerged. Unlike most other snakes, which disappear when cool weather sets in, the cottonmouth may be abroad on warmer days throughout the winter. Its range extends as far north as southern Illinois in the Mississippi Valley and along the Atlantic Coast approximately as far north as the York River in southeastern Virginia.

The cottonmouth so closely resembles the brown water snake that often one must carefully note a snake's markings to know which of the two it is. Both have a stout body, alternating dark and light bands across the body, and a diamond-shaped head. Both can act in a very aggressive manner. In a South Carolina swamp I found myself confronted by a brown water snake that had positioned itself at the base of a large tree. Like the cottonmouth, it coiled as though to strike and then lunged. I beat a hasty retreat. Since the snake did not show a cottony mouth, I knew I was not dealing with a cottonmouth. Still, the brown water snake is capable of inflicting an unpleasant wound if it strikes back on being cornered. It is one of the snakes that sometimes drops into a boat from an overhanging limb; it also may swim toward a small boat instead of away from it. In the habit of sunning itself while loosely draped on a branch anywhere from two to fifteen feet above the water, the seemingly somnolent snake has a way of suddenly dropping from its resting place.

Of the water snakes, which are such a conspicuous feature of the southern swamp, it can safely be said that the brown water snake is the most common species in the East. Somewhere down the list in terms of numbers are the red-bellied, banded, northern, glossy, and green water snakes. Gary Williamson, who makes a practice of counting the number of snakes he sees when taking a canoe trip, has seen as many as thirty-two brown water snakes on a stretch of the Blackwater River in Virginia and twenty-one along an approximately equal stretch of the Northwest River in the same state. Both rivers are in the southeastern portion of Virginia, not far from the Great Dismal Swamp. For those who canoe these and other southern rivers, it may be comforting to know that Gary finds the cottonmouth to be one of the snakes most seldom seen.

A similar situation holds true in regard to numbers in midwestern swamplands. There the diamondback water snake takes the place of the brown water snake. It is similar in appearance to the brown, equally as common, and is the water snake in that region that is most often confused with the cottonmouth. The Midwest has its races of eastern species and also the distinctively western Graham's water snake. Mud snakes, easily mistaken for water snakes, are found in both eastern and western swamps.

Of the larger snakes, no other group is better represented in southern swamps than the rat snakes. Beginning with the black rat snake in more northerly swamps, a number of intergradations based upon color are found from north to south. Rat snakes are expert climbers that spend much of their time in trees. During the nesting season they often prey upon eggs and young of birds. By keeping to trees, rat snakes are able to avoid high water in times of flooding.

Equally at home in the swamp or the uplands are secretive species such as the eastern and midwest worm snakes, the northern brown snake, the red-bellied snake, and the southern ringneck snake. A good place to find almost any of these small snakes is under boards and other debris around vacant hunting and fishing camps. During times of flooding, the smaller snakes, often in company with larger ones, take refuge on floating debris or climb high up into trees and shrubs. On one occasion when the Congaree River was in flood stage, Gary Williamson found a northern brown snake safely coiled in a bush well above flood level. The rough green snake, a common inhabitant of southern swamps, is largely arboreal and therefore completely at home in trees when the water is high.

Snakes that can be classed as occasional visitors to southern swamps include the black racer, the hog-nosed snake, the corn snake, the coachwhip, and the garter snake. The ribbon snake, a close relative of the garter snake, is semiaquatic and almost as much at home in a swamp habitat as are the water snakes. Deserving of its nickname "the Swamp Wamper," the eastern king snake can sometimes be seen swimming rivers and making its way into the dark recesses of cypress-studded islands. The king snakes are cannibalistic in that they frequently prey upon other snakes, including poisonous ones. A king snake in a swamp is probably seeking out other snakes or, another part of its fare, turtle eggs.

For those who are timid about snakes, it must be admitted that the southern swamp has its share of poisonous and nonpoisonous snakes. Besides the cottonmouth, visitors to southern swamps should be on their guard for the copperhead, the canebrake rattlesnake, and, less likely, the pygmy rattlesnake and the coral snake. In years of visiting southern swamps, I have had few encounters with poisonous

snakes other than the cottonmouth. Often one can visit a swamp for days at a time without seeing a snake of any kind. Much depends upon weather and water conditions. Moist, warm late spring weather with periods of sunshine seems to bring snakes out of their hiding places. Whenever there is a big flood, the newspapers are inevitably full of accounts of snakes fleeing to higher ground.

Another worry is biting insects. The tales of past swamp explorers would probably make many persons think twice before visiting a southern swamp. Charles Torrey Simpson, writing in 1920 about a plant-collecting trip in the Cape Sable region of south Florida, told of murderous hordes of mosquitoes that made life almost unbearable for himself and his companions. "The insects," he wrote, "covered the exposed parts of my body until the skin could not be seen, and when I wiped them off blood dripped on the ground. With puffed cheeks and eyelids I could scarcely see and, thoroughly poisoned, I felt stupid with a desire to lie down anywhere and sleep." He went on to tell of well-authenticated cases in Florida and elsewhere of death from mosquito attack.

Today, with our insect repellents and ways of reducing mosquito populations, we will not encounter anything as frightful as the onslaughts described by Simpson. Nevertheless, as I have discovered, those who visit the mangrove swamps in the Cape Sable region, in what is now Everglades National Park, can still expect considerable discomfort during "mosquitoey" times of the year. But much depends upon the swamp and the season. Speaking of more northern swamps, there will be an almost total absence of mosquitoes from about October until mid-April or later. Even after warm weather sets in, mosquitoes in swamps may be no worse than anywhere else or even conspicuous by their absence. As a rule, the less the swamp is altered by man and his livestock, the fewer the mosquitoes. Formerly, when parts of the Okefenokee Swamp were being grazed by cattle, mosquitoes were said to have bred in rain-filled hoof marks left by the animals. There the mosquito larvae were safe from attack by small fishes. C. H. Wharton, writing of Four Holes Swamp in South Carolina, said mosquitoes abounded in recently cut sections. They found ideal breeding places in water-filled ruts made by heavy machinery. On the other hand, he found a striking lack of mosquitoes in uncut portions of the swamp.

When malaria was so prevalent in the South, it was a common notion that the disease had its origin in the swamps. Even breathing the air or vapors that emanated from the swamp was thought to be injurious to one's health. Yet Nathaniel S. Shaler, speaking of malaria in the vicinity of the Great Dismal Swamp in the 1880s, reported that "people who dwell in the interior of the swamp appear to be less affected by such maladies than those who live on the ordinary upland surface of Virginia and North Carolina."

Still another testimonial regarding absence of malaria is

provided by C. T. Trowell in a book on the Okefenokee Swamp. He stated that there is no record of any deaths from malaria or "swamp fever" in the Okefenokee Swamp. He did admit that mosquitoes are sometimes abundant: "Mosquitoes can breed and swarm in overpowering hordes during rainy-warm periods in the swamp. On one night not a mosquito is noted; on the following night millions appear."

I have rarely been bothered by mosquitoes on visits to the Okefenokee Swamp and am tempted to believe that small fishes and aerial predators, such as birds and dragonflies, keep mosquitoes under control except under exceptional circumstances. Thus, it is only when mosquitoes outbreed their predators that are they likely to become serious nuisances.

My greatest tormentors, in the Okefenokee Swamp and several other swamps as well, have been fire ants. Well adapted to wetland habitats, these newcomers to our shores, which appeared back in the 1930s, build their nests on open ground, in rotting stumps, and even on floating vegetation. One day as I was testing one of the Okefenokee's floating islands with a bare foot and my trouser's leg rolled up, I suddenly found my bare skin invaded by swarms of biting ants, each of them injecting an irritating poison with each bite. They left dozens of reddish welts that pained me for days. The welts did not disappear until months later.

If a person watches carefully where he sits and steps, he can avoid these fiery demons. Limited to warmer parts of the country, they are as common in uplands as in swamps. They have an amazing way of adapting to flooding. C. C. Lockwood, writing of the Atchafalaya Swamp in Louisiana, stated that fire ants in times of high water form a floating ball that rolls over and over, permitting the ants to take turns being underwater. Still another description, this one in a letter to me from J. Merrill Lynch, a biologist with the Nature Conservancy, tells of entire colonies of fire ants floating down the Suwannee River during times of flooding. Lynch noted that each individual clung to a neighbor with its mandibles and legs, thereby forming a living boat.

Another form of insect life to watch out for are wasps. Paper wasps (Vespidae) frequently build their nests in low branches a few feet above the water. If a boat passes close to such a nest, the wasps will come swarming to the attack. The Wrights, man and wife, who explored the Okefenokee Swamp early in this century, told of hardships from biting flies during the day and mosquitoes at night. But they reserved their greatest ire for the hidden wasp nests along boat routes and overland trails. The wasps would be right on a person, they state, before he was even aware of their presence.

My review of biting insects would not be complete without some mention of biting flies. Hot summer days when the air is still are apt to bring them out in force. Gary Williamson, writing to me about a canoe trip he took with his son Todd in the Alligator River National Wildlife Refuge in North Car-

olina, stated that they were "almost eaten alive by yellow flies." He was speaking of horseflies or deerflies (family Tabanidae). The blood-sucking females freely attack man and animals.

Everyone has his own recipe for keeping away biting insects. I almost never use an insect repellent. But if biting insects are abroad, I wear a hat and keep my body well protected with clothing. I avoid hair oils, skin lotion, and the like. As a rule, the more one doctors oneself with lotions, the more likely one will be pestered by insects. Apparently an exception to the rule is Skin so Soft, by Avon, a lotion that seems to be an effective mosquito repellent.

Sometimes when biting insects are present in large numbers, the only recourse is to stay away from a swamp. If one waits a few days or weeks, it is likely that a balance will be restored and that he can visit the swamp without being tormented.

For the spiders, which, like other invertebrates, are abundant inhabitants of southern swamps, I have gone to L. L. Gaddy, coauthor of *Common Spiders of South Carolina,* for information. He writes me that the web weavers—especially orb weavers—are the most conspicuous spiders in forested wetlands. Their relatively large size and the size of their webs gain the attention of the canoeist paddling in the black water of a cypress swamp or the hiker on a nearby forest trail. Some orb-weaver webs may be several feet across, and their occupants two to three inches in diameter. These facts, however, need not frighten one away from swamps. The size of the spider bears little relationship to its ability to be a hazard to humans. For example, the black widow (*Latrodectus mactans*) and the brown recluse (*Loxosceles reclusa*), both quite dangerous and generally absent from swamps, are smaller than most large orb weavers. Furthermore, orb weavers rarely bite; instead, they flee when their web is destroyed by the hiker or boater.

Along the Gulf Coast and along the Atlantic Coast north to the Savannah River, the golden silk spider (*Nephila clavipes*) is common in forested wetlands. This beautiful orb weaver may have gold-tinged webs up to six feet across. Gary Williamson and I have encountered it as far apart as the Honey Island Swamp on the Pearl River in Louisiana and the lower Altamaha River in Georgia. We have always been struck by the size of this spider and its web. In inland and more northern swamps, spiders of the genera *Araneus* and *Neoscona* are the dominant orb weavers. The giant *Araneus bicentenarius* may be locally common in some floodplain forests and cypress swamps, and *Neoscona domiciliorum* is abundant in floodplains in late summer. Both species are found in the Congaree Swamp, according to Gaddy, and the latter is ten times as common as any other orb weaver in that swamp. Other orb weavers commonly seen in forested wetlands are the spiny-backed orb weavers of the genera *Micrathena* and *Gasteracantha*. The spines, though they appear dangerous, do not contain toxins; instead they exist to deter predation by birds.

Numerically, the dominant spiders in the floodplain forests are probably the ground-dwelling wolf spiders. In the Congaree Swamp, the false wolf spider (*Schizocosa crassipes*) is ubiquitous in leaf litter. It escapes flooding, according to Gaddy, by scaling trees or running across the surface of the water. In cypress and cypress-gum swamps, fishing spiders (genus *Dolomedes*) are abundant. These large spiders do not build webs but actually dive underwater and capture small prey, including small fish. They are most active at night, when they emerge from stumps and tree cavities. A fishing spider readily runs or walks on the surface of the water. If disturbed, it promptly dives and disappears from sight.

Although a common part of the swampland fauna, the spiders are not a source of danger and, if anything, are an attraction because of their bright coloration and interesting behavior. The only trouble they cause is the minor inconvenience of having their webs get entangled with clothing, glasses, or hands as one brushes against them.

Getting lost is a very real possibility in the swamps. I consider it a greater hazard than anything else I have mentioned so far. Without a compass or the knowledge needed to use the sun as a guide, it is amazingly easy for someone to become lost almost as soon as he leaves a trail or logging road. Upon losing one's way, the tendency is to walk in circles. The winding watercourses that form such a network of channels in many of the swamps offer little help. Charting a course along one of them will often bring the lost person right back to his starting point. A hunter who had been lost for several days in the Congaree Swamp is said to have spent his time following one watercourse after another. Harry Hampton, who did so much to preserve this swamp, said the hunter had become so demented by his experience that he ran away from his rescuers. Although Hampton may have exaggerated, there are more than enough examples of hardships endured by persons who have lost their way among a labyrinth of waterways.

Hampton, who acted as my adviser on my visits to the Congaree Swamp, always insisted that I take a compass and a geological survey map with me on my trips into the swamp. His advice served me well. Only once did I meet with difficulties. Having failed to allow enough time to get back to camp before dark, I found myself struggling through dense growth with scarcely enough light to see my way. Luckily, I came to within earshot of our camp and was guided to safety by friends with flashlights.

The plight of those who get lost in a large swamp and cannot find their way out before nightfall is vividly described by Albert H. Wright, who, with a small party, was exploring the heart of the Okefenokee Swamp in June, 1912. After leaving their small boat near Minnie's Lake, Wright and his friends set out by foot to the northeast. In his notebook he speaks of cutting a trail through tangled vines and briers with a machete. "After a mile or so," he wrote, "we hewed to due west. At 3 P.M. it looked rainy and Bryant climbed a bay and announced himself 'befuddled.' In other words we were lost. We cut boughs and camped on the swamp itself at the base of an immense dead pine. While we were cooking, a pair of pileated woodpeckers stopped nearby. Next we heard the cypress-bay warbler, the Swainson's Warbler, on our trail back. We were eating at 5:48 P.M. in the worst tangle I was ever in. Can not conceive of a wilder place in the U.S.A. than this spot where we are encamped." He goes on to tell of mosquitoes, yellow flies, and the rain. Their supper was corn bread and coffee. But they did manage to pitch a small tent and lie down on a poncho placed over a pile of boughs.

As for getting around in a swamp, a lot depends upon water levels and whether the woods are littered with slash and debris from lumbering operations. If the swamp is flooded, there is no other choice but to use a boat. A boat with a motor is too noisy for my purposes, and in a boat I cannot readily stop to look at birds or plants. But for covering long distances and getting a general overall impression of a swamp, a boat trip can be useful. One can sometimes locate the best stands of trees from a boat and see deer, waterfowl, and large wading birds and their nesting colonies. But if I am going to travel by water, I much prefer a canoe to a motorboat. Canoeing is a much quieter and more thorough way of seeing a swamp. Many of us who explore southern swamps make a practice of putting our canoe into the river or stream at some point and paddling downriver with the current to a convenient spot where we have left a vehicle on which to put the canoe once we disembark.

Travel by foot can be relatively easy if the water is low and one does not mind wading across sloughs and areas with standing water. But much depends upon whether the forest has been opened up by lumbering in recent years and therefore is a tangle of slash, vines, briers, and other new growth. Only with the help of old logging roads can one make much progress in a badly timbered area that is starting to grow back. In time the old logging roads become overgrown, and they, too, are impassable.

During Audubon's day, vast stands of our native bamboo covered stretches of low-lying ground. One such canebrake at the eastern edge of the Great Dismal Swamp was said to cover an expanse twenty miles long. It was an impenetrable morass inhabited by canebrake rattlesnakes, small rodents, black bears, and wild cattle. Grazing and agriculture have made such inroads upon the canebrakes that only relatively small ones remain today. When confronted by these closegrowing bamboos, it is best to find a route around them rather than trying to fight one's way through. One can sympathize with Audubon, who in his account of his trip down the Mississippi, spoke of the difficulty of getting through green briers and canes.

In mentioning the hazards of the southern swamp, I certainly do not want to discourage people from visiting them. By knowing what lies ahead and taking proper precautions, the visitor can have a highly rewarding experience without encountering any hardships. It is important, however, always to carry a compass and, as an extra precaution, a map. For those who want to take advantage of national wildlife refuges, state parks, and nature preserves, there are any number that include swamp habitat that can be viewed conveniently by boat, boardwalk, or nature trail.

From the safety of a boardwalk, one can look down and perhaps view a number of reptiles and amphibians and, the next minute, look up and see a barred owl or pileated woodpecker. That is the easy way to see a swamp, but it is as good a way as any if you are pressed for time and not prepared to slog your way through in the manner of Albert Wright and his friends.

References

Gaddy, L. L., and J. C. Morse. *Common Spiders of South Carolina: With an Annotated Checklist.* Clemson, S.C, 1985.

Lockwood, C. C. *Atchafalaya: America's Largest River Basin Swamp.* Baton Rouge, 1981.

Shaler, Nathaniel S. "Fresh-Water Morasses of the United States." *U.S. Geological Survey Annual Report,* X (1890), 313–39.

Simpson, Charles T. *In Lower Florida Wilds.* New York, 1920.

Trowell, C. T. *The Suwanee Canal Company in the Okefenokee Swamp.* Douglas, Ga., 1984.

Wright, Albert H., and Anna A. Wright. "The Habitats and Composition of the Vegetation of Okefenokee Swamp, Georgia." *Ecological Monographs,* II (1932), 110–232.

In addition to the few bothersome or dangerous species, there are numerous other forms of wildlife that make their home in the swamp. The swamp fauna, in many ways, is as interesting as the cypress tree and the plant life associated with it. Many aquatic species have ancient lineages that can be traced back to Tertiary and Mesozoic times. Examples are turtles, alligators, garfishes, sturgeons, bowfins, and, among the amphibians, sirens. According to Charles H. Wharton and his coauthors, ancient forms mingle with more recent ones, and in many cases the older species have taken refuge in the swamp because of drastic changes in land use elsewhere.

Living side by side with rare species are successful ones that often exhibit an abundance unheard of in other habitats. Their success can be attributed to such factors as readily available food and relative freedom from disturbance by man. C. C. Lockwood, in his book on the Atchafalaya Swamp in Louisiana, wrote of billions of crayfish and of fish hauls containing as much as 1,191 and 1,426 pounds per acre. Studies at Reelfoot Lake, a cypress-fringed body of water in western Tennessee, revealed a surprising variety of insects and fish. For example, twenty-nine waterbug, thirty-five dragonfly, and twenty-eight mosquito species were listed for the lake. Fish were represented by over sixty species. Birds, attracted to the rich habitat by the easily obtainable food, were also abundant.

In western Florida, the lower course of a single river traversing a swamp forest had 118 species of fish, both freshwater and marine. The key to such species' diversity and richness is, according to Wharton and his colleagues, the pulsing of the wet and dry cycle in the floodplain forest. Floodwaters bring nutrients that support food chains beginning with lower organisms and ending, in many cases, with birds and mammals. The dry season permits new plant growth and helps many organisms progress through vital stages of their life cycles. Frogs, toads, and salamanders, for example, with few exceptions, go through an aquatic stage followed by a terrestrial or partly terrestrial stage. In contrast, bottomland communities that are either permanently flooded with slow-moving or stagnant water, or are regularly damaged by unusually high and destructive floods, are not so productive.

The peat lands of the Carolinas, for example, are subjected to little seasonal flooding. As a consequence they have a low nutrient turnover, which, combined with their low pH, makes them much less productive than the river swamps. They do, however, have outstanding value as a home for rare plants and wildlife.

The rest of this chapter provides accounts of forms of wildlife found in most swamp habitats. Some are restricted to swamps; others are found in upland habitats as well. It must also be pointed out that the swamps receive temporary visitors from the outside, particularly migrant birds that stop over briefly in a swamp to feed and rest.

Moths and Butterflies

Southern swamps are astonishingly rich in both moths and butterflies. In part such richness is due to the relatively undisturbed nature of the habitat and, in the case of many species, the presence of larval food plants. The cypress sphinx moth (*Isoparce cupressi*), found from South Carolina southward, lays its eggs on the foliage of the bald cypress. The sweet bay silk moth (*Callosamia securifera*) rears its young on the foliage of sweet bay. The promethea moth uses sweet gum, spicebush, and other plants found in southern swamps.

The zebra swallowtail, one of the common butterflies in many southern swamps, lays its eggs on pawpaw. The palamedes swallowtail, the single butterfly most often identified with swamp habitats, lays its eggs on red bay, sweet bay, and sassafras. The spicebush swallowtail uses spicebush, sassafras, and the bays. The great purple hairstreak chooses mistletoe, an epiphyte that grows much more abundantly, as a rule, in swamps than elsewhere. Hessel's hairstreak uses only Atlantic white cedar and hence has a limited range restricted to swamps where this tree grows. The pearly eye utilizes cane or switch cane, which grows plentifully in swamp habitats but which was once much more widespread. The red admiral, a butterfly that uses a number of larval food plants, is drawn to swamps by the presence of false nettle (*Boehmeria*).

Crustaceans

Crayfish, or crawfish, as they are sometimes called, make up a large proportion of the biomass (the total weight of living organisms) found in southern swamps. For example, crayfish are said to make up one-third of the faunal biomass of the Suwannee River Swamp in Florida. C. C. Lockwood, writing about the Atchafalaya Swamp, stated that Louisiana has twenty-nine species of crayfish and that forty-two million pounds were caught commercially in 1979. He added that crayfish need a dry summer and fall, a winter with standing water, and a spring rise in water level accompanied by warmer temperatures. That is the normal cycle in the Atchafalaya Swamp, and it is one that helps account for the fabulous richness of its wildlife. At the bottom of many food chains, crayfish support organisms from fish to birds and mammals. Birds that feed heavily on crayfish include the barred owl and white ibis. Crayfish feeders among mammals include the river otter and raccoon. A good season for crayfish is likely to mean a good season for a large share of the swamp's wildlife.

Fishes

In keeping with the timeless setting of the cypress swamp are primitive fish that seem as much at home in this environment as they must have been in Mesozoic times, when the dinosaurs flourished. Sturgeons, bony-plated fishes that show their kinship to sharks by having cartilaginous instead of bony skeletons, though greatly reduced in numbers, still ascend some of our rivers. The Atlantic sturgeon, found in the rivers of the Atlantic Coast and the Gulf Coast, seems to be holding its own.

A distant relative of the sturgeon, the paddlefish, with its long paddlelike snout, has the look of a shark but is perfectly harmless. Ranging up to weights of two hundred pounds, paddlefish are found in the Mississippi drainage and some Gulf Coast rivers.

The gars, or garfishes, with an equally long ancestry, are ideally suited for life in swamp waters. Along with the bowfin, another primitive fish common in these waters, they have air bladders that permit them to inhale air at the surface as water levels fall and the oxygen supply becomes depleted. The common species is the longnose gar, which is found in eastern as well as Mississippi Valley waters.

The belief that gars ruin fishing by preying upon game species is largely unfounded. Although they are fierce predators, they do not take a significant toll among fishes prized by anglers. To their credit, they improve conditions for game fishes by weeding out other species that might otherwise deplete food and oxygen supplies. The gars frequently swim close to the surface, churning the water with their bodies.

Sharing swamp waters with the groups already mentioned are the catfishes. From small ones only a few inches long, known as madtoms, to huge ones weighing up to ninety or a hundred pounds, they furnish food and sport to countless fishermen. The flathead catfish and the blue catfishes are the giants, and next come the channel catfish, which may weigh up to fifty pounds. The yellow bullhead is one of the most common and widespread of the catfishes found in southern swamps. It has hemoglobin in its blood, which helps it stay alive when the oxygen supply becomes depleted. When the Everglades dry out, large numbers of yellow bullheads gather in alligator holes.

So long as catfish have not been feeding heavily on human waste products, their flesh is an esteemed table delicacy. From Lake Okeechobee in Florida to Reelfoot Lake in Tennessee there is hardly a dining establishment near fishing grounds that does not serve catfish. Their ability to live in oxygen-poor and even polluted water makes them good candidates for the uncertain water of the southern swamp. Like the carp, American eel, gar, and bowfin, they thrive where many other fish would fail.

When fishermen in the South speak of pike, they do not mean the northern pike but two of its close relatives, the chain and redfin pickerels. Excellent sport fishes, the pickerels—the redfin in particular—are able to adjust well to the murky, often acid waters of the southern swamp.

The sunfish family, represented in southern swamps by such species as the largemouth bass, flier, bluegill, pumpkinseed, black crappie, redear sunfish, and green sunfish, provides even more table fare and sport than do the catfishes. There is a sunfish to fit the taste of every angler. There are small ones that will take almost any bait and large ones, such as the largemouth bass, that will put up a tremendous fight.

Sunfishes are not all equally well adapted to swamp waters. Largemouth bass, living in the clouded, often acid waters of swamps, are usually smaller than those living in more neutral water. But a number of the sunfishes are so well adapted to the swamp that they are seldom found anywhere else. That is true of the pygmy sunfishes, which are only two or three inches long, and also of the flier and warmouth. When a small lake was treated with phosphate in order to raise the pH, bluegills, less tolerant of acid conditions, exploded in numbers, whereas the flier and warmouth were eradicated.

For every larger fish found in swamp waters, there are hundreds, if not thousands, of smaller fishes representing a wide variety of species. To fishermen, who with reasonable accuracy call them shiners or minnows, they are food for larger fishes and useful for bait. Two fishes found in Florida and nearby swamp waters are the smallest in North America. The least killifish, not quite one inch in length, ranks as the smallest fish. Among the places where it is found are the

Everglades, Corkscrew Swamp, and Okefenokee Swamp. The pygmy killifish, only a trifle larger, belongs to another family and is the second-smallest fish in North America.

The mosquito fish, a relative of the least killifish, is famed for its ability to reduce and sometimes eradicate mosquito populations. Also known as gambusia, these fish are only two and a half inches in length. Thousands of them may occupy lily ponds only a few yards wide.

The darters, still other specimens of small fishes, are recognized by their rapid, darting movements and, in many, by their bright coloring. The swamp darter and cypress darter are closely associated with sluggish watercourses in cypress and hardwood swamps. Neither of them reaches over two inches in length. Minnows, relatives of the goldfish and the carp, are easily confused with the darters. Among those to look for in southern swamps are the cypress minnow, eastern mudminnow, and golden shiner.

A final small fish of southern swamps that must be mentioned is the swamp fish, a member of the cave fish family. Only two inches long, nocturnal in habits, and with reduced vision, the swamp fish has adapted to the dark waters of swamps in much the same way that other members of the family have adapted to pools in the dark interiors of caves. Found from southeastern Virginia to southern Georgia, this small fish hides under plant debris during the day and comes out to forage at night. It is seldom seen and rarely caught in nets.

Alligators

In terms of popular interest few of the wildlife forms of the southern swamp can compete with the American alligator. Absent from more northern swamps, this holdover from the Age of Reptiles is presently found from the Carolinas southward on the Atlantic Coast and from southern Arkansas to the Gulf of Mexico in the Mississippi Valley. With the protection that it has received in recent years, the alligator has increased beyond all expectation. Hundreds of them can be seen on a warm winter day in south Florida lining canal and ditch banks. In the Okefenokee Swamp, I have seen as many as 250 in the vicinity of a single lake. Specimens up to fourteen or more feet in length have become tourist attractions at parks and resorts in parts of the South. Old Joe was a much-photographed and highly esteemed "gator" at Wakulla Springs in Florida. Killed by a poacher in 1966, the animal was skinned, and the stuffed specimen is on exhibit in the lobby of the guesthouse. A boat trip at Wakulla Springs on a warm day is a sure way to see—and, if one takes along a camera, to photograph—a great assortment of alligators, large and small. But the largest of the alligators at tourist havens can scarcely compare in size with the largest specimen ever taken. That giant, caught in Louisiana early in this century, measured nineteen feet two inches.

In terms of swamp ecology, the alligator is of first importance. Alligator holes, common in the Everglades and the Okefenokee Swamp, are havens not only for alligators but for fishes and other aquatic forms of life during times of dry weather. Dug by alligators as retreats in swampy terrain, the holes are sometimes the only sources of water left. Should the "gator holes" go dry, a sizable portion of the swamp fauna is faced with disaster.

Alligators make few inroads upon game fishes and instead seek out slower forms, such as garfish and turtles. At wading-bird rookeries, alligators take young birds that fall out of the nest and that would almost certainly die anyway. The presence of alligators keeps predators, such as raccoons and bobcats, from robbing nests, a role that makes the alligator a guardian.

Both male and female alligators roar. It is a sound that, like the staccato of a pileated woodpecker drumming upon a hollow cypress tree, reverberates through the swamp. The sound brings back memories of the time when the alligator was pictured as a ferocious monster with smoke issuing from its nostrils. We now know that alligators are, on the whole, docile, though they are not animals to become intimate with. And they are not to be trusted near dogs.

Turtles

The innumerable turtles seen in swamps on warm days basking on logs and even at the tops of cypress knees and snags are another echo of the past. When one approaches a basking place, the same sequence of events always takes place. The turtles become rigid, and then one by one they leave the log and plop into the water. The name *slider,* which is given to so many of them, is a good one. They push with their legs and slide off of their perch.

Throughout a large part of the area where southern swamps occur, the turtles are the same species as those seen in other freshwater habitats. From five to ten species can be found in most southern swamps. Eight different species, for example, have been recorded in the Great Dismal Swamp. Turtles to look for within their respective ranges include cooters, sliders, smooth softshells, spiny softshells, musk turtles, mud turtles, painted turtles, snapping turtles, and, on higher ground, box turtles. A turtle seen at the top of some "impossible" sunning perch is likely to be one of the mud turtle or map turtle group. To identify with certainty a fair share of the turtles encountered on a typical visit to a swamp requires considerable expertise; some have to be examined in the hand.

In the Deep South, particularly on Gulf Coast rivers, a number of turtles have limited ranges that are closely tied to bottomland swamps. This is true of the Barbour's map turtle and the Alabama map turtle. In both species the female has an enormously enlarged head and is two to three times as large as the male. The Barbour's map turtle is limited in its distribution to the Apalachicola River drainage—a river that

American alligators. This freshwater species is found in swamps
from North Carolina and Arkansas southward.

The eastern coral snake, bright colored and dangerous but seldom seen

(right) *Take heed when the cottonmouth reveals the interior of its cottony white mouth.*

Cornsnake—beautiful and harmless

*Stinkpot turtle, noted for its
ability to climb to the tops
of tall snags*

A spiny softshell turtle

A yellow-bellied slider

The snapping turtle is a minor hazard of the swamp.

Spotted salamander

An opossum hanging by its tail

Gray tree frog singing

*The bobcat—widespread
but rarely seen*

Kentucky warblers and their nest

A pileated woodpecker feeds its young.

Wood storks, an endangered species,
at Corkscrew Swamp nesting colony

*A wood stork at sunset
at the top of a cypress tree*

(above) *The swallow-tailed kite,*
a rare species of
the southern swamps

A snail kite, an endangered
species, brings an apple snail
to its nest in south Florida.
Photograph by Richard Kern

A bald eagle atop its nest
at sunset

A black bear in the Okefenokee Swamp

enters the Gulf of Mexico in the Florida panhandle. The Alabama map turtle is found in the Mobile Bay region of Alabama and other river swamps of this part of the Gulf Coast.

Farther westward along the Gulf Coast, each of three river systems has its sawback turtle. Distinguished by small size and prominent knobs along the midline of the carapace, these turtles, ranging from east to west, are the black-knobbed sawback in rivers entering Mobile Bay, the yellow-blotched sawback in the Pascagoula River, and the ringed sawback in the Pearl River.

The common snapping turtle, ill tempered and with gaping jaws, is found over much of eastern North America. A relative, the alligator snapping turtle, which is generally regarded as the largest freshwater turtle in the world, is more closely associated with southern swamps. Feeding at the bottoms of rivers, lakes, and backwaters, it is found from the Okefenokee Swamp westward into the Mississippi Valley and parts of Texas and Oklahoma. Seldom visible, the alligator snapper eats fish and other organisms, attracting its prey by means of a wormlike lure on the upper surface of its tongue. When something goes to the lure, the turtle suddenly closes its jaws.

Alligator snapping turtles commonly reach weights of a hundred pounds or more. A giant estimated to weigh five hundred pounds was once sighted in an Indiana river. During the course of their lives, some of these turtles are believed to work their way slowly upstream until they reach the headwaters of a river, which explains why some of the largest alligator snapping turtles recorded have been in headwater regions.

Lizards

Although they do not spend any part of their lives in the water, the lizards are among the more conspicuous of the cold-blooded vertebrates found in southern swamps. The green anole, distinguished by its ability to change color, is one of the more common species and often shows itself in areas frequented by people. The skinks, represented by four species, are well adapted to getting around in swamps. Fence lizards, glass lizards, and the six-lined racer are adapted to higher ground at the swamp's edge.

Salamanders

The salamanders are a hidden part of southern swamp fauna. Their presence is often not suspected by visitors. Yet Wharton and his coauthors found that the salamanders are probably the most abundant vertebrates present in the swamps. To find salamanders, one must turn over logs, rake through wet debris, and, for aquatic forms, use a dip net. Fishermen occasionally catch large aquatic salamanders on their lines. They often call them "congo eels" or "conger eels" and believe that they really are eels. These eel-like salamanders

have suitable names, some of them picturesque and others poetic—water dog, mud puppy, hellbender, amphiuma, and siren, for example. Members of a group called the giant salamanders, the "congo eels" are, for the most part, large and decidedly eel-like, with two minute legs in some species, four in others. The two-toed amphiuma is the largest member of the group. A record specimen was almost four feet long.

An array of other salamanders that better fit the popular concept of what a salamander should look like are for the most part smaller and possessed of better-developed legs. Southern swamps play host to such species as the marbled, flatwoods, spotted, eastern tiger, southern dusky, many-lined, and dwarf salamanders. The newts, a largely aquatic group, are also represented.

Tree Frogs, Frogs, and Toads

Compared with the salamanders, the frogs and toads are much more in evidence in southern swamps. They reveal their presence by their loud mating choruses, and with luck, a person may see them before they take refuge at his approach. In many cases the smaller the frog or toad, the louder the chorus. The green tree frog, only an inch or two in length, utters its cowbell-like mating call from March to October. Hundreds or thousands of males may participate at one time. This tree frog, with its bright green body and light stripe running down each side, is probably the amphibian most closely associated with the southern swamp. It is found in every swamp from Delaware and southern Illinois southward and therefore has a range closely approximating that of the bald cypress. It is one of the most abundant small vertebrates of the swamplands.

If there is a second small frog that earns the title of a southern swamp species, it is the bird-voiced tree frog. Smaller than the green tree frog, this tiny species, with its birdlike whistle, is seldom found far from cypress, tupelo, or buttonbush. It is primarily midwestern in distribution, but an eastern race occurs in parts of Georgia and an adjacent part of South Carolina.

The pine barrens tree frog, found in isolated colonies from New Jersey to the Florida panhandle, occurs primarily in Atlantic white cedar and evergreen shrub bog communities. It appears to be absent from the river swamps. In Florida, where it is listed as endangered, it is found in hillside bogs vegetated by bay trees and various evergreen shrubs.

The little grass frog, though a tree frog, is largely terrestrial. Only about half an inch in length, it is North America's smallest frog. A common species, it is found from southeastern Virginia to the southern tip of Florida. Its preferred home seems to be grassy margins of cypress ponds.

The family Ranidae, composed of the true frogs, is best represented in southern swamps by the southern leopard frog. This green or brown frog sprinkled with black dots is found throughout the South and northward to Long Island

and central Illinois. Commonly found in cypress ponds, it sometimes strays considerable distances from water. Many other widely ranging species, including the bullfrog, the river frog (a close relative), the pig frog, and the green frog, can be seen or, more often, heard in southern swamps.

In a category all by itself in the genus *Rana* is the carpenter frog. A sphagnum bog species, with a spotty distribution from the Pine Barrens of New Jersey to the Okefenokee Swamp, it is a wary, seldom-seen frog that sometimes gives away its presence by a sound reminiscent of the noise made by a carpenter driving nails.

For the toads, the swamp is primarily a breeding place where the larvae hatch and from which the tiny subadults begin their journey to higher ground. The three most common and widespread species are the southern toad, Fowler's toad, and the oak toad. The American toad has a range that, overall, is more northern but reaches southward into the Mississippi Valley.

George Porter, in a book on frogs and toads, stated that the southern states harbor a greater concentration of frogs and toads than anywhere else in the United States. The region around Wakulla Springs in Florida, according to Porter, is probably the richest in the country in tree frogs.

Birds

The swamp is an overlooked opportunity for bird watchers. Few habitats offer so many diverse groups in such close proximity to one another, a fact that becomes apparent on even a short trip. For example, when in mid-November, 1986, Gary Williamson, my son John, Jr., and I joined the Paul Wagners for a short boat trip to see something more of the Pearl River in Louisiana, we had little thought of seeing birds. It was late in the day, and we had only time to go downstream in a tour boat and transfer to canoes for a short paddle in a slough. We stopped a few times to look and listen and then made our return.

Thanks to Gary, who has almost uncanny skills in spotting and hearing birds, our short trip was extremely productive from an ornithological standpoint. Although all of us saw larger birds, such as the great egret, great blue heron, wood duck, and belted kingfisher, only Gary could pick out the high-pitched notes of kinglets and blue-gray gnatcatchers. Somewhere in the distance he heard a king rail and, more familiar to most of us, the hoots of a barred owl and calls of woodpeckers. The Wagners, who had been leading boat tours in this area for years, showed us an active bald eagle nest. We rounded out our short trip by seeing a flock of Canada geese, ducks too far away to identify, and flocks of tree swallows.

The lesson to be learned is that for every conspicuous raptor and large wading bird, the swamp offers at least four species of small land birds. The latter are missed if one spends his time touring the swamp in a fast-moving boat. But by stopping now and then and looking and listening, the

visitor to the swamp encounters a great variety of birds. If conditions permit, I do most of my bird-watching on foot. That is by far the best way to see small flycatchers, vireos, and warblers. But one needs the ability of someone such as Gary Williamson if these and other small birds are to be located and identified by ear.

Of ancient bird forms that may have always been a part of the swamp, none is more in keeping with a setting of cypress trees and Spanish moss than the American anhinga, or water turkey. This snakelike bird, which swims with its long neck out of the water, is especially common in Florida swamps.

Herons, egrets, ibises, and wood storks use swamps as nesting and feeding areas. The white ibis enters the interior of the swamp to forage, whereas the yellow-crowned night heron is apt to confine both its nesting and feeding to the interior. Most large waders, on the other hand, are "edge species"—species that nest in colonies in trees or shrubs at edges of lakes and ponds. For the most part, their feeding grounds are open areas of shallow water. As water levels fall, leaving only isolated ponds and ditches as feeding places, the large waders fly in in such numbers that the observer may see hundreds along a few miles of highway.

To see a good variety of large wading birds, it is necessary to visit a number of swamps at different seasons. In Florida and to some extent along the Gulf Coast, large waders can be seen the year round. Farther north, one looks for them from late spring through early fall. In a family all its own is the limpkin, a snail-eating wader whose weird calls are as frightening as any sound heard in the swamps. Florida is the place to see this strange bird.

Swamps that lie in the paths of major flyways are likely to be visited by migrating waterfowl. Large numbers of waterfowl, including Canada geese and a great variety of ducks, winter in Mississippi Valley swamps. The mallard is one of the most common species to do so. In addition, both the wood duck and the hooded merganser nest in tree cavities and are summer residents in many swamps.

The vultures, hawks, and falcons (order Falconiformes) are well represented in swamps. A last retreat for some and a permanent stronghold for others, swamp habitat is vital to the welfare of hawklike birds. The black vulture and the turkey vulture, in habits and appearance the embodiment of everything regarded as sinister in the swamp, are very common. They are often seen perched in dead trees or circling overhead. The importance of swamps for the kites and the short-tailed hawk (to be discussed in Chapter 7) can scarcely be overemphasized. The red-shouldered hawk is the most common hawk of the southern swamp, but its close relative, the red-tailed hawk, is more a bird of the uplands. The swamps furnish both food and nesting sites for the osprey and the bald eagle. Hundreds of bald eagles winter around lakes and bayous in Mississippi Valley swamps. Atlantic Coast swamps also have their nesting and wintering bald eagles.

The American coot, a member of the rail family, is as

much at home in larger bodies of water as are the ducks and geese. Large numbers winter in cypress ponds of Gulf Coast and Mississippi swamplands. Less common, but often present in the same waters as the coot, are two relatives, the common moorhen and purple gallinule. True rails, including the king rail, may be present in open wetlands within a swamp.

Unless marshes and mud flats are present, swamps offer few attractions to shorebirds. An exception is the American woodcock, a member of the shorebird family, which prefers wet woodlands to more open habitat. Its plumage blends in so well with the leaf litter that sometimes one almost steps on the bird before it bursts into flight. The spotted sandpiper, whose habits are more in keeping with those of other shorebirds, is often seen frequenting edges of rivers and swamp ponds. When floodwaters cover the mud flats, this enterprising sandpiper changes its resting place to a dead snag or floating log.

Except for appearing well upstream on waterways that traverse swamps and bottomlands, the gulls and terns are largely absent. The woodlands have nothing to offer them. The mourning dove, on the other hand, utilizes the swamp as a nesting place. Doves confine their feeding to open country.

Owls are very much at home in swamps. Whoever camps for the night in or near a swamp will almost certainly hear more than one species of owl giving what sounds like unearthly screams and hoots. The barred owl, the most common species in nearly every swamp, may startle the visitor by hooting during broad daylight. Less wary than most other species, barred owls will sometimes remain on a tree branch directly over a path as hikers pass below it.

If one's quest is for showy birds, the woodpeckers can be counted upon to oblige. Nowhere are they more abundant or so much in evidence as in a swamp bottomland. The largest and most spectacular one of them all (with the exception of the virtually extinct ivory-billed woodpecker) is the pileated woodpecker. The log cock, as it is sometimes called, reaches population levels in mature swampland that are unheard of elsewhere. Commenting upon the status of this woodpecker in Maryland, Brooke Meanley, in a 1950 issue of the *Wood Thrush,* noted that though three or four can occasionally be seen in a day in some areas, to see as many as fifteen a day is not unusual in the Pocomoke River Swamp. Smaller woodpeckers also abound. The red-headed woodpecker not only nests in many swamps, but in winter large numbers of them concentrate in parts of swamps that offer an abundant supply of acorns. Almost always where there are redheads, there will be red-bellied woodpeckers competing for the same food. The downy woodpecker greatly outnumbers the hairy woodpecker in all of the swamps I have visited. And both the northern flicker and yellow-bellied sapsucker are much in evidence in all of the swamps in winter.

Bird watchers are sometimes surprised to discover that birds they see in towns and cities are equally at home in the wildest parts of the swamps. Still "unreclaimed" by man, the swamp offers perfect habitat to self-sufficient blue jays, Carolina chickadees, tufted titmice, white-breasted nuthatches, Carolina wrens, gray catbirds, brown thrashers, American robins, and northern cardinals. Fall and winter sees the swamp invaded by flocks of robins, ruby- and golden-crowned kinglets, common grackles, American goldfinches, rufous-sided towhees, and white-throated sparrows. Warmer temperatures, food, water, and protection from the wind make the swamp an ideal wintering ground for many birds.

Meanley listed sixty-three species, including ducks, birds of prey, woodpeckers, and small land birds, that can be found on midwinter trips to Maryland swamps. He added that during spring and fall migration the swamp is the best habitat in which to see warblers and other small migrants. Turning to breeding birds, he found that swamps typically support high bird populations. A breeding bird census for the Pocomoke Swamp found that bird populations there had a density of 363 birds per hundred acres (the count was based upon a tabulation of singing males).

The swamps have their endemic bird species. Except for a population in the Appalachians, the Swainson's warbler breeds nowhere else. Wayne's race of the black-throated green warbler is wholly restricted during the breeding season to swamps of the middle Atlantic Coast region. Two nearly extinct species, Bachman's warbler and ivory-billed woodpecker, found a last refuge in the swamps (see Chapter 7).

Finally, the swamps are worth visiting to view a good cross section of North America's colorful wood warblers. A wide variety of them can be seen during the spring and fall migration periods. In winter, the yellow-rumped warbler is the most common species, whereas the orange-crowned, pine, and palm warblers, together with the common yellowthroat, are less in evidence. The brightest colors are seen in spring and summer, the season when a number of warblers use the swamps as a nesting ground. The breath-taking blue and golden yellow of the prothonotary warbler stands out in sharp contrast to the dark cypress sloughs where it is found in greatest abundance. No other brightly colored bird is more representative of the southern swamp. Added color is supplied by other nesting warblers, including the northern parula, hooded, and Kentucky warblers. The American redstart, largely absent from Atlantic Coast swamps, supplies a touch of black and orange. Other warblers and also the vireos blend so well into the shadows of the forest that it is difficult to see them. It takes a keen ear and a sharp eye to pick out the Swainson's, the worm-eating, and the black-and-white warblers, as well as the ovenbird and the Louisiana waterthrush.

Mammals

As is the case for some species of birds, the swamps are a retreat for species of mammals unable to adapt to the drastic changes that have taken place in the uplands. At the same time, certain of the mammals have always been restricted to the swamps. These mammals are called endemic species. The Dismal Swamp short-tailed shrew, regarded as a full species, is restricted in its range to that one swamp. A shrew with an equally limited range occurs in the cypress swamps of Citrus County, Florida. It is the Homossassa shrew, a race of the southeastern shrew. The southeastern shrew is a wide-ranging species that becomes a swamp dweller in southeastern Georgia and Florida.

Some races of fox squirrels are largely or wholly limited to swamp habitat. Examples are the mangrove fox squirrel in southern Florida and the Bachman fox squirrel in coastal Louisiana and Mississippi. Fox squirrels are partial to open pine woods and oak trees. They also frequent cypress trees at edges of swamps.

Mammals that once had much wider ranges but that have retreated to the swamps include the Florida cougar and the nearly extinct red wolf. The Florida cougar, an eastern race of the cougar or mountain lion, in spite of its name, once ranged widely throughout a large part of the southeastern United States. At the present time it is confined to the swamps of south Florida and perhaps swamps in a few other southern states. The red wolf, formerly found in parts of the lower Mississippi Valley and eastern Texas, has virtually disappeared from the wild. What little wild blood is left apparently remains in hybrids between this wolf and the coyote. Red wolves are, however, being bred in captivity. Currently a program is under way to return some of the animals to the wild. The site of this experiment is the Alligator River National Wildlife Refuge in northeastern North Carolina. In view of the fact that this recently acquired 127,183-acre refuge has a wide variety of swamp habitats within its borders, including canebrakes, cypress and Atlantic white cedar swamps, and evergreen shrub bogs, the wolves should feel at home there. Four pairs were released in 1987.

Although they have wide ranges, the black bear, river otter, beaver, and bobcat have become increasingly dependent upon swamp habitats. In the densely populated East, the swamps are one of the few relatively safe retreats left to them. The black bear might easily disappear from our coastal lowlands if it were not for the national wildlife refuges. The largest black bear populations are in the Alligator River, Great Dismal Swamp, and Okefenokee Swamp refuges. Other wetland species that benefit from our refuge system include the swamp rabbit, marsh rabbit, southern mink, round-tailed muskrat, muskrat, and marsh rice rat. Along with these swamp and marsh inhabitants are common, wide-ranging species that frequent both the swamps and the uplands. The opossum, racoon, long-tailed weasel, red fox, gray fox, gray squirrel, eastern fox squirrel, southern flying squirrel, cotton mouse, golden mouse, eastern wood rat, and white-tailed deer belong to this group. Bats of several kinds both visit swamps and use hollow trees for roosting and breeding colonies. Still other mammals, including the eastern cottontail and striped skunk, live at the edges of swamps and venture out into them when the ground is dry enough.

Exotic species found in swamps include the feral hog, nutria, and an invader from the Southwest—the nine-banded armadillo. Moving north from Texas and the Gulf Coast, the armadillo has reached southwestern Missouri in the Midwest and southern Georgia on the Atlantic Coast. If anything, swamps are more vulnerable to invasions by exotic mammals than exotic birds. The European starling and house sparrow are all but unknown as breeding birds in southern swamps.

References

Lockwood, C. C. *Atchafalaya: America's Largest River Basin Swamp*. Baton Rouge, 1981.

Meanley, Brooke. "Birds of the Swamps." *Wood Thrush*, V (Summer, 1950), 105–11.

Porter, George. *The World of the Frog and the Toad*. New York, 1967.

Wharton, Charles, *et al. The Ecology of Bottomland Hardwood Swamps of the South: A Community Profile*. Washington, D.C., 1982.

7 / Vanishing Species

Interwoven into the history of the southern swamp is the real or imagined presence of vanishing or extinct species. It is easy to imagine a flock of Carolina parakeets perched in the branches of a cypress tree or—still a faint possibility in a few swamps—an ivory-billed woodpecker, resplendent in its black and white plumage, pounding upon a limb with its oversized white bill. Allowing the imagination to wander still farther, we can see a male Bachman's warbler at the edge of a canebrake, bringing food to a mate on a nest somewhere in the dense undergrowth. The picture would not be complete without a cougar stalking its prey at the edge of a cypress-filled pond.

Would the extinction or increasing rarity of such species have taken place if the cypress tree and its habitat had been better preserved? That is a difficult question, since the road to extinction can be the result of any one or a combination of several factors. But loss of habitat is often a primary factor, and if it is combined with persecution by man, the results can be disastrous. As Jay Shuler, an authority on the Bachman's warbler, has pointed out, "No animal or plant, no matter how well adapted, can long survive if the habitat for which it evolved is abruptly destroyed."

One factor to be considered in cases of rarity or extinction is whether the species in question was already on a downward path at the time of early settlement by the white man, though the truth is sometimes difficult to find out. Burning of forests and hunting by the Indians could have adversely affected some species. Still other species might have become overly specialized and therefore unable to adapt to changing conditions. Whatever the reasons, several species closely associated with the southern swamp apparently were not thriving even at the time of early settlement.

Thanks to well over a dozen scholarly works by Daniel McKinley of the State University of New York, we have a much clearer picture than that found in older works on the former status and decline of the Carolina parakeet. McKinley has pointed out that the Carolina parakeet was not nearly as abundant or widespread as was thought in the past. He noted that there were no reports of this species from the New England states, only a few from New York to the Carolinas, and, "despite the common name of the species," not many from the Carolinas. In the Midwest, to be sure, there were swarming flocks even in midwinter as far north as the Ohio and Missouri river valleys. But according to Audubon, the species was beginning to show a sharp decline even in his day. In 1831 he wrote, "I should think that along the Mississippi there is not now half the number that existed fifteen years ago." Midwestern birds belonged to a poorly differentiated form known as the Louisiana parakeet. That race was the first to disappear; there were very few sightings after 1880.

It is not difficult to find examples of dependency by the Carolina parakeet upon swamp habitat and cypress trees. Fond of a wide variety of vegetable foods, the Carolina parakeet showed a special preference for the seeds of cocklebur, a common weed often found in the alluvial soils of river bottoms, and cypress seeds. William Bartram told of "hovering and fluttering" by birds in the tops of the trees as they shelled the cypress seed balls to get at the seeds.

There are few reports on the nesting habits of the Carolina parakeet. Audubon had as much to say as anyone on the topic. He stated that the birds deposit their eggs in the bottoms of cavities in trees and that many females deposit their eggs together. He was of the opinion that the normal clutch was two eggs. Probably little credence can be given to reports from northern Florida around 1890 stating that the birds built open nests on outer twigs and branches of cypress trees. Whole colonies of birds were said to build flimsy nests of cypress twigs at these exposed sites. Whatever the truth may have been regarding these reports, the birds were known to roost in hollows in trees. Cypress and sycamore trees were frequently selected for that purpose.

Over much of the year, the Carolina parakeet traveled widely in flocks, appearing for a few days in one locale and then moving on to another. They visited almost any kind of habitat, including orchards and farming country. Although much was made of the bird's supposed destructiveness to fruit and grain crops, McKinley was unable to find much evidence supporting these claims. The occasional damage the birds did apparently was greatly exaggerated.

The bird's nomadic tendencies seem to have obscured the fact that the real home of the Carolina parakeet was primarily

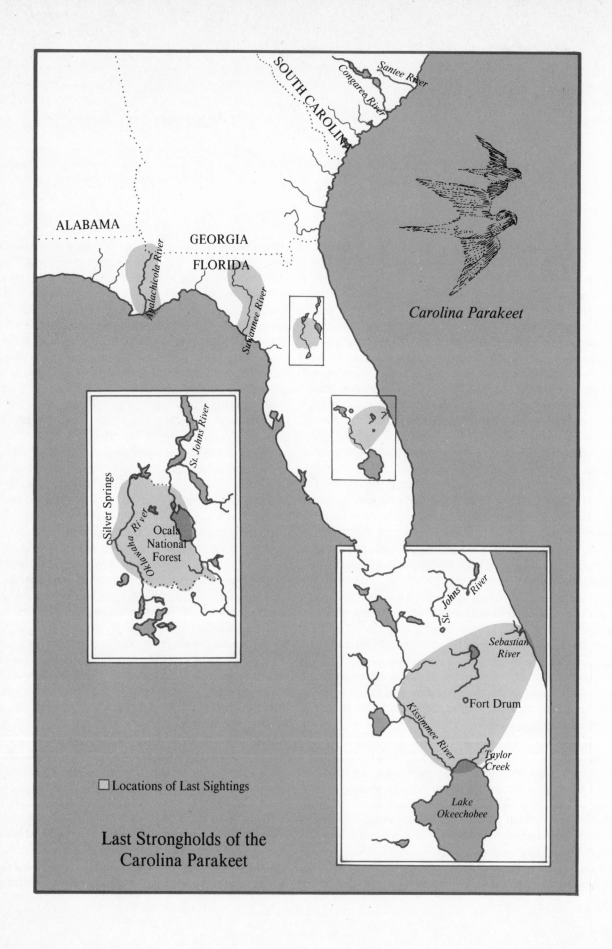

SOUTH CAROLINA

Santee River

Congaree River

Carolina Parakeet

ALABAMA

GEORGIA

FLORIDA

Apalachicola River

Suwannee River

St. Johns River

Silver Springs

Oklawaha River

Ocala National Forest

☐ Locations of Last Sightings

Last Strongholds of the Carolina Parakeet

St. Johns River

Sebastian River

Kissimmee River

Fort Drum

Taylor Creek

Lake Okeechobee

the southern swamp. Not only do many early accounts tell of its presence in swamp habitat, but during its last days nearly all sightings were made in swamps deep in the South, usually in ones with cypress trees. In South Carolina, for example, early sightings, as reported by McKinley, were in river swamps along the Santee, Coosawhatchie, Combahee, and Congaree rivers. The Congaree, noted in recent years for its big trees, was visited in 1782 by Enos Reeves, an army officer from Pennsylvania on an exploratory trip into the South. As he approached McCord's Ferry on the Congaree River, he observed Carolina parakeets. He also noted alligators in the river.

But the stronghold of the Carolina parakeet was the cypress-bordered lakes and rivers of Florida. McKinley has provided a detailed account of the history of the Carolina parakeet in that state down to the time of the last few sightings. Most of the information available on the bird in Florida came from persons who were shooting or trapping the birds for one reason or another. Toward the end of the last century, museum collectors, anxious to obtain specimens before the bird became extinct, were particularly active. A collector named August Koch was busy shooting the last of the birds in the lower part of the Apalachicola River floodplain during the 1890s. That area is one of the greatest reservoirs of rare plant and animal species in North America. Another collecting ground was along the beautiful Oklawaha River in north-central Florida, a river that has its source in Silver Springs. To the southeast, the St. Johns River had attracted naturalists and collectors since the time of William Bartram. It, too, supplied a share of specimens for the insatiable man with a gun.

The last and most important stronghold of the Carolina parakeet was a wide region stretching from Lake Okeechobee to portions of the Kissimmee River on the west and the Sebastian River on the northeast, which flowed toward the Atlantic. Names that stand out in the final history of the Carolina parakeet are Taylor Creek, a stream flowing into the northeastern portion of Lake Okeechobee, and Fort Drum and Fort Drum Swamp, some twenty miles to the north of Lake Okeechobee. The last accepted sighting of the bird was in February of 1920, when a competent observer named Henry Redding reported seeing a flock of about thirty near Fort Drum.

But the history of the Carolina parakeet did not come to a neat and tidy end with this final sighting. There have been numerous reports since 1920, but they are all highly suspect simply because they came after the species was supposed to be extinct. Some of these reports are, of course, spurious, but others are better documented than earlier sightings that were often accepted without question. A reasonably well documented later report was supplied by Charles E. Doe, curator of birds at the University of Florida. He reported finding three pairs of parakeets in the spring of 1926; they were said to be nesting in an oak hammock in the Kissimmee Prairie. He did not harm the birds, and he took five of their eggs, which are presently in the Florida State Museum in Gainesville. The eggs, however, were not accepted as sufficient proof of the parakeets' presence. Other members of the parrot family were beginning to become established in Florida at that time, and the eggs of most species are hard to tell apart.

Eyebrows were raised in ornithological circles when some ten years later Carolina parakeets were reported in South Carolina. Not only had South Carolina dropped out of the running many years before, but the reports were much more recent than the latest ones from Florida. A game-bird expert named George Malamphy had released wild turkeys on the lower Santee and had seen, from baited blinds on numerous occasions, so he said, parakeets that flew in to join the feast. His reports soon brought a number of skeptical ornithologists to the area. Of those who investigated the reports, only Alexander Sprunt, Jr., had the temerity to declare that the birds were indeed Carolina parakeets and stick to this conclusion. Others either did not see anything that excited them, or they later changed their minds. Ludlow Griscom, a dean of American ornithology at that time, was critical of the whole affair. Sprunt, however, went on to become equally well known and trusted for his bird identifications. I knew Sprunt in the 1940s when he was leading field trips for the National Audubon Society. When I asked him about his parakeet sightings, he said he had observed a flight line of as many as eight parakeets and that he believed that they had been Carolina parakeets. I thought it was significant that, unlike some enthusiasts who have sighted rare birds, he did not maintain that they were definitely Carolina parakeets.

Far less attention has been paid to a 1937 filming of parrotlike birds in or near the Okefenokee Swamp in Georgia. A movie taken by a guide showed three birds that, according to those who have viewed the film, could have been Carolina parakeets. Whatever one may make of these last two reports, there can be no question about the fate of the Carolina parakeet as of the present. It is extinct.

The ivory-billed woodpecker, on the other hand, has been far less obliging. It has a habit of reappearing just when nearly everyone has given up on it. Unlike the Carolina parakeet, the ivorybill is not a gregarious species that readily shows itself before all humanity. Persecution by man caused it to retire ever deeper into the great swamps of the South. From the time of its discovery early in the eighteenth century, it has been an elusive, retiring bird, becoming if anything warier and harder to find over the years. I know from long experience how difficult it is to see or hear one.

I began looking for the ivorybill with my friend Davis Crompton of Worcester, Massachusetts, in the late 1940s. On a trip to the mountains of eastern Cuba in April, 1948, we had success beyond our wildest dreams. The Cuban race of the ivorybill had been thought extinct since about 1920. But on a remote mountain ridge dominated by pine woods, we found an active nesting site with three adult birds in attendance. I returned from the trip with photographs and the skull of a long-dead specimen.

This success whetted my appetite all the more to find the American ivorybill, a larger bird that, so far as is known, is confined to southern swamps but sometimes appears in pine woods. When I launched my search in 1950, the ivorybill was in one of its shadowy periods when most people thought it was extinct. The most recent sightings had been in the Singer tract in north-central Louisiana where James Tanner, a graduate student at Cornell, conducted a life history study of the species in the 1930s. Unlike the Carolina parakeet, the ivorybill had outlasted the days of ruthless collecting and was now being studied instead of shot. But the eight pairs or so in the eighty thousand acres of virgin bottomland timber making up the Singer tract did not stay put. Many of the birds drifted away before heavy cutting took place there about the time of World War II. Nomadic in habits, especially when looking for food, the ivorybill moved to wherever there were fresh supplies of recently dead timber. Whether the trees were killed by fire, insect attack, or wind made no difference. Under the bark of such trees, the birds could almost always uncover the larvae of certain wood-boring beetles. The bird's huge bill was a powerful implement for uncovering these rich food supplies.

In the fall of 1950 I joined veteran ivorybill searcher Whitney Eastman of Minneapolis on a two-day trip in the Chipola River Swamp in northwestern Florida. A tributary of the Apalachicola River, the Chipola shares much of the distinctiveness of the wilderness along the larger river. Unfortunately, I gave up the search too soon and went back to the University of Florida, where I was a graduate student. Shortly after my departure, Eastman and others with him reported seeing a pair of ivorybills. Returning to the Chipola River on my own in April, 1951, I had the good fortune to hear the distinctive tin-trumpet call notes of the ivorybill toward dusk one evening. The calls were apparently made by a bird returning to a roost hole for the night.

Not until 1965 was I again in what looked like good ivorybill country. Over the years South Carolina had supplied few ivorybill records. Arthur T. Wayne, a South Carolina ornithologist of the late nineteenth and early twentieth centuries, spent a lifetime hunting down rare bird species and collecting their eggs and skins for museums. In spite of much searching, he never found an ivory-billed woodpecker in South Carolina. For this species and the Carolina parakeet, he went to Florida, where he contributed his share to the decimation of both. But Alexander Sprunt, Jr., and his colleagues did see ivorybills when searching for the Carolina parakeet in swamp forests along the lower Santee River in 1936. A few years ago, I visited Wadmacaun Island in the Santee, one of the locations where both the ivorybill and

suspected Carolina parakeets had been sighted during the period of Sprunt's investigation. The heavily timbered island seemed as wild and unvisited as in Sprunt's day. It was easy to believe that it had once held two of North America's rarest birds.

Beginning in October of 1966, I started looking for the ivorybill under the auspices of the World Wildlife Fund. My first assignment was to search the northwest corner of the huge Eglin Air Force Base in northwestern Florida. Two bird watchers from Chicago had provided me with a detailed account of their sighting of a pair of ivorybills in pine trees at the edge of a small tributary flowing into the Yellow River. Years later I explored the Yellow River with Gary Williamson and Gray Bass of the Florida Game and Fresh Water Fish Commission. Nowhere in northwestern Florida had I seen a wilder, more untouched river than this one. A blackwater stream that flows into Pensacola Bay, the Yellow, with its dark water, is poorly named. The river is flanked by cypress swamps and could easily have harbored ivory-billed woodpeckers at the time of my visit in 1966 and perhaps even today has a remnant population. Swallow-tailed kites were one of the rewards on my most recent visit.

But in 1966 I spent my time searching the general area where the Chicago bird watchers had made their sighting. Nowhere else in my search for the ivorybill did I ever encounter such difficult and tortuous terrain. The country consisted of alternating ridges and low ground. The ridges were dominated by pine, whereas the low ground was filled with impenetrable thickets containing closely growing titi and buckwheat trees (*Cliftonia monophylla*). After battling my way through one of these thickets, with its web of intertwining greenbriers, I would sometimes emerge scratched and bleeding. On one occasion, after penetrating such a thicket, I found myself at a secret weapons-testing site where some men were preparing to fire a projectile of some kind. I do not know if they were more surprised to see me or I to see them. They could not believe that I had penetrated the growth that surrounded the site on all sides. However, there was a road leading into the site, and after explaining the innocence of my mission, I was allowed to leave by it.

After two weeks of searching, I left the base without having seen a sign of the ivorybill. I had probably been searching the wrong areas. I should have spent my time in the swamp forests along the Yellow River. Nevertheless, it is not improbable that ivorybills would leave the swamp to seek beetle grubs under the bark of dying pine trees. Many of the pine trees were victims of attacks by the pine-bark beetle. The ivorybill, with its chisel-like bill, is capable of scaling off bark from tree trunks well before the tree is dead. In this regard it has an advantage over other woodpeckers, with the possible exception of the pileated woodpecker. When much of eastern North America was clothed with mature timber, there were always ample supplies of dead and dying trees to meet the needs of woodpeckers. The ivorybill, with its bark-scaling habit, had an abundant supply of food at its disposal. Not a generalized feeder like the pileated, the ivorybill clung to its specialized feeding methods as the forests became fragmented. Inability to adapt is thought to be a main reason for its decline.

In late November of 1966, I was in the Big Thicket of eastern Texas, where there seemed to be a better chance of finding the ivorybill. A bird watcher named Olga Lloyd had given a good description of an ivorybill she had seen seven months earlier. The sighting area was a flooded swampland on the Neches River above a large reservoir. To reach the fishing camp where she and her husband were staying, Mrs. Lloyd was accustomed to driving miles of sandy backwoods roads; near a spot where vehicles forded a stream, she had seen from her car window a bird she took to be an ivorybill. Clinging to the trunk of a tree, the bird allowed her a good look before it flew away.

After I had been shown the exact spot where she had made her sighting, I made a reconnaissance of the area. Sizable oak and sweet gum trees abounded on slightly higher ground. Toward the Neches River, to the east, there was a maze of winding sloughs, or bayous, as they are called in Texas. A strange never-never land of cypress trees clad with beard lichens (*Usnea*) and also Spanish moss, the bayous, at that season of the year, were the home of wood ducks, mallards, and anhingas. Woodpeckers abounded. Rarely had I seen larger numbers in such a short time. As a reminder of how far west I was, I saw a roadrunner every so often in the oak and hickory woodlands.

Almost from the start, I found evidence of ivorybill presence. Toward dusk on December 3, a few days after I began my search, I heard the loud tin-trumpet call of an ivorybill not far from where Olga Lloyd had made her sighting. But heavy rain during the next few days delayed my return to the area. I was intensely excited and could not wait to resume my search. On December 10, after having spent two days exploring a heavily forested area across the river, I was back at the original sighting place. It was a crisp, sunny day, and the woods were alive with birds. This would be the big day, I told myself.

But as the morning wore on without any signs to give me hope, I felt discouraged. After making perhaps the third circuit of a route that took me through wet woodlands and along the edge of a bayou, I started out for one last try. I had reached a spot about halfway along the path when, like a phantom, something rose from the forest floor and headed for a big cypress tree standing in the dark waters of the bayou. It was an ivory-billed woodpecker!

The white was where it was supposed to be, and the flight, straight and deliberate, was definitely not the bouncing up and down of the pileated woodpecker. The head was away from me, so that I saw little of the bill and crest. The bird was noticeably larger than the pileated, and the wings struck me as substantially longer. After alighting in the cypress tree, the bird hitched its way around to the other side of the trunk and soon flew off across the bayou into the woods that lay beyond.

I followed as best I could. After failing to find a log lying across the bayou, I removed my clothing and, wading out into the chilly water, found myself first up to my waist and then up to my shoulders. But I made the crossing, holding my binoculars and clothing high over my head. After dressing on the far bank, I set out in the direction the bird had taken. I soon found it again. This time it was perched on a stump with wings outspread, making a threat display, or so it seemed, aimed at a pair of pileated woodpeckers feeding nearby. That was my last sighting of the ivorybill.

Perhaps I should not make too much of this notion, but I have long felt that competition for food and perhaps also nesting sites from pileated woodpeckers has contributed to the downfall of the ivorybill. Both species had reached rarity status by the end of the nineteenth century. The pileated made a surprising comeback. The ivorybill, on the other hand, continued its decline, in spite of dramatically reduced persecution by man.

Except for photographs taken in the Singer tract, there have been no satisfactory shots of the North American ivorybill. Controversial photographs made on May 22, 1971, of an ivorybill high in a tree in the Atchafalaya Swamp in Louisiana failed to gain acceptance by some of the ornithologists who viewed them. Yet the photos, taken by a man training his hunting dogs, were good enough proof for the late George Lowery, Louisiana's foremost ornithologist. Knowing the man and the circumstances surrounding the event, Lowery dismissed as ridiculous the contention that there was anything fraudulent about this episode.

After once again hearing ivorybill call notes in this area, I returned to my home in Virginia. Over the next year and a half, I spent most of my time in the Big Thicket, hoping for further sightings and, most of all, hoping for a chance to learn more about the mysterious woodpecker that for the last century has demonstrated such a remarkable capacity for dropping out of sight and then showing itself again. With help from my wife, Mary Alice, and our friends Peter and Ruth Isleib, who shared a cabin with us, I expanded my search to cover most of the Big Thicket. Soon reports of possible ivorybill sightings were reaching us every few days. Many, if not most, were from well-wishers who all too often had confused the ivorybill with the pileated and even, in a few cases, with the much smaller red-headed woodpecker. Yet it seemed advisable to check into every report, which took up most of our time.

In the meantime I had no further luck at the original sighting area. Bird watchers had learned about the location and were visiting there in some numbers. A few reported making ivorybill sightings. However, I was having second thoughts about the publicity that was surrounding our search. A shy, retiring species like the ivorybill might well avoid a part of its territory where people were combing the woods. The harm, should a nesting site be discovered and visited, could well be disastrous. The opposite argument, and the one we were subscribing to at the moment, was that a modest amount of publicity might lead to more information about the bird and help with its protection and preservation of its habitat.

As we searched the Big Thicket on foot, by car, by canoe, and even by small plane, we seemed always on the point of seeing or hearing an ivorybill without ever quite doing it. The bird, it seemed to us, was always around the next bend in the river or curve in the road. When we got there, it would be gone. By now my estimate of perhaps five or more pairs in the Big Thicket had been lowered to no more than two or three. But other woodpeckers were everywhere. I had never seen so many pileated woodpeckers—sometimes I would see fifteen or twenty in a day. Attracted by abundant mast supplies and large numbers of dead trees, red-headed woodpeckers could be seen by the dozens in some parts of the Big Thicket. The red-bellied woodpecker, the downy woodpecker, the flicker, and the sapsucker were also plentiful.

On February 25, 1968, our luck returned. Geraldine Watson, a local naturalist who knew the birds and plants of the Big Thicket as well as anyone, called us one evening to say she had had a fleeting glimpse of a bird that she was sure was an ivorybill in a heavily timbered area on Village Creek, a tributary of the Neches River. Early the next morning, carrying a tape recorder and accompanied by Mary Alice and Ruth, I approached a wooded bluff overlooking the creek. We had hardly entered the woods before there came, loud and clear, the trumpetlike calls of an ivorybill. I recorded several sequences of notes; then there was silence. Our vision blocked by pine trees, we failed to see the source of the call notes.

The tape has since been analyzed by J. William Hardy at the sound laboratory of the Florida State Museum. Although almost 100 percent sure that my recording was of a genuine ivorybill, he could not completely rule out the possibility that the sounds were made by a very clever blue jay. On February 16, Geraldine Watson again saw an ivorybill in the same area. That time she had a better look and was more convinced than ever of her identification. The sighting was followed by call notes a few days later suggestive of one bird calling to another and being answered.

Until the mid-1970s, reported sightings of ivorybills were coming from South Carolina, Florida, Louisiana, and Texas. Occasionally they were backed by something more than visual identification. Besides the photographs from Louisiana that I have already mentioned, there was a feather taken from a woodpecker roosting hole in a wooded area in Highlands County, Florida, that was identified at the Smithsonian Institution as belonging to an ivory-billed woodpecker.

But in recent years reports have become fewer and fewer. I attribute this to two factors. First, habitat, mentioned by Jay Shuler as a prime requisite in the case of declining species, was especially important to the survival of the ivorybill. By 1975 conversion of forested land into agricultural fields had reached such serious proportions in the ivorybill's dwindling range that few large tracts were left. In the words of John K. Terres, the ivorybill's decline has been caused chiefly "by lumbering of vast forests in southern United States, including hardwood forests of river bottoms, and areas of dead and dying trees." Whether illegal shooting was a factor is not known. For several years such heavy penalties have been on the books that no one will admit shooting an ivorybill or any other endangered species.

The second cause of the decrease in reliable reports is fear of ridicule. No one wants to experience the kind of inquisition that awaits anyone who does not have incontrovertible proof of a sighting. In former days proof lay in displaying a freshly killed specimen. Although that kind of proof is now unthinkable, standards for accepting the presence of a nearly extinct species are as rigid as ever, a fact that has led to an unfortunate impasse. If no qualified person will accept your testimony, why go to the trouble of searching for the rare species? Second, if the rarity were found, why risk one's reputation by reporting it? Although novices, who continually confuse the pileated woodpecker with the ivorybill, still report sightings, today few serious bird students would dare state that they had seen or heard an ivorybill.

Its status hidden by a cloud of secrecy and its habitat ever more compressed, the ivorybill faces an unpromising future. I feel reasonably confident that a few are left in Louisiana. But the Big Thicket has been so badly cut over in recent years that it would be almost a miracle if any are still holding on in its diminished woodlands. There is little hope for South Carolina. Florida is a big question mark.

The third member of the triumvirate, the Bachman's warbler, has demonstrated an even greater capacity than either the Carolina parakeet or ivory-billed woodpecker to drop out of sight and reappear years later. Discovered on the Edisto River in South Carolina in 1832 by Audubon's good friend, the Reverend John Bachman, this small warbler promptly disappeared for fifty years after becoming known to science. However, for a ten-year period from about 1886 to 1896, it became almost common. Rediscovered in 1886 near Lake Pontchartrain in Louisiana by a collector names Charles G. Galbraith, it began to be recorded in some numbers. Galbraith, obtaining all his specimens near Mandeville on Lake Pontchartrain, shot thirty-eight during spring migrations from 1886 to 1888. He obtained still more specimens in 1891. On March 3, 1889, twenty-one birds struck the lighthouse at Sombrero Key in Florida. And not to be outdone, Arthur T. Wayne, whom we met in connection with the unbridled collecting of Carolina parakeets and ivory-billed woodpeckers in Florida, was busy shooting Bachman's warblers in 1892 and 1894 along the Suwannee, Wacissa, and Aucilla rivers in Florida. His score was fifty specimens for the Suwannee and a total of eight more for the other two rivers.

After this brief return to prominence, the tiny warbler once more nearly dropped out of sight. Nevertheless, the indefatigable Wayne had the luck to find a nesting colony in a swamp only twelve miles northeast of his home in Mt. Pleasant, a suburb of Charleston. The swamp, known as I'On Swamp, is partially within Fairlawn plantation and borders Mayrant's Reserve, a body of water formerly used as a reservoir for irrigating rice fields. It was in this area that for a period of about fifteen years, Wayne succeeded in finding the elusive warbler. Between 1906 and 1918, Wayne found thirty-two nests, a huge number considering the fact that only five other nests have ever been found. The number of nests found by Wayne was tabulated by Jay Shuler, who carefully searched through Wayne's old notebooks. Wayne, however, was more interested in obtaining eggs and skins for museums than in studying the life history of the rare bird.

Wayne must be admired for his perseverance in searching for and finding this warbler's nests under difficult circumstances. Hal H. Harrison, who, like myself, has looked for the Bachman's warbler without success at Fairlawn, described the hazards in his book on warblers. Snakes, ticks, chiggers, and mosquitoes are only a part of the discomfort. Nests found by Wayne were in the midst of dense tangles of thorny shrubs, cane, and scrub palmetto and often over water. Although all of Wayne's nests were only one to four feet from the ground, the adults, when not engaged at the nest, were usually high in the tops of trees, where they were difficult to see. Wayne said the male usually sang from the top of a cypress or sweet gum. As Harrison pointed out, Wayne was willing to endure the trying circumstances for the sake of the $150 he received for each set of eggs.

Besides nests found by Wayne, two were found in swamp habitat in Dunklin County in extreme southeastern Missouri in 1897 and 1898; another was found in Kentucky in 1906; and two more were discovered in Alabama in 1920 and 1937. Although no more nests were found in South Carolina following those found by Wayne, the birds did return to the Fairlawn area for a good many more years. Their nesting range also included adjacent parts of I'On Swamp in the Francis Marion National Forest. Bachman's was sighted occasionally in this general area from 1948 through 1953, and there have been a few reports since then. One of the most recent sightings was in April, 1973, when two local bird watchers, Ted Beckett and Stan Langston, reported seeing a singing male.

The last sighting of Bachman's warbler, according to Harrison, was of a female seen by five observers in Cuba in 1980. Bachman's is known to winter in Cuba and, less commonly, in parts of the South. There have been several December reports from the Okefenokee Swamp in Georgia.

What little information there is on the requirements of Bachman's during the nesting season indicates that it needs a specialized habitat that is transitory in nature. In his book *Alabama Birds,* Thomas A. Imhof stated that the warblers nest along borders of swamps, especially where the forest crown is open and blackberry bushes are plentiful. The nest is usually in blackberry, he added. Summing up Imhof's and Wayne's descriptions, one can say that Bachman's seems to require a heavily forested swamp or swamp edge where standing water is present and where there are openings containing blackberry bushes and other low, shrubby growth.

Although there would seem to be no shortage of this kind of habitat, available information is too limited to pinpoint the bird's exact requirements. It should be remembered that Bachman's disappeared from sight for fifty years after its discovery—an interval during which the southern swamps were not, for the most part, being drastically altered through logging and drainage. But in an article published in 1986, James V. Remsen, Jr., raised the interesting question of whether the decline of the Bachman's warbler was not related in some way to the decline in our native cane, or bamboo. As I have already noted, for a long period in our history the great stands of cane seen in Audubon's day were being destroyed by agriculture and grazing. Lacking, however, is any strong evidence that the Bachman's warbler relied upon cane as an integral part of its nesting habitat or for any other reason.

It would appear that the cause or causes for the decline and possible extinction of the Bachman's warbler are unknown. But it should be remembered that not many people visit southern swamps looking for this small bird. As was pointed out by Alexander Sprunt, Jr., the Bachman's is one of the most difficult of all birds to find in the dense growth where it makes its home. Like the ivorybill, it is still much too early to write off this small, elusive bird as extinct.

The importance of the southern swamp to the survival of rare and endangered species can scarcely be overemphasized. Among birds, besides these three species whose existence by about 1900 dangled from the slenderest of threads, could perhaps be added the passenger pigeon. But that now extinct bird, whose population was once in the countless millions, was more northern in its nesting distribution and apparently utilized upland forests far more than the river bottoms for finding food.

The snail kite (or Everglade kite) is another possible worthy addition. Far more an inhabitant of freshwater marshes than swampland, it does, however, resort to trees as places to rest and devour its food. A restricted diet, composed almost entirely of a single genus of freshwater snails, is the main factor behind the bird's rarity. With the drainage and development that has overtaken so much of Florida, the snail kite has been deprived of much of its food supply. Now listed as an endangered species, with a population ranging somewhere between one hundred and two hundred birds, the snail kite in Florida (other populations exist in countries to the south of us) is extremely dependent upon habitat in national wildlife refuges and the Everglades National Park. In recent years one of the best places to see these birds has been open marshes around the Shark Valley visitors' center in Everglades National Park. Formerly the stronghold of the snail kite was the Lake Okeechobee area, where at one time it must have shared some of its range with the now extinct Carolina parakeet.

From a standpoint of rarity, the more common swallow-tailed kite is hardly in the same class as the snail kite. This kite is more graceful in flight and has a spectacular forked tail. Restricted in its breeding range almost entirely to southern swamps, the swallow-tailed kite is found in larger swamps from the middle Mississippi Valley and South Carolina southward. Formerly the bird ranged as far north as Minnesota. Alexander Sprunt, Jr., in his book *Florida Bird Life,* said that the swallow-tailed kite is especially common in that state's Big Cypress Swamp, and that is as true today as when Sprunt wrote the book over twenty years ago. Sprunt stated that the nests are fifty to a hundred feet from the ground in pines or cypresses and nearly always near a cypress swamp.

The best place to find the Mississippi kite, still another of the graceful birds that at times hover in the air like a kite, is the southern swamp. It also ranges westward into parts of the southern and central Great Plains. In my experience in swamps from South Carolina to Louisiana, the Mississippi kite is always much more common than the swallow-tailed kite. Moreover, it is rapidly expanding its range and sometimes nests in residential districts of towns and cities. Like the other two kites, it is a bird highly sought by bird watchers.

The short-tailed hawk, a tropical species that reaches Florida, is another bird closely associated with cypress swamps. With two color phases—the first is black and the second black and white—the short-tailed is a small hawk seen in winter in the Everglades National Park and the Big Cypress Swamp. During the breeding season, it ranges as far north as the Suwannee River and lower Apalachicola River. Sprunt calls it a lover of deep cypress swamps and observes that the nest is usually placed in cypress trees thirty to ninety-five feet above the ground. In Florida the short-tailed hawk is listed as a rare species. (Species in more precarious situations are listed as *endangered,* and those somewhere between endangered and rare are listed as *threatened.*)

The bald eagle, listed as threatened in Florida, is partly dependent upon cypress trees in the more southern portions of its nesting range. In Florida, where the largest population exists outside of Alaska, the birds confine their nesting largely to pines and cypresses. The trees can be living or dead. The bald eagle population in Florida, as elsewhere in the forty-eight contiguous states, fell to dangerously low

levels during the era when DDT was in heavy use. Thinning of eggshells, as a consequence of the eagles' eating pesticide-contaminated food, was at the heart of the problem. Today, after the banning of this chemical compound in 1973, the bald eagle is slowly making a comeback. The largest nesting concentrations in Florida are in the Everglades National Park. Other important nesting areas exist along the state's west coast as far north as the mouth of the Suwannee River and along the St. John's River in eastern Florida. Even inland the bird is now fairly common in some places; over twenty pairs, for example, nest today in the lake country of Alachua County in north-central Florida. Present limiting factors in Florida, and in many other areas where this eagle is present, are destruction of coastal nesting habitat and disturbance of nesting eagles by man. Also, acid rain, by harming organisms on which bald eagles feed, could pose a threat to the birds.

In the mid–Mississippi Valley hundreds of bald eagles spend the winter in the vicinity of bodies of water that are part of wildlife refuges. They feed primarily upon fish and injured waterfowl. The birds are present in significant numbers at Reelfoot Lake National Wildlife Refuge in Tennessee and at the Big Lake, Wapanooka, and White River National Wildlife refuges in Arkansas.

Somehow it is the gregarious species that nest in colonies that sustain the most precipitous declines and seem most prone to extinction. Examples are the passenger pigeon and Carolina parakeet. Today, many years after those two species were in the throes of irreversible decline, the wood stork seems to be headed in the same direction. Our only stork and the largest of our long-legged wading birds, the wood stork in this country is generally thought of as a southern Florida species. Although that is basically true, the birds are found locally from South Carolina to Florida and west to Texas and range southward from our borders to southern South America.

It is ironic that the wood stork survived the days of plume and market hunting quite well only to become a victim of southern Florida's recent water management policies. Its earlier success was a matter of happenstance. Not having beautiful plumes and not being good to eat, it was spared during the latter part of the nineteenth century and early years of this one. For example, a colony in the Big Cypress Swamp of southern Florida contained up to 8,000 nests when it was visited in 1912 and 1914. But the population in Florida declined from some 75,000 breeding pairs of wood storks during the early 1930s to only about 4,500 pairs in 1984. Small colonies in Georgia and South Carolina boosted the overall figure in 1984 to about 5,000 pairs. The marked decline, which had accelerated in the 1960s, was good reason for the wood stork to be declared an endangered species in 1984.

The cause of the wood stork's decline, in the words of John C. Ogden of the National Audubon Society, is degradation of freshwater wetlands. A specialized feeder requiring an abundance of small fish during the nesting season, the wood stork has been unable to adjust to man's drastic manipulation of southern Florida's water system. In most years, at the outset of the breeding season, which is in winter in southern Florida, the birds cannot find large enough supplies of small fish near nesting colonies to maintain young and adults alike. Fishing is best when the prey is concentrated in shallow pools that are in the process of drying up. But in some years the season is too dry, and in others there is too much water. Absence of suitable water levels is sometimes an act of nature, but more often it seems connected with drainage schemes and changed hydroperiods that are the works of man.

At the largest wood stork nesting colony, which is located at the National Audubon Society's Corkscrew Sanctuary in southwest Florida, there have been only ten years since 1957 when two thousand or more young were fledged. The birds nest in the tops of the huge cypress trees that dominate a portion of the sanctuary. As early as 1969, experiments were begun at the sanctuary aimed at providing artificial ponds where the birds could feed. Eight ponds with a total of thirty acres were constructed. Although the ponds were utilized, they were not of a sufficient size to provide for a colony as large as the one at Corkscrew.

In other parts of Florida, where the larger cypress trees have been cut, the wood stork is hard pressed to find suitable nesting sites. Nesting by this species in Florida is largely confined to large cypress trees and, in coastal areas, to red mangroves. In recent years, according to Ogden, some colonies in Florida have been in tall trees standing in water in man-made impoundments.

The one slightly encouraging trend, in what otherwise would seem to be a bleak outlook for the bird in this country, is somewhat better nesting prospects in more northern wood stork colonies in recent years. As Ogden has said, "An interesting and possibly short-term phenomenon is the slightly improved reproduction that recently has been seen in colonies located between central Florida and Georgia, while the historically large south Florida colonies continue to decline." A flourishing colony, for example, was discovered in 1980 in eastern Georgia near Millen in Jenkins County. Although only about 150 to 200 pairs nest there, the reproduction rate has been encouraging. The birds nest in tops of pond cypresses located in a large Carolina bay. With Gary Williamson, I visited this colony in May, 1986, and we saw for ourselves the extraordinary measures that are being taken to ensure the success of the nesting birds. A large part of the Carolina bay has been acquired by the Nature Conservancy. As at Corkscrew, the National Audubon Society is establishing managed fishponds where the birds can feed.

Of the nine bird species with close ties to the southern swamp discussed in this chapter, one, the Carolina parakeet, is extinct; two, the ivory-billed woodpecker and the Bachman's warbler, appear to be on the brink of extinction; two others, the snail kite and short-tailed hawk, are precariously dependent upon wild habitat in south Florida; another, the wood stork, is in the throes of a precipitous decline; and the remaining three—the swallow-tailed kite, the Mississippi kite, and the bald eagle—are presently doing well enough but are highly vulnerable to any harmful changes in the environment that man may make.

Similar examples of extinction or near extinction can be found among the swamp's mammals. Two southern swamp species, the Florida cougar and the red wolf, are listed as endangered. The only remaining red wolves are thirty captive animals, some of which are being released in the Alligator River National Wildlife Refuge in North Carolina. Among reptiles, the American alligator, under rigid protection, has increased so substantially in portions of its range that in these areas it is no longer listed as endangered. Although not closely associated with southern swamps, the eastern indigo snake of Florida and southeastern Georgia is another declining species closely dependent upon habitat and listed as endangered. Among fishes, the shortnose sturgeon, which ascends the Altamaha and other rivers in the Atlantic coastal plain, is listed as endangered.

In our attempts to save endangered species and at the same time prevent still more forms from becoming rare or threatened, we should give highest priority to two goals—saving habitat and combatting pollution. Channeling streams by deepening and straightening them is one of the most significant factors in loss of habitat for waterfowl and other wetland species. Channelization also impairs or destroys the ecosystems where it takes place, as stated by Charles H. Wharton: "Drainage, channelization and levee building are highly destructive of natural systems." Clear-cutting and replanting in pine or other trees is another destructive practice that can be tolerated in relatively sterile uplands but not in wetlands that are drained for that purpose. Wherever it occurs, it is harmful to wildlife and flies in the face of recreational and scenic values.

The biggest losses to swamp habitat, however, come from agriculture. In 1984 John Madson wrote in a *National Geographic* article that few original wetlands have been hit harder than the great hardwood swamps and timbered bottomlands of the South. He noted that in the Mississippi Valley from southeastern Missouri to the Gulf of Mexico, nearly seven million acres of hardwood forests and their associated wetlands have been drained in the past fifty years. Almost nine-tenths of Arkansas' original hardwood swamps have met such a fate. The great hardwood forests Madson speaks of have been replaced by immense fields of corn, cotton, soybeans, and other crops, which contribute ever greater surpluses to the nation's farm programs.

In a press release in 1985, the United States Fish and

Wildlife Service reported that of the original 215 million acres of wetlands in our country, less than half remains. And 87 percent of this loss has been due to conversion of wetlands into agricultural land. But the release did contain one note that gave cause for hope. The farm bill passed by Congress in 1985 denies farm program benefits to any person who in the future converts wetlands to agricultural production. The wetlands, according to the press release, are valued for four main reasons: 1) the diversity of their wildlife; 2) the natural flood control they provide; 3) the fact that they act as filters for removing impurities from the water supply; and 4) their replenishment of groundwater levels.

Swamp wetlands, as well as marshes, are vital for safeguarding a long list of rare, threatened, and endangered forms of animal life. Besides keeping such forms from disappearing altogether, the swamp is a last retreat for the black bear and river otter, which are presently holding their own but would otherwise disappear from large sections of the country.

Not to be overlooked is the need to keep our rivers and streams as free as possible from pollution. To do so is particularly important in regard to fish and other aquatic forms. Acid rain is a type of water pollution that is especially insidious because it slowly depletes aquatic resources without our knowing it. The harm it does to life forms that require non-acidic water is difficult to assess, but examples of losses among such plants and animals have been demonstrated.

Thanks to the work being done by state, federal, and private agencies in assisting rare and endangered species and in protecting their habitats, the picture today is brighter than it was a few years ago. Had the era of protection come earlier, we might still have the passenger pigeon and Carolina parakeet with us. Also, a number of others might not today be on the brink of extinction.

References

Bartram, William. *Travels Through North and South Carolina, Georgia, East and West Florida*. Edited by Mark Van Doren. New York, 1928.

Dennis, John V. "The Ivory-Billed Woodpecker (*Campephilus principalis*)." *Avicultural Magazine*, LXXXV (Spring, 1979), 75–84.

———. "A Last Remnant of Ivory-Billed Woodpeckers in Cuba." *Auk*, LXV (1948), 497–507.

———. "Tale of Two Woodpeckers." *Living Bird Quarterly*, III (Winter, 1984), 18–21.

Griscom, Ludlow, and Alexander Sprunt, Jr. *The Warblers of America*. New York, 1957.

Harrison, Hal H. *Wood Warblers' World*. New York, 1984.

Imhof, Thomas A. *Alabama Birds*. Montgomery, 1962.

Kale, Herbert W. II, ed. *Birds*. Gainesville, Fla., 1978. Vol. II of Peter C. Pritchard, ed., *Rare and Endangered Biota of Florida*. 6 vols. to date.

McKinley, Daniel. *The Carolina Parakeet in Florida*. Florida Ornithological Society Special Publication No. 2. Gainesville, 1985.

———. "Historical Review of the Carolina Parakeet in the Carolinas." *Brimleyana*, I (March, 1979), 81–98.

Madson, John. "North American Waterfowl: A Lot of Trouble and a Few Triumphs." *National Geographic*, CLXVI (1984), 562–99.

Ogden, John C. [Account of Wood Stork.] In *Audubon Wildlife Report, 1985*, edited by Roger L. Di Silvestro. New York, 1985.

Peattie, Donald Culross, ed. *Audubon's America*. Boston, 1940.

Remsen, James V., Jr. "Was Bachman's Warbler a Bamboo Specialist?" *Auk*, CIII (1986), 216–19.

Shuler, Jay. "Bachman's Warbler Habitat." *Chat*, XLI (Spring, 1977), 19–23.

———. "Clutch Size and Onset of Laying in Bachman's Warbler." *Chat*, XLIII (Spring, 1979), 27–29.

Sprunt, Alexander, Jr. *Florida Bird Life*. New York, 1954.

Tanner, James T. *The Ivory-Billed Woodpecker*. National Audubon Society Research Report No. 1. New York, 1942.

Terres, John K. *The Audubon Society Encyclopedia of North American Birds*. New York, 1980.

Wharton, Charles H. *The Natural Environments of Georgia*. Atlanta, 1978.

8 / The Great Dismal Swamp

The first reliable authority on the Great Dismal Swamp was George Washington. At the age of thirty-one, he made the first of his six visits to the swamp. Unlike others who had ventured into this supposedly forbidding realm of biting insects, gloomy forests, and impenetrable canebrakes, Washington liked what he saw. He described the swamp as a "glorious paradise," with good soil, abundant wild fowl, and plentiful game. Moreover, his early training as a surveyor helped him understand the topography of the swamp. He regarded it as "neither plain nor hollow, but a hillside."

Earlier visitors to the Great Dismal Swamp, oppressed by the dark waters and the long shadows cast by the trees, found the place frightening. They imagined unseen perils threatening them from all sides. It was a sinister place, and *dismal* seemed the most appropriate word to describe it. But whether the term was first applied to the swamp by the Indians or by the early white settlers is not known.

The most outspoken critic of the Great Dismal Swamp was William Byrd II. Taking on the assignment of leading a crew of rough frontiersmen to survey a disputed section of boundary between Virginia and North Carolina, Byrd might have seemed out of his element. He was a witty, well-educated Virginia planter with literary ambitions. Although he did not endure the hardships lightly, he was a good leader who took his assignment seriously. When in 1728 the party began its work, Byrd took the precaution of taking along an ample supply of wine and rum for himself and his men. As the party slowly made its way through the treacherous mire and tangles that bordered the swamp, Byrd became more and more scathing in his denunciations. "Rum, that cordial of life," he stated, "was never found more necessary than in this dirty place." He wrote that the "swamp's fowl damps . . . rendered the air unfit for respiration." According to Byrd, there was no wildlife. Not even a turkey buzzard would fly across the swamp, he said.

Before taking Byrd's descriptions at face value, one should realize that he was making the most of whatever drama each situation afforded. He was to turn the often bawdy adventures of his men into an entertaining volume that can be read with pleasure today. His *Histories of the Dividing Line Betwixt Virginia and North Carolina* has the flavor of a work by Rabelais.

Of all the difficult country that the expedition passed through, only the Great Dismal Swamp completely daunted Byrd. There were no women, no high ground—nothing but an endless wilderness of trees and canebrakes. Leaving his men after getting them started through the quagmire, he made a long detour around the swamp. Yet he seems to have had second thoughts about the "horrible desart," as he called it. Years later he was thinking of adding portions of the swamp to his already large holdings.

Even though George Washington took delight in the swamp, in 1763 he formed two companies to undertake an ambitious drainage project. The result was a five-mile-long ditch from the western rim to Lake Drummond in the heart of the swamp. Washington's Ditch, as it came to be called, still pours its wine-colored water into the lake. But it was totally inadequate for the purpose for which it was dug. The peat soil and the roots of plants growing in it hold water like a sponge. Only a network of canals could appreciably affect the drainage.

Disappointed over the outcome, Washington and his associates tried timber cutting as a source of revenue. Apparently it was not very remunerative, since Washington was soon trying to sell his one-twelfth share of the operation. In 1796 he appeared to have a purchaser in Harry Lee, father of Robert E. Lee. But Lee was unable to raise the necessary funds. When Washington died in 1799, his share of the business passed to his heirs.

The name of still another famous American figures in the history of the swamp. In 1787 Patrick Henry, who was then governor of Virginia, succeeded in getting the state's General Assembly to authorize work on an interstate canal that would bisect the swamp from north to south. Again the idea was to drain the land for growing crops. Since Henry was a major landowner in the swamp, it is not necessary to look far for his motive.

Patrick Henry probably did not realize any benefits from the project. Not until 1805 was the canal open to small-boat traffic, and only after decades of digging canals and ditches did parts of the swamp begin to yield to drainage. Today Henry's canal is known as the Dismal Swamp Canal. It serves not only for drainage but as an artery for small boats plying between Hampton Roads and the coastal waters of North Carolina. Motorists traveling U.S. Highway 17 between Norfolk and Elizabeth City follow the canal for approximately twenty-five miles.

While the edges of the swamp were gradually giving way to agriculture, the deeper recesses for a long time remained as unchanged and enduring as the wilderness of William Byrd and George Washington. But J. W. Chickering, in a paper published in 1873, stated that much of the swamp had been cleared and partly drained. Although he found cypress, white cedar, tulip poplar, sweet gum, and swamp tupelo growing in profusion, he reported that most of the large trees either had been cut or had fallen victim to the frequent fires that raged through the swamp.

Most people would probably prefer the more pristine swamp of Byrd's day to the one described by Chickering. But deep within the swamp, there was still Lake Drummond, as lonely and mysterious as ever. The lake was named after William Drummond, who was the sole survivor of a hunting party that had entered the swamp when it was almost completely unexplored. Drummond is remembered as the first colonial governor of North Carolina and for having been hung, drawn, and quartered for the part he played in Bacon's Rebellion.

Lake Drummond remains today much as it always was. As dusk falls, the gnarled cypress trees that stand in shallow water along the shore cast ever longer shadows. A green-backed heron flaps its way awkwardly to a perch where it will pass the night. Before settling down, it utters a strange squawk as though dissatisfied with its lodging place. Somewhere in the shadows, a figure appears at the lake's edge but quickly vanishes in the darkness. Could it be the ghost of William Drummond, the lake's discoverer? Perhaps it was only a deer coming to the lake for a final drink before bedding down for the night. The next apparition is more startling. The moon, emerging from behind a cloud, bathes the lake in its silvery light. But there is still another light—flickering, eerie, apparently coming from a small craft gliding along the smooth surface of the lake. Is it the sorrowful Indian girl in her canoe searching for her lover? One of the most poignant legends of the swamp relates to an Indian maiden who died shortly before her wedding was to take place. Her bereaved lover plunged into the swamp and was reunited with her in death. Yet, according to the legend, the maiden in her canoe occasionally appears at night on Lake Drummond. Her way is guided by a lantern filled with fireflies. The story is retold by the Irish poet Thomas Moore in his poem "The Lake of the Dismal Swamp," which appeared in 1803. Foxfire, a luminescence given off by fungi in decayed wood, offers a different explanation for strange lights in bogs or swamps at night. Many ghost stories and legends have their origin in this phenomenon.

Another theme that for a time captured the attention of writers prior to the Civil War was the experiences of the runaway slaves who sought refuge in the swamp. Many were fugitives from the hard labor of digging drainage ditches. The swamp offered few comforts, and often the sound of the bloodhound told of armed men in pursuit of the hard-pressed black man. Longfellow told of the plight of the fugitives in one of his poems. So does Harriet Beecher Stowe in her writings. Nevertheless, many of the runaways did eke out a living in the Dismal Swamp, trading cypress shingles for various necessities.

But the abolitionist writers, wishing to charge their tales with every possible ounce of melodrama, once again depicted the swamp as a fearful place where nature conspired with the white man to make life unbearable for the fugitive. The abolitionists contributed much to the negative image of southern swamps during the nineteenth century.

During the Civil War, Union soldiers made several raids into the Dismal Swamp to procure a product that at first glance one would hardly think was worth risking one's life for. This product was the antiseptic swamp water that is colored by the decaying plant matter and the brown-colored peat through which it drains. The Great Dismal Swamp is the largest peat formation of its kind in North America, and as we shall see, peat provides the best clue to the age of the swamp and how it was formed. The brown-to-amber-colored swamp water had long been in demand as drinking water for use on sailing vessels. It never went bad.

At least one visitor found the swamp exhilarating and cheerful. In his youth the American poet Robert Frost had a book of poems rejected by a woman who seems to have been more than an editor in his eyes. In despair Frost made his way to the swamp with the intention of committing suicide. After hiking along a towpath bordering the Dismal Swamp Canal, his spirits revived, and he was once again ready to face the world. The happy ending is that Frost not only became famous but won Elinor White, the editor, as his wife.

By 1970, drainage had reduced the swamp to about a third of its original size. During Washington's day the swamp may have contained about one million acres, but no two authorities seem to agree on either the swamp's past or present size. But in 1970 there could be little doubt that unless steps were taken, soon there would be no swamp. The situation had become so grave that conservation groups around the nation were increasingly alarmed and were seeking ways to save what was left. But little concrete progress was made until an eleventh-hour announcement by the largest lumber company with holdings in the swamp. In 1973 Union Camp announced that it was turning over 49,213 acres to the Nature Conservancy.

A young wood duck looking out of a nest hole

Lake Drummond in the Great Dismal Swamp

*The green-backed heron, one of
the five species of herons that
breed in the Dismal Swamp*

*The common grackle, which formerly
roosted in huge numbers in
the Great Dismal Swamp*

The wild turkey flourishes in the Congaree Swamp.

(left) *Aerial view showing the pronounced meandering of the Congaree River*

A fallen tree in Congaree Swamp with earth clinging to its roots

Devil's-walking-stick

*A record swamp chestnut oak
in the Congaree Swamp*

*The snakelike twisting of
the supplejack* (Berchemia scandens)

The edge of Blake's Reserve, a reservoir
that once held fresh water for the
cultivation of rice

Great blue herons have been nesting at Blake's Reserve ever since the beginning of the nineteenth century.

Partly submerged alligators look like logs.

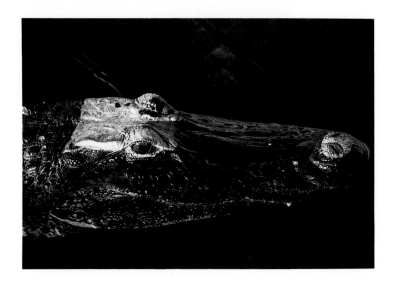

Green-fly orchid (Epidendrum conopseum)

The buttressed base of this cypress tree in the Beidler Forest is heavily encrusted with lichens.

*Pitcher plants and other insectivorous plants
commonly grow in Carolina bays.*

*Flocks of white ibis visit
the Four Holes Swamp.*

Xeric or dry-soil vegetation grows in the sand ridges that surround Carolina bays.

(right) *An aerial view of a Carolina bay bisected by a power line*

The eastern tiger salamander, one of the rarer species sometimes found in Carolina bays

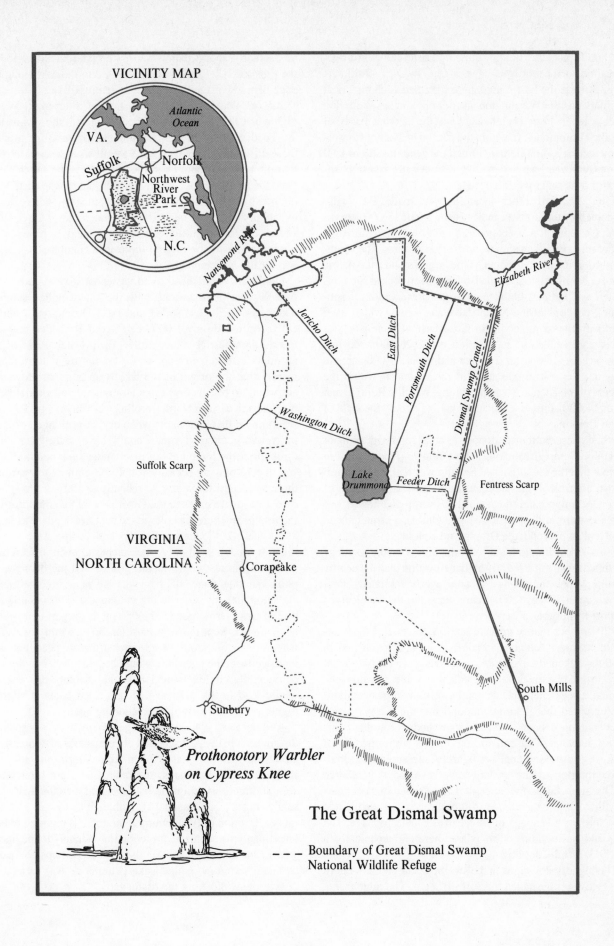

VICINITY MAP

Atlantic Ocean

VA.

Suffolk

Norfolk

Northwest River Park

N.C.

Nansemond River

Elizabeth River

Jericho Ditch

East Ditch

Portsmouth Ditch

Dismal Swamp Canal

Washington Ditch

Suffolk Scarp

Lake Drummond

Feeder Ditch

Fentress Scarp

VIRGINIA

NORTH CAROLINA

Corapeake

South Mills

Sunbury

Prothonotory Warbler on Cypress Knee

The Great Dismal Swamp

- - - Boundary of Great Dismal Swamp
National Wildlife Refuge

A solid tract, this holding stretched from the North Carolina line to the northern edge of the swamp. Within its confines were the best remaining timber and such historical landmarks as the Washington and Jericho ditches, both dug by slave labor. Equally significant was the fact that nearly all of Lake Drummond lay within the tract. The Nature Conservancy, acting as middleman, turned the generous gift of land over to the U.S. Fish and Wildlife Service for the establishment of a national wildlife refuge.

Soon afterward, other donations were made. Especially welcomed by the Conservancy was the gift of 13,000 acres in North Carolina. It was not generally realized that a little over half of the original swamp lay in North Carolina. The southern portion in that state contains the largest stands of Atlantic white cedar in existence and also large evergreen shrub bogs known as "lights." Only through the preservation of substantial portions of the North Carolina swamp, which were rapidly disappearing, could the Great Dismal Swamp be preserved as a viable entity. By 1985, some 26,000 acres had been preserved in North Carolina and about 80,000 acres in Virginia. Some 106,000 acres of the swamp is within the borders of the Dismal Swamp National Wildlife Refuge, and about 14,000 acres is a sanctuary maintained by the state of North Carolina.

When conservationists stopped to consider the meaning of the Union Camp gift and others that followed, they awoke to the fact that the Great Dismal Swamp was really not so well known after all. Important questions, such as the origin of Lake Drummond and the age of the swamp and how it was formed, were still open to debate. One L. Lesquereux in 1853 had compared Lake Drummond with the raised bogs of Europe. According to his theory, the lake was like a sponge holding its water at a slightly higher elevation than the nearby swamp. When the sponge became overly saturated, it released some of the water. Years later, the theory received support from other observers.

Still another theory appeared before the end of the nineteenth century. Nathaniel Shaler, in a paper published in 1890, had likened Lake Drummond to lakes in the North that were originally much larger bodies of water but that had gradually been encroached upon by surrounding vegetation. He suggested that Lake Drummond was the last vestige of what had once been a much larger body of water. This theory, like that of the convex bog, has not withstood the test of more painstaking analyses. Careful measurements of altitude throughout the swamp have revealed that George Washington was correct after all: Lake Drummond occupies a shallow basin on a hillside. Although a very gentle hillside to be sure, it had enough of a slope to affect the drainage. The lake and surrounding swamp are therefore technically a perched, or hillside, bog.

The highest elevations in the swamp occur on the western side below a ridge called the Suffolk Scarp. The ridge marks an ancient seacoast dating back to an interglacial period of the Pleistocene. Lowest elevations are to the east along the edge of a low ridge known as the Fentress Rise.

Anyone who has observed the flow of water in the Washington and Jericho ditches on the west side of the swamp and the Feeder Ditch on the east side can observe for himself these differences in elevation. Water flows by way of the first two ditches into Lake Drummond. The Feeder Ditch flows from the lake into the Dismal Swamp Canal to the east. Most of the swamp's drainage is to the southeast, where rivers eventually take the acid-stained waters into the coastal sounds of North Carolina. On the other hand, portions of the northern part of the swamp drain into Hampton Roads by way of the Nansemond River.

Donald R. Whitehead, who has exhaustively studied the past history of the swamp with the aid of pollen samples taken from peat, has stated that Lake Drummond "apparently originated only 4,000 years ago." He added that it is *not* the last vestige of an earlier, open-water phase of the swamp. Offering no explanation of his own, he remarks merely that the origin of the lake is an enigma. However, according to one theory, Lake Drummond and similar peat-bog lakes in eastern North Carolina were created by fire. It is well known that peat burns when dry. A prolonged drought in recent geological times could have made peat beds throughout the region tinder dry. Under such conditions, it would take only an occasional bolt of lightning to start fires that might burn for years. As recently as 1923, a fire spread over 150 square miles of the Great Dismal Swamp, destroying timber and burning holes in the peat to a depth of as much as six feet. At the present time, peat deposits in the swamp range from depths of only a few inches to about fifteen feet.

Exponents of the theory that fire caused the depressions point out that many of the lakes are at a slightly higher elevation than the surrounding swampland. This is said to be true of Lake Drummond. They go on to suggest that peat at lake edges is kept moist because of the proximity of water. But during conditions of extreme drought, peat that is a distance from the lakeshore would become dry enough to be combustible. If fire burned only the outlying dry peat, it would lead to the existence of rain-filled lakes at slightly higher elevations than the surrounding land.

Another theory holds that a huge meteorite shower at some distant time in the past scooped out thousands of depressions along the Atlantic coastal plain from Virginia to Florida. Known as Carolina bays, the depressions are oriented in similar directions, elliptical in shape, and surrounded by low sandy ridges (see Chapter 12). Although this is not an accurate description of Lake Drummond, there is reported to be a large magnetic center of attraction immediately to the northwest of the lake. Still another theory, and perhaps not one to be taken seriously, is that Lake Drummond was formed by beaver dams blocking the drainage.

Peat, by preserving objects that become embedded in it, is a calendar of past biological events. Whitehead has said that peat first began accumulating in the area of the Great Dismal Swamp about 9,000 years ago. There was no swamp at that time, only a huge, shallow depression bordering the sea-coast. Deposition may have taken place in a lagoon behind dunes or barrier islands. The sea was rising at that time, causing marsh development to proceed inland. Indications are that the marsh was originally brackish. There may have been a reinvasion of salt water and then gradual change to a freshwater marsh. That phase was followed by an invasion of tree growth. Over 8,000 years ago, according to pollen samples, the dominant trees were beech, hemlock, and birch. The presence of the latter two suggests that the climate during the period was considerably cooler than it is today. During a period between 3,500 and 8,200 years ago, oaks, hickories, and sweet gums were the dominant species. By then the climate seems to have been much like it now is. But a subtle change was taking place. The region was gradually turning into the typical southern swamp we know today, with its cypresses, water tupelos, and other southern species. Whitehead believes that the change can be explained by changes in climate. But he leans to the view that, as the swamp became filled with peat, the hardwoods mentioned earlier gave way to plants better suited to acidic, peaty soil. So it was that the swamp became clothed primarily with acid-loving plants of southern origin.

These plants would still rule today if it were not for changes brought about by man. In a period of two hundred years, according to Whitehead, man has caused changes in the composition of the swamp that under purely natural conditions would have taken from two to three thousand years. The question now is whether he can reverse the process and reinstate the cypresses and white cedars that once were such a dominant part of the plant life of the swamp.

Although not everyone may agree with Whitehead, it is generally accepted that the same plants that have grown in the swamp for hundreds of years are still present. What has changed is their numbers and distribution. Instead of a plant community dominated by one or two species covering hundreds of square miles, there is now a hodgepodge made up of many diverse communities. Within the original borders of the swamp can be found pure stands of Atlantic white cedar, evergreen shrub bog communities, brier thickets, cane-brakes, loblolly pine barrens, gum (tupelo) swamps, cypress swamps, and mixed swamp forests consisting of red maple, swamp chestnut oak, tulip poplar, sweet gum, sweet bay, and red bay.

If any one tree has emerged as dominant, it is the red maple. The changed conditions have favored this adaptable tree. The most common tree of the Union Camp tract, it occurs with other hardwoods or in solid stands throughout much of the swamp. Where logging once occurred, it is a common sight to see red maple saplings growing in decayed stumps. In time a single tree will be left, its roots tightly embracing the stump as they reach down into the moist earth below. When the stump finally disintegrates, the red maple is left standing on its stiltlike roots. Amercian holly, pond pine, and other swamp plants commonly gain a footing on decayed stumps and logs. No other seems to thrive as well on those platforms as does the red maple.

Where cane forms dense cover, it is a favorite retreat of the black bear. Less dense stands are an important nesting substrate for the Swainson's warbler. The golden mouse, near its northern limits in the Great Dismal Swamp, also occurs in cane thickets and uses old or deserted Swainson's warbler nests for its home, and the Creole pearly eye, a southern butterfly at its northern range limits, is associated with this habitat. In moister sections of the hardwood forest, sweet pepperbush or white alder is usually the most important understory plant.

But it is the vines, almost as much as the cypress and water tupelo, that separate the southern swamp from more northern ones. The Great Dismal shows its distinctive southern character in the variety and abundance of its vines. Some twenty species can be called common. The vines fall into two general classes—those that twist their way up into trees and those that climb straight up the trunk. Among the twisters are laurel greenbrier, yellow jessamine, and supplejack. Supplejack is a strangler as well as a twister. Its serpentlike stems, up to four or five inches thick where wrapped around tree trunks and one another, seem to be squeezing to death whatever they clasp. That is sometimes true, and when the support dies and rots away, the supplejack is left dangling like a twisted rope, its uppermost branches clinging to a treetop. In contrast, the crossvine and climbing hydrangea—two of the more common southern species—climb straight up the trunks of trees without doing any damage.

The Atlantic white cedar, which was such an important part of the swamp during earlier times, is now largely confined to tracts on the North Carolina side of the state line. There one can walk along old lumbering roads and see solid stands of these tall, straight trees. Prior to the 1930s, there was over a hundred thousand acres of white cedar, or juniper, as it is sometimes called, in the Great Dismal Swamp. Today only about ten thousand acres is left. The trees depend largely upon fire for regeneration. Without fire or some other disturbance to prepare a seedbed, there is no new growth.

Over much of the swamp, white cedar, as well as gum and maple swamps, give way to wetter woodlands dominated by bald cypress. Unlike in earlier days, when cypress was one of the most common trees, the cypress growth today consists largely of a few acres here and there of young trees that have sprung up since periods of heavy lumbering in the 1950s and earlier. There are also occasional giants that were spared because they were hollow or otherwise defective. One of the largest of the survivors is a partially hollow tree two and a half miles from the western edge of the swamp that has a breast-high circumference of twenty-two feet nine inches. That tree is estimated to be six hundred years old. Although it has been struck by lightning three times, it appears to be vigorous and capable of sustaining still more harsh treatment at the hands of the elements.

Like so many other swamps where cypress was once abundant, the Great Dismal has its share of cypress logs embedded in peat or covered over by water. Many have been unearthed during the course of digging ditches and canals. Other logs, equally well preserved, lie on the bottom of Lake Drummond.

Wildflowers that grow commonly on the damp forest floor include Indian cucumber root, jack-in-the-pulpit, crane-fly orchid, Solomon's seal, atamasco lily, and jewelweed. Lizard's-tail, a common swamp wildflower from our more northern states southward, can often be found growing in solid stands in shallow water. The swamp is one of the strongholds of the rare dwarf trillium. Blooming in late March, this tiny trillium has predominantly purple flowers and reaches only one to three inches above the leaf litter.

Ferns are abundant in the Dismal Swamp, being represented by no less than thirty species. In more open woodland, large areas are covered by the netted chain fern. Although some ferns, such as this one, grow profusely in moist soil, others seem more at home on stumps, decaying logs, and even cypress knees. The royal fern is a good example of a species that thrives on a woody substrate. The resurrection fern, whose fronds look withered and brown in dry weather but turn fresh and green when it rains, grows plentifully on trunks and branches of trees. It is most often seen growing on tupelo (black gum). A relatively rare fern of southern swamps present as far south as Georgia was first discovered in the Great Dismal Swamp—the log fern (*Dryopteris celsa*). Nowhere is it more common than in the swamp where it was first found.

One plant of the swamp that the visitor will quickly learn to respect is the devil's-walking-stick. Armed with sharp spines on its trunk and branches and the midribs of its leaves, this shrub or small tree is a formidable barrier wherever it grows. In few places is it more abundant than in the Great Dismal Swamp. Solid stands clothe canal banks, edges of roads, and other relatively open areas. It grows less profusely in the shade and is absent from very wet areas.

The same restrictions that limit the number of plants growing in the swamp apply equally to the wildlife. This generalization is well illustrated by the fish fauna. Only fishes that can adapt to murky water high in tannic acid and hence with a low pH are able to thrive in the swamp. It is not surprising, therefore, to find a member of the blindfish family (largely inhabitants of caves) occurring in the swamp's waters. Proponents of the Great Dismal Swamp call it the Dismal Swamp fish. But the swamp is only the northern limit of this two-and-one-half-inch fish that ranges southward into Georgia.

Some twenty-five species of fishes, including the two-inch sawcheek darter, have been recorded in Dismal Swamp waters. The acidic water seems to favor more primitive fish such as the longnose gar, the bowfin, and catfishes.

A study conducted in 1984 showed that only three species of interest to fishermen could be called common in Lake Drummond. The yellow bullhead, a catfish offering sport as well as good eating, was the most plentiful of the three. Next on the list was the yellow perch, of equal interest to the fisherman. Third in numbers was the flier, a small sunfish— too small, as a rule, to be of much interest. But enough of them will make a tasty meal; moreover, the flier helps clear swamp waters of mosquito larvae.

The 1984 study produced two unexpected conclusions: first, indications that fish in Lake Drummond grow at a rate equal to or better than the average rate of fish from other lakes in Virginia, and second, that the yellow bullhead appears to prey upon the eggs of the black crappie, thereby preventing that species from reaching suitable numbers. Other sport fishes in the lake were the white catfish, brown bullhead, chain pickerel, bluegill, and pumpkinseed sunfish. Although the fisherman may not catch prize specimens in Lake Drummond or the many canals and ditches that crisscross the swamp, he is not likely to return home empty-handed.

The waters of the swamp are ideal breeding places for mosquitoes and biting flies. Those small pests, however, are not the ever present menace that they are pictured to be in more lurid accounts of southern swamps. The same waters that produce bothersome insects are also a home for forms of life that prey upon insect larvae. Nevertheless, I would advise visitors to the Great Dismal Swamp during the summer months to prepare for possible assault by biting insects.

To see butterflies, the ideal time to visit the swamp is April and May. On a day in late May when I was exploring the Corapeake Ditch area along the state line with my naturalist friend Gary Williamson, we saw literally hundreds of palamedes swallowtails collected around mud puddles in old logging roads, busily engaged in siphoning up water. The larva of this common butterfly of southern swamps feeds on leaves of red bay, sweet bay, and sassafras. The second-most common species, in my experience, is the zebra swallowtail. The larva of this spectacular black-and-white butterfly with elongated "tails" feeds upon the leaves of pawpaw (*Asimina triloba*). Brooke Meanley, who has written extensively on the natural history of the Great Dismal Swamp, advises looking for butterflies along spoil-bank roads and in the evergreen shrub bog communities. He normally records between ten and twelve species on visits to the swamp during the spring or fall. I manage to do almost as well, and consider the swamp to be one of the best for butterflies.

Neophyte visitors to southern swamps are always anxious

about poisonous snakes. Only three poisonous species—the eastern cottonmouth, the canebrake rattlesnake, and the copperhead—occur in the Great Dismal Swamp, and of these three, only the copperhead can be considered at all common. Meanley, over the course of his many visits to the swamp, has observed fifteen species of snakes, including the three poisonous ones. But on one four-day visit to the swamp in June his only sighting of a snake was of an unidentified species being carried off in the talons of a red-shouldered hawk. On trips with Gary Williamson, whose specialty is herpetology and who is forever turning over logs in search of snakes, I have never seen more than three species during a day's outing in the swamp. On a trip to Lake Drummond in May, our tally of snakes sighted was two eastern worm snakes, a black rat snake, and a southern ring-necked snake. Yet, more species of turtles and snakes have been recorded in the Great Dismal Swamp than of toads and frogs. David E. Delzell, in a recent tabulation, gave the following figures for number of species of reptiles and amphibians definitely known from the swamp: toads and frogs, 19; salamanders, 8; turtles, 8; snakes, 20; and lizards, 7.

Turtles are common and, on the whole, much more in evidence during the warmer months than are snakes. The spotted turtle is one of the most common species, but the painted turtle, mud turtle, and snapping turtle are also abundant. The yellow-bellied turtle is at its northern range limits. In drier sections, the eastern box turtle is reasonably common. That turtles are more visible than snakes is illustrated by Brooke Meanley's record of having seen all of the Dismal Swamp turtles but only three-fourths of its snakes.

An unusually large number of species of toads and frogs are at or near northern range limits. The list includes the oak toad, southern toad, squirrel tree frog, little grass frog, southern cricket frog, and Brimley's chorus frog. The little grass frog, the smallest frog in North America, is fairly common in the swamp.

The lizards are represented by four kinds of skinks, the northern fence lizard, and the green anole. However, the anole, known for its ability to change color from green to brown and back again, is basically more southern and a rarity this far north. A better-known denizen of the southern swamp, the American alligator, has a much less certain claim to the Great Dismal Swamp than does the green anole. Although alligators have been sighted in the murky waters of the swamp, most evidence suggests that they were individuals released by man. The natural range of the alligator begins about thirty-five to fifty miles south of the swamp.

Turning to birds, one finds that the swamp does not offer enough aquatic foods to attract large numbers of water birds. Nevertheless, a good variety of water birds use Lake Drummond as a resting area and, to some extent, find food in its waters. Among the visitors that are seen from time to time are loons, grebes, whistling swans, Canada geese, and a large variety of ducks. In some respects a better habitat for water birds, the many canals and ditches that transect the swamp attract herons, egrets, pied-billed grebes, and waterfowl. Migrating shorebirds are sometimes seen on exposed mud flats when water levels are low. Now and then gulls, mainly ring-billed and herring gulls, are seen winging their way across the swamp.

Five species of herons have been known to breed in the swamp—the great blue, green-backed, little blue herons, and the two night herons, the black-crowned and yellow-crowned. The mallard, black duck, blue-winged teal, and wood duck have been known to breed there, as has the belted kingfisher. Other large, spectacular breeders include the red-shouldered hawk, barred owl, turkey and black vultures, and pileated woodpecker. An interesting departure from normal breeding habits is seen in the chimney swift. In the Great Dismal, as well as the Congaree Swamp in South Carolina, chimney swifts prove that they have not been completely won over by chimneys; in those two swamps, and probably others, the birds nest communally in hollow trees, as they did before the days of settlement.

The chief lure that brings bird watchers to the swamp is the warblers. Not only do many warblers pass through during spring and fall migration, but there are no less than sixteen resident breeding species. Two of the breeders are warblers that are difficult to find elsewhere and, for that matter, not so easy to locate in the Great Dismal Swamp in spite of their reasonably good numbers. The Swainson's is a southern warbler that reaches its northern limits in the Pocomoke River Swamp of Maryland and Delaware; the other rare warbler is the Wayne's warbler, a race of the black-throated green warbler. Nowhere very common, Wayne's is found only within a narrow coastal strip from about Charleston, South Carolina, to the Great Dismal. In the wet woodlands of this swamp, it seems to reach its maximum density as a breeding bird.

Meanley, who has studied the breeding habits of both species, noted that each has its special niche where it conducts all of its activities. The Swainson's is most often found in black-gum swamps that years earlier had been subjected to lumbering and partial drainage. A bird of the understory, it frequents dense thickets of greenbrier and sweet pepperbush. The nest is placed in these tangles and also in cane growth. In contrast, the Wayne's warbler ranges much higher. It is seen, as a rule, twenty to forty feet from the ground and is often found in the same black-gum swampland as that occupied by the Swainson's warbler.

The two warblers have different arrival schedules. Wayne's is one of the first of the resident warblers to arrive in the spring. Its appearance during the last week in March, only a few days behind the yellow-throated warbler, is before trees are well in leaf. The Swainson's, on the other hand, is the latest of the resident warblers to arrive, reaching the swamp sometime after mid-April.

Bird watchers from April onward should have no trouble

finding the prothonotary warbler, whose blue and golden plumage stands out so vividly against the darker shades of the swamp. Along with the red-eyed vireo, that much-sought warbler is probably the most abundant breeding bird of the swamp's wet woodlands. It is often seen on low branches hanging over water.

Four U.S. Fish and Wildlife breeding-bird surveys along a twenty-five-mile route in late May and early June of 1978–1981 indicate that the ten most abundant breeding birds in the section covered were, in order of abundance, the prothonotary warbler (sixty-six were seen in 1981 along the twenty-five-mile route), the hooded warbler, the red-eyed vireo, the ovenbird, the common yellowthroat, the wood thrush, the Acadian flycatcher, the Carolina wren, the great-crested flycatcher, and the white-eyed vireo. In the heavily cutover second growth along the Corapeake Ditch, I suspect that the prarie warbler, gray catbird, and bobwhite would have figured importantly in such a census. But in solid stands of Atlantic white cedar, I have found little else but the crested flycatcher during the breeding season.

In winter the swamp is a gathering place for birds that take advantage of abundant food supplies found within the swamp or sometimes in fields well beyond its borders. Robins and cedar waxwings are often present in huge flocks. The birds feed avidly upon the fruits of holly, Japanese honeysuckle, poison ivy, mistletoe, and greenbrier. Often feeding with them are occasional fruiteaters such as the eastern bluebird, hermit thrush, mockingbird, and pileated woodpecker. The Atlantic white cedar, so birdless during the summer months, in the winter may be visited by large flocks of pine siskins. The birds are attracted by the winged seeds that are beginning to be released from the tree's small cones. One winter Brooke Meanley estimated that he saw as many as ten thousand pine siskins feeding in a stand of white cedar.

For many years the greatest spectacle of all was the huge flocks of birds that streamed into the swamp toward dusk to roost and then departed early in the morning. Feeding upon unharvested corn and peanuts in nearby fields during the fall and winter, common grackles and red-winged blackbirds, together with lesser numbers of brown-headed cowbirds, rusty blackbirds, and starlings, used the swamp as a "bedroom community," commuting to the fields each day. At one time as many as twenty-five million individuals occupied a well-known blackbird roost in the Corapeake Ditch section. That roosting area was the largest of its kind in the country. But about 1976, owing to changing agricultural practices, the huge roost was abandoned.

Approximately 225 species of birds have been reported in the Great Dismal Swamp. Of these, 85 have supplied breeding records. Although the list is impressive, there are some conspicuous gaps. For example, Kentucky and parula warblers and the brown-headed cowbird are nearly absent as breeding birds. The osprey does not nest, and most water birds are scarce or absent. Among birds of prey, a swallow-tailed kite that appeared in May of 1980 afforded an exceptional record. That bird is normally found from South Carolina to Florida and westward along the Gulf Coast to Louisiana.

The mammals call for different techniques than the birds. Often the only indications of their presence are footprints in soft earth, fecal matter, claw marks on trees, and sounds and movements behind curtains of underbrush. An entire day in the Great Dismal Swamp may yield only two or three mammal sightings. But Brooke Meanley, by remaining perfectly quiet in one spot, has observed river otter families playing only yards away; he has also been rewarded by sightings of black bear, muskrat, raccoon, mink, bobcat, and white-tailed deer. My biggest thrill was seeing a mother black bear with two cubs on two consecutive days in late October of 1983. Steve Maslowski was with me on both occasions.

The black bear is the swamp's best-known mammal. Writing in 1890, Nathaniel S. Shaler stated that as many as several hundred were killed in a single season by hunters. He stated that local people told of ferocious battles between bears and wild cattle. He heard of one case in which a bull and a bear died battling each other.

The number of black bears presently in the Great Dismal Swamp is unknown. However, a bear-tagging program begun by the Fish and Wildlife Service in 1984 is supplying much-needed information on the numbers and habits of the bears. By August, 1985, sixty bears had been tagged. It now seems reasonable to believe that the bear population is well over a hundred. Only swamps along the Alligator River in North Carolina and in the Okefenokee Swamp in Georgia have East Coast populations that can compete with the one in the Great Dismal.

It has been learned that not all of the Dismal Swamp bears hole up for the winter; some remain active the year round. Denning occurs in large cavities in black gums and bald cypresses and also in dense tangles in white cedar swamps. Females give birth to two cubs in February. The cubs leave the den with the mother in late April. When danger threatens, the mother sends her cubs up a tree; meanwhile she stands guard at the base. Bears in the Great Dismal Swamp represent no threat to people. They quickly retreat when they see someone approaching.

The swamp offers a number of other mammals that are much more secretive than the black bear and that generally are of interest only to the mammalogist. At the top of the list is the Dismal Swamp short-tailed shrew (*Blarina telmalestes*), discovered by A. K. Fisher in 1895. It is an endemic species, found only in the swamp that gave it its common name. The golden mouse, at its northeastern range limit, was discovered near the swamp. The swamp is also the home of three subspecies that were discovered within its limits: the Bachman's shrew, the southern bog lemming, and a muskrat (*Ondatra zibethicus macrodon*).

After so many "swamp celebrities," the chipmunk, at the

southeastern extremity of its range in the swamp, and the marsh rabbit, at its northern limit, seem hardly worth noting. The bat most likely to be seen in the swamp is the evening bat. That species, as well as the northern red bat and eastern big-eared bat, was discovered years ago roosting in hollow cypress trees at the edge of Lake Drummond. The Great Dismal Swamp has thirty-two mammal species. That is somewhat fewer than the forty-eight recorded in the Oke- fenokee Swamp, but it must be remembered that the Great Dismal is smaller in area and does not have as many dis- tinctive habitats.

Motorists can obtain a passing look at the Great Dismal by driving along U.S. Highway 17 at the eastern edge of the swamp. The highway follows the Dismal Swamp Canal. Although one can see typical swamp plants, such as the devil's-walking-stick, red bay, sweet bay, titi, sweet pepper- bush, and switch cane, the country there has been greatly altered by drainage and clearing.

Taking the White Marsh Road (State Road 642) from Suffolk and driving southward, one will find roads leading into the western part of the swamp. The roads are clearly marked and lead to parking areas where one can get out and hike to such points of interest as Jericho Ditch and Wash- ington Ditch. The refuge headquarters is located at 3216 Desert Road on the west side of the swamp. To reach it, follow U.S. Route 32 south from Suffolk and look for brown signs pointing to the headquarters. For information about entering the refuge and taking advantage of guided tours, one should write to the Dismal Swamp National Wildlife Refuge, Box 349, Suffolk, Virginia 23434.

References

Chickering, J. W. "The Flora of the Dismal Swamp." *American Naturalist*, VII (1873), 521–24.

Delzell, David E. "A Provisional Checklist of Amphibians and Reptiles in the Great Dismal Swamp Area, with Comments on Their Range of Distribution." In *The Great Dismal Swamp*, edited by Paul W. Kirk, Jr. Charlottesville, 1979.

Meanley, Brooke. *Swamps, River Bottoms, and Canebrakes*. Barre, Mass., 1972.

Shaler, Nathaniel, S. "Fresh-Water Morasses of the United States." *U.S. Geological Survey Annual Report*, X (1890), 313–39.

Whitehead, Donald R. "Developmental and Environmental His- tory of the Dismal Swamp." *Ecological Monographs*, XLII (1972), 301–15.

9 / The Big Rivers

Traveling south from the Pocomoke River, one meets ever larger swamps and the rivers that nourish them. Unlike the blackwater streams, which rarely flood to any great degree, the large rivers begin spilling over their banks whenever there has been sufficient accumulation of water in their drainage basins. Floodwaters are the lifeblood of the big river swamps. Transporting nutrients from fertile farmlands and upland slopes to the swamps, the floodwaters nourish the plant life and the small organisms that furnish food for higher forms. In these wet bottomlands, the bald cypress reaches its maximum size and grows faster than elsewhere.

The typical big river becomes sluggish when it reaches the coastal plain. No longer hemmed in by high banks, it easily spills over into low ground and almost as easily changes its course. It is constantly in a state of flux. The river carves out wide floodplains and, at the same time, builds up rich alluvial deposits. Cutting away at one side, building up on the other, deepening its channel in one place, filling it in in another, the river moves on its uncertain course, taking perhaps twice the distance that is necessary to reach the sea. As if to make up for such extravagance, it now and then takes a short cut. After transcribing one huge loop after another, the river, with the next big rush of floodwater, may take a shorter route, leaving behind loops that become oxbow lakes.

Over the centuries the floodplain becomes dotted with oxbow lakes. For the most part, they are crescent-shaped, conforming to the previous curve in the river. Stagnant or partly stagnant through much of the year, they are commonly called "dead lakes." But every time the river floods, they become rejuvenated—refilled with living organisms. Oxbow lakes are often superb fishing grounds.

Some of the silt the river carries is deposited at the river's banks. Building higher ground, the silt forms levees or terraces, which, like dikes built by man, follow the two sides of the river as it makes its way to the sea. The levees serve to keep the water in the river at a higher level than water in the swamp behind the levee. But there are always gaps in the levee where tributaries enter the river. When the river is low, the tributaries flow into the river; on the other hand, when the river is high, there is a reverse flow, as the river's water flows by way of tributaries and smaller arteries, known as sloughs or guts, back into the swamp.

Often choked with logs and seeming to lead nowhere, the slough is the key to a natural flood control system. Man could scarcely improve upon it even if he wanted to. Like a safety valve, the slough drains off some of the floodwater and takes it into the interior of the swamp. Within the swamp, the water is held as if by a sponge. Some is absorbed by trees, some evaporates, and whatever is left begins a return passage through the sloughs when the river returns to normal level.

The swamp ecosystem is without parallel in taming floodwaters. Besides its usefulness in flood control, the swamp filters out harmful chemicals and other waste products. The dikes, dams, and channels that man builds at great expense reclaim some land for his special uses, but they also harm or even destroy systems that have been working perfectly for ages. We maintain our systems only through constant repair and dredging. So long as we do not interfere, nature controls and regulates the systems it has evolved over the ages. Our systems break down; nature's never do.

The first of the truly big rivers one meets after leaving the southeastern portion of Virginia is the Roanoke. Along with the Chowan River, immediately to the north, the Roanoke flows into Albemarle Sound. The lower part of the Roanoke is a labyrinth of islands and winding watercourses where the highly acidic waters of blackwater streams mix with the more neutral water of the Roanoke. During times of flooding, the Roanoke carries a heavy load of silt, some of which goes into building levees along its banks. Great and Goodman islands, at the mouth of the Roanoke, are preserves acquired by the Nature Conservancy. There the silt-laden waters of the Roanoke mingle with the dark water of blackwater streams, such as the Cashie River, to produce a diverse plant community and rich fauna. At the mouth of the Roanoke, which fits the description of a drowned estuary, evidence of rising sea level can be seen in the many cypress trees standing well out in the water, even far out in the sound itself. Cypress must have dry land to become established, and thus the trees first sprouted when the sea level was lower. Under the present flooded conditions, no more cypress trees will spring up in the wide waters of the lower Roanoke.

On a canoe trip on the lower Roanoke with Gary Williamson in March of 1985, I became better acquainted with the offshore stands of bald cypress and the birdlife of the estuary. Ospreys were common, using bald cypress trees as nesting sites. Out best sighting of the day was an adult bald eagle that we observed cruising about at treetop level; every so often it stopped to perch on the dead limb of a cypress tree. Later we learned that a pair were nesting in the area—only the second known nesting for North Carolina since the eagle population plummeted during the 1960s. The estuary also offered birds seldom seen upstream. Among such birds were the double-crested cormorant, the red-breasted merganser, and the scaup.

The lower Roanoke is a wild region indeed. After launching our canoe at a highway bridge, we did not see a single human habitation on our ten-mile paddle. Except for the small-boat traffic, it would have seemed that we were back in the days of the American Indian. Even the black bear has fared quite well in this area. Soon after landing at the mouth of the river, we came upon a large cypress tree with numerous bear-claw marks on its trunk. About twenty feet up, we could see a sizable hollow that might well have been a bear's denning cavity.

On a second Roanoke canoe trip, in August, 1985, we had an even more genuine wilderness experience at a point higher up on the river. During a day's paddle, we did not see another boat or another person. Always in view were walls of cypress and water tupelo at the water's edge. On rounding a bend in the river, we were generally greeted by a pair of wood ducks serenely floating on the water. At our approach they would take flight, uttering their piercing calls as they did so. From time to time we saw herons and egrets. Once a flock of seventeen white ibis flew up from a dark slough.

The large wading birds that we saw were not unexpected, since the Roanoke floodplain contains seven known heronries, or almost a third of the inland heronries in North Carolina. The two common breeding species are the great egret and great blue heron.

The Roanoke has a high priority in the Nature Conservancy's program of saving river bottom swamps. Some 14,000 acres and more than 20 miles of the river are now under protection; further acquisitions of swampland are expected. The floodplain of the lower and middle reaches of the Roanoke varies from 3.5 to 4.5 miles in width and contains about 150,000 acres of bottomland forest.

The river's wooded bottomlands support a wealth of bird and mammal life. At the end of 1985 the bird list had 214 species; of these, 88 were known to breed. Of special interest are disjunct bird populations, that is, breeding populations outside the normal range limits of the species. The Roanoke has two such populations. One is a colony of cerulean warblers along the river about a mile downstream from the town of Halifax, and the other is the northernmost breeding colony of Mississippi kites on the Atlantic coastal plain. The kites are found in the same general area as the cerulean warblers.

The Roanoke offers the fisherman not only the expected catch but fishes for which the river is especially noted. In spring the striped bass, an anadromous fish, enters the river to spawn. The falls of the Roanoke at Weldon are a famous spawning ground for this species. Above the falls the river offers a resident species, the Roanoke bass. Along with the Roanoke log perch, the Roanoke darter, and the orangefin madtom, the Roanoke bass is one of several species limited or largely limited to the Roanoke watershed in distribution.

The rivers, with their bottomland swamps, are such a prominent feature of the coastal plain that the motorist, taking a major highway south, can expect a river crossing every twenty to thirty miles. Beginning with the Chowan and Roanoke, one meets in quick succession the Tar, Neuse, Northeast Cape Fear, Black, Cape Fear, and Lumber rivers in North Carolina. Near the coast, there is the Waccamaw, which flows south into South Carolina.

In South Carolina, the river crossings are just as numerous. They begin with the Little Pee Dee, Great Pee Dee, Lynches, and Black rivers. About halfway across the state, one comes to South Carolina's biggest river system—the Santee. I devote the last part of this chapter to that system, which includes the Congaree River. With its big trees and, until recently, almost untouched wilderness, the Congaree is a river indelibly imprinted upon my memory. Chapter 11 treats Four Holes Swamp, a small swampland watercourse lying south of the Santee; like the Congaree, it is noted for its big trees. Four Holes flows into the Edisto and is followed in quick order by the Combahee, Coosawhatchie, and Savannah. The Savannah, a large brownwater river having its source in the Appalachians, forms the boundary between South Carolina and Georgia.

With its bottomland swamps and high bluffs, the Savannah River was well known to William Bartram, who called it a river of pleasing vistas and untrammeled beauty. Except at highway crossings, its beauty at the present time is largely hidden. The Savannah National Wildlife Refuge is one of the few places where the motorist can stop and see something of the swamps and marshes that border the river. The refuge, which lies in South Carolina, is easily reached from U.S. Highway 17 before the highway crosses the Savannah River above the city of Savannah. About half of this 26,580-acre refuge is in diked marsh, and the other half is in bottomland swamp containing mixed hardwoods and cypresses. The refuge is one of the easiest and best stops the bird watcher can make when traveling the coastal route.

Like the Great Dismal Swamp in Virginia, the Savannah drainage is a dividing line between more northern plants and animals and more southern ones. The ogeechee tupelo (*Nyssa ogeche*), the saw palmetto (*Serenoa repens*), and the pinckneya (*Pinckneya pubens*) are woody plants of the Deep

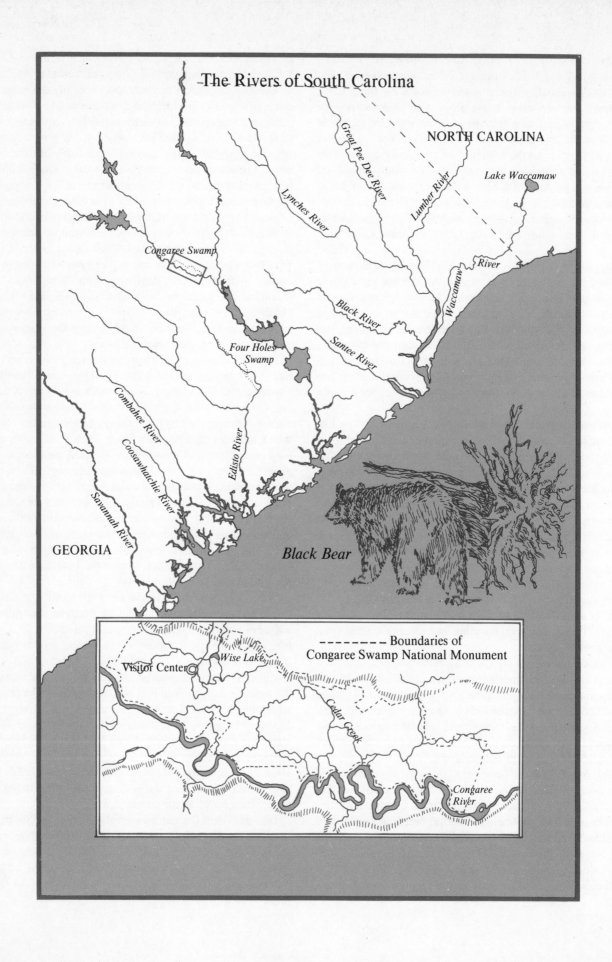

The Rivers of South Carolina

NORTH CAROLINA

Great Pee Dee River

Lumber River

Lake Waccamaw

Lynches River

Congaree Swamp

Black River

Waccamaw River

Four Holes Swamp

Santee River

Combahee River

Coosawhatchie River

Edisto River

Savannah River

GEORGIA

Black Bear

Visitor Center

Wise Lake

- - - - - - - Boundaries of Congaree Swamp National Monument

Cedar Creek

Congaree River

South that barely make it across the dividing line into South Carolina. Among reptiles and amphibians, no fewer than four species, like the plants just mentioned, barely cross the river into South Carolina. The four are the gopher tortoise, the northern mole skink, the eastern indigo snake, and the eastern bird-voiced tree frog.

Well inland in the coastal plain of Georgia, the Oconee and Ocmulgee rivers join to form the Altamaha, which is the next big river after the Savannah. With a bottomland swamp five and a half miles wide at Jessup, Georgia, and wider yet downstream, the Altamaha is a challenge to anyone wishing to search out its natural wonders. There is no easy way to explore the swamps along the river. Gary Williamson and I found that a canoe was the best conveyance for reaching wilder areas along the lower river. And there is always the option of stopping at highway crossings to have a look.

The Altamaha has a special claim to botanical fame. In the fall of 1765, John Bartram and his son William discovered a new tree species near the site of Fort Barrington on the lower reaches of the river. John named the plant franklinia in honor of Benjamin Franklin. On subsequent trips they collected plants and seeds, which were propagated in the Bartram garden in Philadelphia. The new tree (it could also be called a shrub) proved to be a member of the tea family (Theaceae) and a close relative of the loblolly bay. But following a visit in 1790 to the discovery site by the botanist Moses Marshall, the tree was never again found growing in the wild. The plant became known as "the lost franklinia." If it had not been for specimens saved by the Bartrams, the plant in all likelihood would have become lost forever. Nevertheless, everyone with an interest in botany who explores the Altamaha bottomlands carries a faint hope of rediscovering the plant. I myself have explored the region around the site of old Fort Barrington without making any exciting finds.

In an article that appeared in 1937, Francis Harper and Arthur N. Leeds shed light upon the probable habitat in which the plant grew. Using the clue that the Bartrams found franklinia growing with pinckneya, they came to the conclusion that the discovery site was a sandhill bog near the river and not the river swamp proper. They based that assumption upon the fact that pinckneya is a bog species adapted to acidic soil. The river, they pointed out, is on the alkaline side. That finding in no way disqualifies franklinia from being a member of a cypress-dominated plant community. The sandhill bogs in the region are likely to contain pinckneya, bay trees, tupelos, and cypresses.

Although franklinia has completely disappeared and no one knows why or knows even exactly where it was once found, the river and its swamplands still contain many other treasures. The lower part of the river is sometimes visited by the West Indian manatee, or sea cow, a grotesque-looking seal-like mammal that maintains a foothold in Florida waters. Of even greater interest are the river's freshwater clams, or mussels. No fewer than six endemic species have been discovered. Members of the family Unionidae, the clams have larvae that require certain fish as their hosts during early developmental stages. The most curious of the clams is the spiny clam (*Elliptio spinosa*), whose shell is armed with from one to four spines on each valve. A relict species, the clam was discovered about 160 years ago and, like a number of other species, has had a way of becoming lost to science. Ivan R. Tomkins, a Georgia naturalist, rediscovered the spiny clam in 1954, when the river was very low. Appropriately, he found the clams on a sandbar in the river a short distance from Fort Barrington of lost franklinia fame.

Lewis Island, a large wooded island in the river a few miles upstream from the town of Darien, contains sizable numbers of virgin bald cypresses that somehow escaped cutting during earlier days. Gary Williamson and I reached the island after a hard paddle upstream by canoe and at once began a search for the big trees. None were visible from the river. But after hiking a short distance, we suddenly came upon one of the giants, its presence screened by a dense growth of much smaller trees. We continued to find more of the big trees as we stumbled about in soggy bottomland. They were widely scattered and lacked tall knees or prominent basal bulges. Some were little more than hollow shells, but they were nevertheless still alive and outwardly sound. On our trip we did not see another person or even a boat. We were reminded of the lower Roanoke, where we also had the river all to ourselves.

During the latter part of the nineteenth century, the Altamaha, like so many other rivers of the East Coast, served as an artery to float out cypress logs and other timber. In an account that appeared in the Savannah *Morning News* in February, 1884, mention is made of a boat called a snag puller that cleared the Altamaha of obstructing driftwood so that rafts of logs could be floated out more easily. "Petrified tree trunks were removed," according to the account, and "a big gum tree 10 miles upriver was finally moved."

The Altamaha and other big rivers of the East Coast must have been exquisite sights before the advent of lumbering. Lewis Island gave Gary and I a hint of what their forests were probably like. But the Congaree Swamp in South Carolina provides an even better example. A large tract of timber along that river escaped the thorough cutting that overtook most of the bottomland swamps around the turn of the century.

A part of the Santee watershed, the Congaree begins where the Broad and Saluda rivers meet at Columbia. There, at the edge of the fall line, rapids give way to the winding, comparatively sluggish river, the kind so characteristic of the coastal plain. The Congaree takes sixty miles of meandering to cover a distance of thirty miles as the crow flies. It then joins the Wateree to form the Santee.

I first became aware of the Congaree River in 1965. Richard Pough, conservationist and author of bird guides, called to ask me if I would accept an assignment with the Charleston Museum to explore a large tract of virgin timber where he and others hoped that I might be able to find the nearly extinct ivory-billed woodpecker. Pough said that though no reliable sightings of the bird had been made in the Congaree Swamp, it was the only large tract of virgin bottomland timber left in the East and, as such, might contain the rare bird, since the ivorybill was generally thought to be dependent upon the few large stands of mature timber still in existence. Of some sixty thousand acres of bottomland timber within the floodplain of the Congaree Swamp, no fewer than fifteen thousand acres, all in a single tract, was what could be considered virgin or nearly virgin timber. To account for the presence of such a large stand so close to Columbia, the capital of South Carolina, it is necessary to trace the history of the river and its swamp. John Cely provided me with an account of the swamp, including the reasons why its big trees were spared when nearly everywhere else the forests were being leveled.

Originally, a tribe of Indians named the Congarees lived in the region. They obtained much of their sustenance by fishing and hunting in the swamp. At that time cougars, bears, elk, and wolves were still plentiful in the swamp and its environs. Mounds tell of the Indians' long tenure in the bottomlands. But by 1740 the white settlers had arrived; their ways and their diseases spelled the doom of the aborigines.

At the time of the American Revolution, some of the land along the river was being cultivated. However, the cost of clearing land and erecting dikes to protect crops from flooding was prohibitive. As a result, very little of the bottomland was reclaimed for agriculture. Indigo and corn were the chief crops of the region. After the Revolution, rice, primarily a tidewater crop, replaced indigo.

In 1825 in a publication entitled *Statistics of South Carolina,* a writer named Robert Mills echoed a sentiment toward swamps that goes back to William Byrd II and is still the prevailing view. Referring to the large amounts of unreclaimed and undrained swampland in Richland County, where the Congaree Swamp is located, he wrote, "What clouds of miasma, invisible to sight, almost continually rise from these sinks of corruption, and who can calculate the extent of its pestilential influence?" Mills reported that of the 403,000 acres in Richland County, only 25,000 acres were being cultivated in 1825. Probably a minuscule amount of swampland was under cultivation at that time.

Around 1840 a planter named James Adams was using slave labor to build a dike at what is now the northern boundary of the Congaree Swamp National Monument. Large trees grow on the dike today. Apparently the project was never completed. For the most part, it was easier to grow crops in the uplands while allowing cattle and hogs to roam the swamps. To provide safe havens for livestock during times of high water, large mounds called "cattle mounts" were

constructed by the slaves. The three or four cattle mounts that I have visited in the Congaree Swamp were covered with large trees. Instead of typical swamp plants, the mounds supported hickory, tulip poplar, and flowering dogwood. One of the larger cattle mounts was fifty feet wide, ninety feet long, six to seven feet high, and roughly circular in shape.

Adams and other landowners of his day must have experienced difficulty in herding their livestock to these mounds in time of high water. The Congaree rises so rapidly that even today advance warnings are provided to hunters, fishermen, and others so that they will allow ample time to leave low-lying areas. In just a few hours the river can cover the bottomlands with four or five feet of swirling muddy water. Although the river is most prone to flooding during the spring, high water can occur at any time of the year. On an average the swamp floods ten times during the course of a year.

From the end of the Civil War until the beginning of this century, the swamps along the Congaree appear to have been little used except for fishing, hunting, and running cattle. In 1895 the Santee River Cypress Lumber Company, owned by the Beidler family of Chicago, began acquiring choice tracts of swampland in South Carolina containing cypress. By 1905 the company held over a hundred thousand acres in the bottomlands of the Congaree, Wateree, and Santee rivers. The harvesting of cypress began with the land purchases.

It was not easy to reach the trees or, once they were cut, to remove them from the swamps. The first step was to girdle the trees by ax, so that, after a period of time, the wood would be dry enough to float. The next step was to fell the trees and haul them to creeks and rivers where they could be floated to sawmills. According to Harry Hampton, who did so much to save a large portion of the Congaree Swamp, about half the cypress cut in the Congaree was too green to float and sank to the bottoms of waterways where it remains to this day. John Cely stated that logging took place only along the waterways, sloughs, and ponds where the cypresses grew. No roads were built to haul out the logs, and none of the hardwood trees were cut. He added that some magnificent cypress specimens escaped cutting and are still standing today. The average age of the trees at the time they were cut, according to Beidler sawmill records, was between five hundred and seven hundred years!

By 1915 the logging ceased in the fifteen-thousand-acre Beidler holding in the Congaree Swamp. The swamp again became a faraway place, little visited and virtually unknown except to the hunters and fishermen who went there. For many years the Beidler family showed no interest in removing any more of the trees. Except for the cutting of the cypress and previous small-scale grazing and agricultural ventures, the swamp was almost as wild and untouched as when the Congaree Indians had been there.

When, in 1965, I first visited the swamp, South Carolina was in the throes of one of its infrequent winter ice storms—a time when every tree and road surface is coated with ice. On the evening of my arrival, Harry Hampton took me to a frigid clubhouse within the Beidler tract used by members of a hunting club. With help from an open fire, I managed to get through an uncomfortable night. The next morning, with the sun out and ice glittering from every tree, I found myself in a wonderland. Birds were flitting about, woodpeckers were calling, and the ice, loosened by the rays of the sun, was raining down in small particles from the big trees. The awesome size of the trees was what most impressed me about the swamp. Those who are used to calling a tree big if it has a trunk diameter of three feet have a hard time getting used to trees with diameters of five or six feet. Were trees of this size commonplace in our early forests, or was the large size due to the fertility of the soil and good growing conditions? I will return to this question toward the end of the chapter.

As I set out on my first hike, I was impressed by the openness of the terrain below the big trees. I could walk for long distances without encountering tangles of impeding growth. Open, parklike stands, as I knew, are typical of virgin timber. The only serious obstacle to my progress was the many small watercourses that wound everywhere through the wooded bottomlands. I was reminded of a description given by John Lawson, an explorer and naturalist who in December, 1700, visited the upper part of the Santee where it joins the Wateree and Congaree. He spoke of coming frequently upon "small brooks or runs of water" that were two or three feet deep. He wrote, "You meet dry land for another space, so another brook, this continuing." Lawson's brooks were the many sloughs or guts that weave such an intricate pattern throughout the length and breadth of the Congaree Swamp and other swamps as well. But under the guidance of Hampton, who knew the swamp better than almost anyone else, I discovered that if one follows a slough for a short distance, he almost invariably comes upon a fallen tree that bridges the stream bed. Although slippery and often covered with moss, the tree trunks made convenient crossing places. But unless the swamp was unusually dry, there were always low areas that could be crossed only by wading in water that might be ankle- or knee-deep. Lawson also found that he and the others in his small party had to resort to wading. He wrote of wading in freezing weather through "a prodigious wide and deep swamp, being forc'd to strip stark-naked," and having "much a-do to save ourselves from drowning in this fatiegue."

Later, as I explored the swamp on my own or with Harry Hampton, I experienced the same difficulties as did Lawson and his party. When encountering wide, inundated stretches of the swamp, known as *flats,* I had no choice but to plunge in and try to reach the opposite side. Sometimes, like Lawson, it took "much a-do" for me to reach my objective. On more than one occasion, as I hiked in the swamp with Hampton after darkness had fallen, I found that we were obliged to make our way over uneven, vine-studded terrain. Not all of the swamp is open and parklike. That is particularly true at the edges of sloughs and rivers and where trees have fallen. The extra sunlight at such places promotes the growth of canebrakes as well as of tangles composed of shrubs and vines. Only through Harry's uncanny ability to find his way without compass or flashlight in pitch darkness were we able to get back to our campsites.

Harry and my friend Gary Williamson were with me one day when, without warning, a giant tree directly in front of us crashed to the ground. I later learned that in a mature forest that is not a totally unexpected event. After having lived its full life-span, a tree, weakened by age, will suddenly topple over. Loud splintering sounds fill the air as the tree begins to fall; then a great boom echoes through the forest as it hits the ground. It is an awesome sight to witness the final collapse of an ancient tree. Strangely, the event is likely to take place on a windless day when the tree is in full foliage.

The gap in the forest made by the fallen giant is soon filled with vigorous young growth responding to the entry of sunlight. Eventually the old tree will be replaced by one or more younger ones. Thus, trees in a mature forest are far from having uniform ages. Such a forest is made up of trees of different ages, all competing with one another for space and sunlight.

The trees that fall slowly decompose. Ants, beetles, and centipedes work their way into the wood, and at the same time, fungi, feeding upon decay, cover portions of the outer surface. The Congaree Swamp, as is true of other swamps, plays host to a wide variety of fungi, each with its distinctive shape and coloring. Eventually the fallen tree turns into soil, leaving behind mounds that are not unlike primitive human burial sites. The overturned roots at the base of the tree form the largest mounds. Hampton told me that these mounds are called *hurricanes*—a reference to the fact that in hurricanes many trees become uprooted and slowly decay.

The Congaree Swamp is noted for a tree species that, unlike others, has little opportunity for regeneration. The tree, the loblolly pine, requires open ground to become established. It is therefore surprising to find large stands of mature loblolly pine growing in a forest that has not been open to any substantial degree since white settlement took place in the region. The pines represent different age groups. A few are extremely old, far surpassing the 200 years usually given as the age limit for the loblolly. Dr. Wade T. Batson, professor of botany at the University of South Carolina, counted 320 annual growth rings on the stump of a Congaree loblolly. L. L. Gaddy has said that the loblollies range in height from 140 to 170 feet and that there are three with a breast-high circumference of over 15 feet. Others are not so large and seem to range in age from about 180 to 200 years.

Each year lightning kills a few of the pines, and others die of old age. Sadly, a pine bark beetle infestation during the last few years has led to the demise of great numbers of the survivors from an earlier time.

How the loblolly got its start in the swamp is a mystery. It has been suggested that during a series of drought years the swamp became dry enough to allow the entry of fire. Large conflagrations may have opened up parts of the swamp. Taking advantage of openings, seedlings could have gotten a start. As is evident today, the trees grew on higher ground that is covered by water only when the swamp is flooded.

Depending upon whose study one goes by, there are as few as eleven plant communities in the Congaree Swamp and its borders or as many as seventeen. Based upon slight differences in elevation, the communities range from cypresses and water tupelos in areas that are nearly permanently flooded, to pines, oaks, hickories, and pawpaws at higher sites known as old river terraces. Cypress is most common at borders of sloughs, edges of oxbow lakes, and other low places. Large trees date back to the era of cypress cutting and earlier. Gaddy stated that there are more than twenty cypress trees in the swamp with a circumference of over twelve feet and several over twenty feet.

One day when exploring a remote part of the swamp with Harry, I came upon a giant living cypress that was nothing more than a shell. Boosting myself up ten feet, I was able to look through a hole into the cavernous interior of the tree. As my eyes became accustomed to the dim light, I could make out long rotting strands of wood that hung like stalactites from inside walls of the tree. I could barely see the bottom of the cavity. It was five or six feet below ground level and contained enough space to pitch a tent. I crawled through the hole part of the way into the interior cavity and then began examining the walls around me to see if there were any bats or other forms of wildlife in the dark refuge. Before I knew what had happened, a huge chunk of rotten wood that I had somehow jarred loose fell squarely on my head and shattered into dozens of smaller pieces. Owing to the fact that the wood was well decayed and light, I escaped injury. Slightly dazed, I climbed back out into daylight and lowered myself to the ground.

In 1978 L. L. Gaddy wrote that the fifteen-thousand-acre Beidler tract and adjacent holdings have accounted for twenty-two state and national champion trees. The national champions (six in all) were possum haw holly, laurel oak, overcup oak, sweet gum, swamp tupelo, and swamp privet. However, champion trees keep their titles only until some other tree exceeds them in number of points scored. The champion laurel oak in the Congaree Swamp, for example, has since been surpassed by one in Georgia. But a 1984 listing of big trees of South Carolina gives the Beidler tract and adjacent holdings twenty-five state champions and cochampions; of these seven were national champions.

Since 1978 the swamp had gained a national champion shumard oak and Carolina ash. Therefore, if anything, the swamp's reputation for big trees is now on firmer ground than ever.

Gaddy observed that in this forest of big trees one loses all sense of size. A sweet gum that looks small turns out to be three feet in diameter, and a "short tree" is a hundred feet tall. He added that all of the canopy trees are giants in comparison with the trees of other forests. The girth of the trees is not the only feature that impresses the visitor to the swamp. Competition for light has produced a canopy that ranges from 110 to 160 feet in height! Gaddy's examples of giant trees include a loblolly of 168 feet, a willow oak of 158 feet, a persimmon of 110 feet, and an American holly of 99 feet.

One cannot help but wonder whether trees of this size were typical of the early American forest. I can only make the conjecture that the Congaree Swamp, with its rich soil and ample moisture, probably contains larger trees than were generally found in the uplands. But most southern swamps, especially those enriched by the waters of brownwater rivers, may well have had trees whose sizes compared favorably with those presently found in the Congaree Swamp. Even today there are a few swamps other than the Congaree where sizable numbers of very large trees, including state and national champions, can be found.

For example, Gary Williamson, along with another big-tree enthusiast, Byron Carmean, measured trees along the Nottoway River in southeastern Virginia and discovered eighteen state champions and cochampions and several national champions. Their greatest triumph came in 1985, when they discovered an American elm in the Nottoway Swamp that surpassed in size the famous Louis Vieux Elm in Kansas, which was honored by being made the centerpiece of a one-tree state park. Like the Congaree River, the Nottoway is a brownwater river and therefore yearly receives a quota of rich soil from the uplands. But the Congaree River excels in having a much larger floodplain and a far greater expanse of mature timber.

In 1969, while a campaign was under way to save the Congaree Swamp, cutting began again in the Beidler tract. Looking at the threat from a philosophical standpoint, John Culler, editor of an outdoor magazine, wrote, "We must remember that the Beidlers are in the lumber business, and the very fact that they have owned the area for all these years and not cut it is the only reason it is still there now." Fortunately, an intense campaign, headed by the LeConte Chapter of the Sierra Club, to save the Congaree Swamp and its big trees was ultimately successful. In 1976, by an act of Congress, a Congaree Swamp National Monument was established. The monument consists of the entire 15,135-acre former Beidler holding, and presently an additional 3,900 acres is slated for acquisition. The swamp is not as pristine today, however, as when I explored it in 1965. Lumbering roads have been built, and during the course of the most recent lumbering operation, approximately 700 acres in the Beidler tract were clear-cut and 2,000 acres selectively cut.

I am very grateful for the many months I spent in the swamp and the lessons I learned from the late Harry Hampton, an experienced woodsman, a true sportsman, and the prime mover in saving the Congaree Swamp. Although my search for the ivory-billed woodpecker in the swamp was unsuccessful, I did obtain clues that the bird might be present. Reports I received from hunters and fishermen seemed suggestive of occasional appearances of one or more of the woodpeckers, which seem so perfectly suited for a swamp with so many large living and dead trees. A member of Harry's hunting club said he had seen a big woodpecker flying across the Congaree River with "what looked like a large white cigar in its mouth." That report, and another of a big woodpecker with a black crest, sounded convincing. The ivorybill's large white bill could be compared with a white cigar, and the female ivorybill is the only North American woodpecker with a black crest. The male ivorybill and both the male and female pileated woodpeckers have red crests.

Even though a few species are missing, the Congaree Swamp today, as when John Lawson visited it in 1700, has its rare species and its larger, more spectacular ones. Lawson found the sloughs "well stor'd" with fowl, including a multicolored bird that almost certainly was the wood duck. Wood ducks abound in the swamp today. He also spoke of large numbers of woodcock and "gangs" of up to several hundred wild turkeys that came down from their roosts to feed upon acorns at early dawn. The woodcocks are still in the swamp, and Harry Hampton, an inveterate turkey hunter who loved to tell how the turkeys usually outsmarted him, would have been glad to vouch for the presence of these magnificent birds. Other wildlife forms of special interest found in the swamp today include the pine woods snake, swallow-tailed kite, Mississippi kite, Swainson's warbler, bobcat, river otter, marsh rabbit, and fox squirrel.

Thanks to its present status as a national monument, the once largely inaccessible Beidler tract can now easily be visited by the public. With the help of guided tours, canoe trails, a boardwalk, and twenty-five miles of primitive hiking trails, the sights of this great forest are open to anyone who is willing to hike or paddle. About twenty miles southeast of Columbia, the swamp can be reached by way of State Highway 48. Watch for signs marking the entrance road. There is a visitors' center at the park entrance. Information about the park can be obtained by writing to the superintendent of the Congaree Swamp National Monument, P.O. Box 11920, Columbia, South Carolina 29211.

References

Cely, John. "Is the Beidler Tract in Congaree Swamp Virgin?" In *Congaree Swamp: Greatest Unprotected Forest on the Continent.* Sierra Club Publication. Columbia, S.C., 1974.

Gaddy, L. L. "Congaree: Forest of Giants." *American Forests,* LXXXIV (April, 1978), 51–53.

Harper, Francis, and Arthur N. Leeds. "A Supplementary Chapter on *Franklinia alatamaha.*" *Bartonia,* XIX (1937), 1–13.

Savage, Henry. *River of the Carolinas: The Santee.* New York, 1956.

Tomkins, Ivan R. "Altamaha's Spiny Mussel." *Nature Magazine,* XLIX (1956), 415–16.

During the heyday of rice culture, which began around 1800, the low country of southeastern North Carolina, South Carolina, and Georgia was a quiltwork of rice fields. Fresh water, essential for growing rice, was often obtained by damming small streams. The impoundments behind the dams could be tapped whenever water was needed. Known as reserves or backwaters, they sometimes supported large stands of cypress. But nearly everywhere else along the coast cypress and other trees were destroyed to make more room for rice growing. Charles H. Wharton has written that, using slave labor, plantation owners completely destroyed the great cypress and other timber by burning or burying the trees and that extensive dikes and canals occupied the entire floodplain for several miles upstream along the rivers. According to Wharton, huge buried cypress logs dating back to that period are still occasionally found.

Around 1800 a rice planter named John Middleton had acquired large holdings of both marshland and higher ground on the south side of the Santee River near its mouth. Called the Washo plantation, this tract, like so many others, was an intricate network of canals, dikes, and reserves for storing water. One of the reserves eventually became famous as the last large nesting colony of herons and egrets during the grim days of plume hunting at the end of the nineteenth century. During Middleton's time, the reserve was beginning to receive attention because of its teeming wildlife. A reporter from the Charleston *Courier,* visiting the reserve in April, 1823, wrote a glowing account of what he saw.

He described the reserve as a swamp over ten miles long, filled with cypress and other trees growing so close together that the proprietor had had to cut a path for boats and canoes. Every dead log had its sunning alligators, and the tops of the trees were filled with nesting birds. The reporter spoke of seeing "great American herons, white cranes, and fish hawks." He added that "the darter of Wilson, a bird so imperfectly known, may be seen in flocks in the air, or perched on trees." He concluded, "In this magnificent repository the naturalist . . . will find ample field for his researches."

The reporter's great American heron was the great blue heron, his white cranes were egrets, and his fish hawk was the osprey. Finally, "the darter of Wilson" was the anhinga. The sights that so impressed the reporter can still be seen today thanks to a long succession of benign owners who have protected the rookery over the years.

The next owner, Arthur M. Blake, held title to twenty-five thousand acres and at one time owned nine hundred slaves. Rice growing was enormously profitable, as seen by his income and those of the area's other planters. Blake was said to have earned as much as $250,000 in one season from his rice fields. It is no wonder that today, in spite of ravages of war and time, many beautiful antebellum homes still exist in the low country. Blake, who died in 1881, spent his last years in England. The rice reserve, where so many birds nest among the cypress, is called Blake's Reserve or, sometimes, the Washo Reserve.

By 1900 a new use had been found for the diked marshes. Rice growing had slowly become a thing of the past. Following the Civil War, many of the plantations were abandoned, and the impoundments and ditches fell into disrepair. Nevertheless, in the face of great odds, a few planters restored the rice fields and began growing rice again. But by the 1870s, rice could be grown more profitably in Louisiana, Texas, and Arkansas. Besides facing stiff competition from the western rice fields, growers along the Atlantic Coast suffered from the effects of a series of devastating hurricanes that demolished the old rice fields and their dikes. Finally, the planters had to contend with the bobolink, a member of the blackbird family. During the spring, migrating bobolinks, or ricebirds, as they were often called, would descend upon the rice fields and eat the grain while it was still in the milk stage. In late summer, on their return flight, the birds would eat mature grain. Efforts to ward off the birds by shooting had little effect.

But birdlife of a different sort, it turned out, came to the rescue of the stricken plantation owners. Northern sportsmen had discovered that the diked marshes were a paradise for ducks and geese. Banding together and forming shooting clubs, they purchased the best of the old rice plantations and maintained the intricate systems of ditches, dikes, and impoundments. Instead of rice, the impoundments now produced freshwater food plants that would entice waterfowl.

In 1898 a group calling themselves the Santee Club (later known as the Santee Gun Club) purchased a portion of the former holdings of Arthur M. Blake and built a large club-house. One of the early members of the club was President Grover Cleveland, who, with his bulky frame, must have had trouble reaching duck blinds out in the marshes. Over the years the club expanded its holdings from the original two thousand to three thousand acres to over twenty-three thousand. Adhering strictly to game laws of their own and to those later imposed by state and federal governments, the club gained a reputation for good sportsmanship. During its early years the club's outstanding achievement was to provide protection for the teeming rookery at Blake's Reserve.

The services of the club were greatly appreciated by ornithologists and bird lovers of that day. Herbert K. Job, one of the visitors to the reserve, told of paddling about all day and reveling in the sights and sounds of "the largest, and perhaps the only large egret rookery in North America." His visit was followed by that of another noted ornithologist, Frank M. Chapman, who took delight in the new lacelike foliage of the cypress trees draped with Spanish moss. He regarded the reserve as the birds' last refuge from the plume hunter.

Members of the Santee Gun Club had new challenges to face as the century wore on. During the Dust Bowl years of the 1930s, waterfowl and waterfowl shooting were facing an uncertain future. There was concern that there would no longer be good shooting in the old rice fields. A sharp decline in waterfowl was followed during the winter of 1941 by a severe freeze in the South that decimated the population of the common snipe. Until then, snipe shooting had been a favored sport of club members.

In June of 1974, the Santee Gun Club, in one of the most magnanimous offers in recent conservation history, donated its holdings to the Nature Conservancy. With the exception of Blake's Reserve and its immediate environs, the land was then promptly turned over by the Conservancy to the state of South Carolina for use as a wildlife management area. The Conservancy, as in most such cases, reserves the right to reclaim jurisdiction if, for any reason, management is not in the best interests of its preservation goals. The property is now called the Santee Coastal Reserve. It can be reached by leaving U.S. Highway 17 just south of where it crosses the Santee River south of Georgetown and then driving about two miles to the east. Signs point the way.

For the most part, the bird rookeries at Blake's Reserve have prospered. But Alexander Sprunt, Jr., pointed out as long ago as 1964 that, although the threat of the plume hunter was a thing of the past, it was necessary to protect the colony from bird lovers. "So many people," he wrote, "had heard of this great rookery and were visiting it that the birds were constantly disturbed." Bird photographers were the worst offenders. As a result of so much disturbance, the rookery

population began to fall off drastically. Sprunt went on to say that the area was finally completely closed by the Santee Gun Club except to those who had received special permission. A policy of not allowing visits to the area during the nesting season is being maintained by the Nature Conservancy.

Sprunt told of magnificent cypress trees rimming the lagoon and staining the water with their tannic acid, thereby making it a dark wine color. He also spoke of small floating islands composed of bushes, saplings, and grass that shifted from one location to another "at the whim of the wind." On long-dead stubs of ancient trees, he reported, there were nests of ospreys, and on logs, or half submerged, there were alligators. He also saw anhingas and the same members of the heron family mentioned by the reporter from the Charleston *Courier*. There were also bird species not mentioned in the 1823 account. In 1947 the state's first nesting of the glossy ibis was recorded at the Blake Reserve. Nesting white ibis, Louisiana herons (tricolored herons), little blue herons, and black-crowned and yellow-crowned night herons were also reported by Sprunt.

On visits to Blake's Reserve during the spring, summer, and early fall of 1975, I failed to see the glossy ibis, the Louisiana heron, or, another bird mentioned by Sprunt, the swallow-tailed kite. But ospreys, other large waders, woodpeckers, chimney swifts, belted kingfishers, and prothonotary, northern parula, yellow-throated, and hooded warblers were very much in evidence. By that time the cattle egret, a relative newcomer to North America, had become one of the most common nesting species at the rookery. Also present in good numbers were nesting great egrets and great blue herons. The most impressive sight, aside from the wading bird rookery, was the many osprey nests precariously placed at tops of dead and living cypress trees. Anyone approaching the reserve is greeted by the screaming cries of the ospreys. There are some fifty nests in all, with about three-fourths of them occupied in any one nesting season. Occasional empty nests are patronized by nesting great horned owls. Some of the ospreys stay on into the fall after the nesting season is over. I saw around half a dozen on a visit on September 14 and about twice as many on a mid-February visit.

The dead trees also lure wood ducks, which nest both in hollows and in wood duck boxes, and such other cavity nesters as woodpeckers, crested flycatchers, titmice, and prothonotary warblers. The wood ducks are joined during the fall and winter by other waterfowl. In some years as many as five thousand American wigeons have been counted on lagoons in the reserve. Smaller numbers of American coots are present at that time of year and, along with them, pied-billed grebes and common moorhens. A new chapter in the reserve's ornithological history commenced with the first nesting of the bald eagle in 1982.

As a rule, cypress swamps do not play host to so many fish-eating birds. But large rookeries are sometimes present

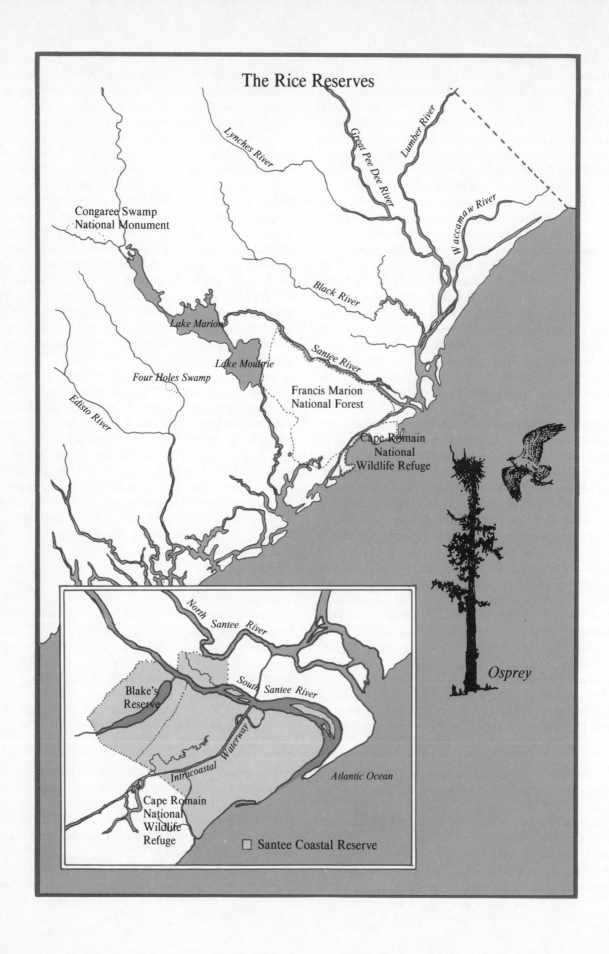

The Rice Reserves

Lynches River

Great Pee Dee River

Lumber River

Waccamaw River

Congaree Swamp
National Monument

Black River

Lake Marion

Lake Moultrie

Santee River

Four Holes Swamp

Edisto River

Francis Marion
National Forest

Cape Romain
National
Wildlife Refuge

Osprey

North Santee River

Blake's
Reserve

South Santee River

Intracoastal Waterway

Atlantic Ocean

Cape Romain
National
Wildlife
Refuge

☐ Santee Coastal Reserve

if the swamp is near freshwater or brackish marshes. That is very much the case at Blake's Reserve. Only a short flight away are the old rice fields, now impoundments maintained for waterfowl. The Santee River, along with numerous creeks and small estuaries, provides additional feeding grounds. Plentiful food supplies, as well as years of protection, have made Blake's Reserve the outstanding bird mecca that it has been for nearly two hundred years.

Like the birdlife, the cypress tree has played an important role in the history of Blake's Reserve. The presence of hollow hulks of trees up to three and a half feet in diameter indicate that cypress was there at the time the area was flooded. Where deep flooding took place, the original cypresses, it is safe to assume, either died within a few years or were left in a moribund condition. It is these dead trees that presently furnish so many sites for nesting ospreys. I measured the water depth in a part of the reserve where the largest number of dead cypress trees are present. The water was between eight and nine feet in depth, too deep for the survival of cypress trees. In somewhat more shallow sections, many cypresses are living but seem stunted in growth; some were dead. In those moderately deep sections, I found no knees protruding above the water level. In shoaler water around the perimeter of the reserve is a belt of young cypress trees that had sprouted during dry years when water levels were low. Those trees ranged from only five to twenty feet in height. Nests of large wading birds were either in cypresses or button bushes. Both pond cypress and bald cypress are present and also swamp tupelo, water tupelo, and water ash. Small green wood-orchid and water-spider orchid are plentiful in wetter parts of the reserve, the latter even growing in masses of floating water weed. Except for larger lagoons, the summer months see the waters of the reserve so choked with coontail,

frog's-bit, and other aquatic plants that it is impossible to paddle a canoe in many places. During fall and winter, ducks and coots clear away some of the floating plants by eating them.

The history of Blake's Reserve is duplicated in the low country by other reserves that at first were impoundments to supply water for rice fields and then came under the ownership of large shooting preserves. The reserves are of two types—those that are wooded and those that are open bodies of water. Examples of wooded reserves are Blake's Reserve and, to the southwest not far from Charleston, Penny Dam Reserve on Fairlawn plantation. Penny Dam, like Blake's, is filled with cypresses and over the years has supported flourishing colonies of wading birds. The wood stork nested here in 1928. A second rice reserve on Fairlawn plantation has the distinction of being one of the last known haunts of Bachman's warbler. Known as Mayrant's or Myrant's Reserve, it is an open body of water surrounded by swamp forest.

It is something of a paradox that the rice reserves, a by-product of intense deforestation related to rice growing, should become safe havens for cypress trees and many rare or spectacular forms of birdlife. The Santee Coastal Reserve, besides having its famous rookeries, contains Carolina bays, a habitat rich in rare plants as well as reptiles, amphibians, and other wildlife (see Chapter 12).

References

Sprunt, Alexander, Jr. *Carolina Low Country Impressions.* New York, 1964.

Wharton, Charles H. *The Natural Environments of Georgia.* Atlanta, 1978.

Driving south in the Atlantic coastal plain, the traveler with an interest in swamps soon discovers that there is a good selection of them to visit. If there is only time enough to visit one, I would be inclined to choose the Four Holes Swamp in South Carolina. Near interstate highways and owned in part by the National Audubon Society, Four Holes has everything one could wish for in a southern swamp. Foremost in interest is the nearly 1,800 acres of virgin bottomland timber that miraculously escaped cutting during the era of heavy timbering. The Audubon Society sanctuary, appropriately named after the man who spared the timber, contains some of the largest and oldest bald cypress trees in existence. Known as the Francis Beidler Forest, the 3,660-acre sanctuary has interpretative facilities, a long self-guided boardwalk into the swamp, and guided tours.

Unlike the Congaree, Four Holes is not a brownwater swamp. It has a narrow watershed and little seasonal flooding. The water that reaches it comes from nearby slopes and numerous springs. A gentle drainage system with its headwaters south of the Congaree River, Four Holes takes a southeasterly course through the low, hilly country of the coastal plain and, after nourishing the Beidler Forest, makes an abrupt change in direction and flows to the southwest. It is believed that the change in direction was due to an ancient sandbar, a relict of the pre-Pleistocene sea, that blocked the course of the old Four Holes drainage and caused the water to find a new outlet to the sea. The swamp drains into the Edisto River, a parallel stream that, like Four Holes, also makes a shift in direction as it approaches the coast, turning southward to enter St. Helena Sound.

Four Holes Swamp was well known to the Indians and also to Francis Marion, the Revolutionary War commander who earned fame as the Swamp Fox. Marion and his forces are said to have crossed the swamp many times, but he apparently did not use the swamp as a retreat. Skirmishing between the patriots and the Tories took place in the region during the Revolution. Like so many other southern swamps, Four Holes was a haven for runaway slaves. But for the most part, history bypassed the secluded swamp, and the existence of the virgin timber was for a long time a guarded secret. The name *Four Holes,* according to some,

was derived from the presence of four fishing lakes in the swamp used by the Yamasee Indians. Another guess is that there were four passageways—openings or "holes"—that were used by early settlers to cross the swamp.

When the big lumbering interests, having cut off the virgin timber in the North, moved into South Carolina in the 1890s, the Beidler family of Chicago acquired the best cypress timber that could be found in the state. The cypress in Four Holes Swamp was one of the Beidlers' smaller acquisitions. For reasons that are unclear, no lumbering was conducted in this holding. Did the owner think the trees were too beautiful to be cut?

It is known that the Beidlers had a relatively benign attitude toward cutting. This attitude can be traced to the philosophy of Francis Beidler, the member of the family who directed the lumbering operations. In 1875, at the age of twenty-one, he toured the West, visiting Old Faithful and other natural wonders. He was sufficiently inspired by what he saw to dedicate himself to the preservation of our natural heritage. Later he took courage from the examples of Theodore Roosevelt and Gifford Pinchot, the foremost conservationists of his day and persons whom he greatly admired. Francis Beidler was not opposed to judicious cutting of timber. At the same time, he probably had good reasons for leaving portions of his holdings untouched. After he died in 1924, the Beidler family carried on in his tradition.

But the Beidlers' happy policy of leaving large tracts untouched was interrupted by a hydroelectric project in the 1930s that left most of their holdings underwater, embittering the owners as well as conservationists throughout the nation. The Santee-Cooper Project, as it was called, flooded a large portion of the Santee River bottoms along with its best cypress trees. According to a Beidler forester named Fred Seely in a letter to Henry Savage that is in the South Carolina archives, the cypress in the river basin had an average age of between 500 and 700 years; one tree was 1,600 years old. Seeley, very bitter about the project, said he would like to break the dam and let the swamp grow back again.

Having had their land condemned and having received what they saw as inadequate compensation, the Beidlers henceforth looked with suspicion upon interference with private holdings on the part of government or power companies. Some of the cypress was harvested before flooding occurred, but the trunks of many trees were left behind on the bottoms of two lakes. Salvage efforts to obtain those logs have been under way for a number of years.

Damage from the Santee-Cooper Project was not limited to the destruction of the swamp. About 88 percent of the Santee's flow had been diverted to the Cooper River, a sister waterway that empties into Charleston Harbor. As a result of that diversion, the Cooper River is choked with silt and must be dredged at great cost almost annually; at the same time, the Santee, deprived of a large share of its water and sediment, no longer enriches the duck marshes at its mouth, a fact that caused consternation among members of the Santee Gun Club. To overcome the damage, they were obliged to construct many miles of dikes to create freshwater impoundments containing marsh plants favored by waterfowl.

Unaffected by these events, the big cypress trees in Four Holes Swamp added more rings to the many that already told of their great age; other plants and the wildlife continued to exist in much the same way that they always had. Aside from cutting an occasional cypress tree to provide wood for making shingles, local farmers used the swamp only for fishing and hunting. Otherwise Four Holes was left to itself. Any changes that took place were those of nature. They were the inevitable changes that come with dry or wet years, with fire from lightning, and with destruction from wind, ice storms, or insect attacks. Those changes were modest indeed compared with the ones induced by man. With his engineering skills, man can quickly convert a swamp into a lake or, the opposite extreme, into dry land.

In 1969 the Beidler family, in the process of liquidating their holdings, authorized the cutting of a block of virgin timber in Four Holes Swamp. Conservationists in Charleston, only forty miles away, learned of both the cutting operation and the fact that, unknown to them all these years, there was still an untouched swamp in their neighborhood. They were quickly jarred into action. Peter Manigault of the Charleston *News and Courier* looked for support from conservation organizations. It was at this juncture that I was asked by the National Park Service to conduct a study of the swamp. During the last half of 1969 and early 1970, I was in Four Holes much of the time, often up to my knees in water, measuring trees, identifying plants and animals, and recording whatever seemed worth taking note of. It was much like my days in the Congaree Swamp. A smaller swamp, Four Holes was easier to comprehend, and there was also less danger of becoming lost. Less awesome than the Congaree, it nonetheless impressed me with its picture-book beauty—reflections of trees upon the still surface of black water, sunlight filtering through the foliage of immense trees, cardinal flowers at the edge of moss-covered banks, flocks of white ibis feeding among grotesquely shaped cypress knees.

One day I set out with Eliot Porter, the famous nature photographer, to find one of the largest and most impressive cypress trees in the swamp. The tree was in a little-explored part of the swamp where there were few landmarks to tell me how to reach it again. Even though he was weighted down with heavy camera equipment and had to wade every step of the way, Porter was game for making the search. Finally, we found the tree, its huge buttressed base dwarfing everything else in sight. At the base of the tree Porter assembled his camera equipment. Placing a dark cloth over his head and the camera, he studiously positioned himself for a shot. But strangely enough, he had the camera pointed away from the tree, not toward it. Apparently finding a tree of such size an impossible subject, he focused upon a colorful leaf floating in the water.

The outstanding feature of the swamp is the cypress trees. Many are 1,000 years old or older, and one giant, as mentioned earlier, was estimated by David Stahle to be between 1,500 and 2,000 years old. It was the oldest tree he discovered in his survey of ages reached by the bald cypress. This ancient giant can easily be viewed from the 6,500-foot-long boardwalk that traverses a portion of the swamp. The tree touches the very edge of the boardwalk. Other cypress trees in the swamp are as large or larger. Upstream, well outside the Beidler Forest, is the largest cypress tree recorded in South Carolina. That one reaches a height of 122 feet and has a circumference of 29 feet 9 inches.

It is no longer necessary to wade in deep, murky water to see the sights of Four Holes Swamp. In the spring of 1974, a tract of 3,415 acres of the former Beidler holdings was dedicated as a National Audubon Society sanctuary. The sanctuary was named the Francis Beidler Forest in honor of the man who, far ahead of his time, had the vision to preserve such a sizable portion of his swampland holdings in South Carolina. Now, stepping in to take his place, the National Audubon Society and the Nature Conservancy, through their combined efforts, were able to raise $1.5 million for the purchase of the Beidler holdings in Four Holes Swamp. In the years immediately following, such improvements as an entrance road, parking area, visitors' center, and boardwalk were constructed in the sanctuary. And 254 acres was added to it.

From the boardwalk the visitor can see a fine sample of the cypress forest. The largest trees are bald cypresses, but water tupelos, with their swollen bases and their trunk diameters of between three and four feet, give their codominants stiff competition for space in the almost permanently flooded environment. Everywhere are cypress knees, like forests of ninepins, rising to heights of three to five feet and taking on a variety of sizes and shapes. Some look like animals or human figures. A knee near the boardwalk reminded me of a rabbit, with two ears rising from a rounded head. Another looked like a large wave cresting before it was about to break and roll up on the beach.

The cypress knees in the swamp, to my eyes, seemed to fall into two recognizable types. There are, first, the relatively thin, conelike knees that taper to a rounded top. Often several of them are linked together and rise to different heights. The second group of knees are moundlike and resemble a mountain whose sharp edges have been worn off by glaciers. The breaking wave that I mentioned is an example of that type.

Many of those who visit cypress swamps are struck by the cathedral-like atmosphere of these dimly lighted forests. This effect comes partly from the knees and partly from the massive trunks of the trees that rise like columns from the black water of the swamp. When viewing such a setting, one should speak only in whispers. Many of the visitors to the Beidler Forest are careful not to raise their voices. By maintaining a near silence, they can better appreciate the awesome beauty of the cypress forest, and at the same time, they increase their chances of seeing wildlife.

Sharing wetter parts of the swamp with bald cypress and water tupelo is a third water-loving tree species—the Carolina ash. Those three are the only trees in the swamp adapted to semipermanent flooding. Cypress, the tallest, forms the canopy. Water tupelo is a subcanopy species, while Carolina ash, a small tree, is a part of the understory. Other plants, both woody and herbaceous, also grow in the wet, shaded parts of the swamp. But they require a substrate of some kind as a lodging place and only rarely are able to establish themselves in the permanently wet soil. Common substrates are floating logs, decaying stumps, cypress knees, and enlarged bases of cypress and tupelo. Richard D. Porcher, whose many botanical studies in South Carolina have sometimes taken him to Four Holes Swamp, has listed some of the trees in the swamp that grow on cypress knees and enlarged bases of cypress and tupelo. They include not only red maple (a species to be expected) but laurel oak, sweet gum, American elm, and spruce pine. He pointed out that trees growing on these often impoverished sites never reach a large size. On the other hand, many of the shrubs are well adapted to such sites and do as well on them as they would anywhere else. Those that seem particularly well adapted include Virginia willow (*Itea*), possum haw holly, swamp dogwood, American snowbell, buttonbush, and two species of fetterbushes.

Porcher recognized five plant communities in the Beidler Forest. A hardwood bluff slope community, with characteristic forms, including American beech and tulip poplar, occupies the bluff slope on either side of the swamp. A second community, the seepage bog, is found in places along the bluffs and below them. That community is composed of aquatic plants found in springs. Porcher estimated that there were over a hundred springs with bog plants on the eastern side of the swamp alone. A third plant community, which he called the swamp forest, is the one I have already discussed—the lowest, wettest level, containing bald cypress, water tupelo, Carolina elm, and plants that use tree buttresses and other high niches as substrates. Islands of higher ground within the swamp forest contain a fourth plant community, which Porcher called the hardwood bottom. It is only occasionally flooded. Oaks, red maples, sweet gums, American elms, and an occasional bald cypress are among the trees represented in the canopy. Dense stands of dwarf palmetto occur in the shrub layer. A fifth community, which Porcher called the ridge bottom community, is slightly higher than the hardwood bottom and includes the most diverse assemblage of plants of any of the communities. Before reaching the swamp forest by way of the boardwalk, the visitor passes through a wide belt of the ridge bottom community.

As viewed from the boardwalk, the ridge bottom seems to contain every tree, shrub, and vine found in the swamp, as well as a wide variety of wildflowers. About the only missing component is bald cypress and other members of the swamp forest community. Replacing the cypress is a tree that could almost belong to the northern spruce forest. Recognized by its smooth bark, very small cones, and often crooked trunk, spruce pine grows abundantly at Four Holes, which is one of its northern outposts. It thrives along sand banks of slow-moving southern rivers. Often growing side by side with spruce pine at Four Holes is the familiar loblolly pine. Some of them are quite large, but they cannot compete with the giant loblollies of the Congaree Swamp. The pines lend a somewhat somber look to what would otherwise be one of the brighter communities of the swamp.

Wildflowers in the ridge bottom community are represented first of all by flowering shrubs. Flowering dogwoods, red buckeyes, and azaleas are in bloom in late March and April. For a time they dominate the scene. But atamasco lilies, coming into bloom about Easter time, will provide the biggest thrill for those lucky enough to see them. Large stands of these lilies are present in the ridge bottom community but may not always be spotted from the boardwalk. Even if one misses the lilies, there will be a chance of seeing other early bloomers, including painted trillium, bloodroot, yellow star-grass, and mayapple. Present, but with such small blossoms that it is easily overlooked, is the rare dwarf trillium (*Trillium pusillum*), a candidate for endangered species status. Only one population is known in the Beidler Forest, and it is close to the boardwalk.

Unlike the Congaree Swamp, which has a wide floodplain, Four Holes Swamp is only a mile to a mile and a half in width and has no well-defined watercourse through most of its length. In the words of Richard Porcher, "The water flows slowly through a series of small runs and streams that crisscross the floodplain and join and separate in a pattern that seems to have no purpose or identity." He goes on to say that the smaller runs and streams become deeper and wider where two or three of them merge to form lakes of various sizes.

Among the larger ones in the Beidler Forest are Mellard's Lake, Goodson Lake, Canoe Lake, and Singletary Lake. The lakes are beauty spots that offer the visitor ample opportunities for seeing wildlife, including river otters and the birdlife of the swamp. Birds are everywhere and abundant year round, but they are easier to see in areas of open water, where one's vision is not obstructed by trees.

The small lakes are a haven for wood ducks and are visited by the pied-billed grebe, anhinga, black duck, and mallard. White ibis appear in small flocks throughout the swamp in spring and summer when the water is low. They are attracted by the many crayfish found in the swamp, which are a major item in their diet. The most common herons are the little blue and yellow-crowned night herons. The bird list for the Beidler Forest contains 140 species, and it should grow as observers report their findings.

The fact that the Beidler Forest is a National Audubon Society sanctuary containing one of the few remaining stands of virgin cypress has attracted students from a wide variety of natural history disciplines. As a result, the flora and fauna of this swamp have, in just a few years, become better known than that of many of the other southern swamps. Comparisons have been made between the fauna of the cut and uncut portions of the swamp. Alligators, for example, are much more common in the lower part of the swamp, where the most recent cutting has taken place, than they are in uncut portions. On the other hand, the virgin swamp contains a higher density of nesting birds than cut portions. Cavity-nesting birds are particularly abundant in the virgin tract, making up 32 percent of the species there.

Whether the Four Holes Swamp fits any of the common classifications given swamps is questionable. It is not the typical, highly acidic blackwater swamp and not a brown-water swamp. The water in Four Holes, neutralized by limestone outcrops, has a pH that ranges from about 6.7 to 7.1, which is about at the neutral point. As a result, the swamp is richer in aquatic forms than it would be if the water were highly acidic. The soil is also neutral, which makes for good plant growth. The towering cypress trees supply good evidence of the richness of the environment. Although Four Holes can pass as a blackwater swamp, it differs considerably from most of those found along the Atlantic Coast.

The sanctuary is open daily from 9 A.M. to 5 P.M. except on Mondays. To reach the sanctuary from Charleston, take Interstate 26 west to Exit 187, go south (left) on South Carolina Highway 27 to U.S. Highway 78, go west (right) on 78 to U.S. Highway 178, and follow the Beidler Forest signs from there to the sanctuary. From Interstate 95 or Columbia, take Interstate 26 east to Exit 177, go south (right) on State Highway 453 to U.S. Highway 178, go east (left) on 178 through Harleyville, and follow the Beidler Forest signs from the edge of town to the sanctuary.

References

Brunswig, Norman L., and Stephen G. Winton. *The Francis Beidler Forest in Four Holes Swamp*. National Audubon Society visitors' guide. New York, 1978.

Porcher, Richard. "The Vascular Flora of the Francis Beidler Forest in Four Holes Swamp, Berkeley and Dorchester Counties, South Carolina." *Castanea,* XLVI (1981), 248–80.

When J. F. D. Smyth, the ever inquisitive, widely traveled Britisher, visited the coastal plain region of North Carolina at the end of the American Revolution, he said the flat countryside was covered in a thousand places with "stagnated water," which "without doubt must be extremely unhealthful." Continuing his unflattering description, he added, "Nothing can be more dreary, melancholy, and uncomfortable than the almost perpetual dreary pines, sandy barrens, and dismal swamps, that are met with throughout the whole of that part of the country."

Although Smyth had a keen eye for geological features, he failed, as did so many others, to notice that certain of the wetlands with "stagnated water" were of a particular shape and were laid out essentially in the same direction. But that was difficult to notice from horseback or on foot. These peculiar wetlands and many similar boglike communities are called *pocosins*. Filled with dense, almost impenetrable vegetation, they could not be crossed in those days without hacking one's way through. They were places to be avoided at all costs.

Not until the middle of the nineteenth century did anyone suggest that there was a special type of pocosin in the Carolinas that differed from others and that had a unique origin. What formed these depressions no one could say with assurance, and the subject is still being debated today. But in 1847 Michael Tuomey, state geologist of South Carolina, reported upon certain depressions in his state that had an artificial appearance. Their uniform shape and rounded outlines reminded him of semicircular tracks used for horse racing. The only explanation he could think of for their symmetry was that at some period in the past they had been shaped by wave action.

Tuomey, surprisingly enough, in his brief account, had hit upon an explanation that is highly regarded by many students today. The Carolina bays, as the depressions came to be called, did not receive further notice until almost the end of the century. In 1895 they were mentioned in an article by an amateur geologist named Leonidas E. Glenn. He sketched several of the bays he had observed in the vicinity of Darlington, South Carolina, and described their soil structure. At a loss as to their origin, he offered the suggestion that they were formed by the motion of currents at a time when the region was covered by the ocean. In 1931 another South Carolina investigator, Laurence L. Smith, compared the bays with limestone sinkholes and wondered if they, like the sinkholes, had been formed by leaching action.

In 1933 South Carolina, the focal point of what little interest there had been in Carolina bays, suddenly became the center of a sweeping investigation into the whole question. Two professors, on viewing aerial photographs of terrain in the vicinity of Myrtle Beach, were struck by the large number of bays in that area and by how they conformed to the same pattern. They were elliptical in shape, aligned on a northwest-to-southeast axis, with the smaller end of the ellipses pointing to the southeast. The bays varied in size. Some were only one hundred or two hundred yards in diameter; others had diameters of up to six or seven miles. Not infrequently the bays overlapped each other, as seen in outlines of smaller bays in the basins of larger ones. As seen to good advantage in aerial photographs, the bays were contained within sand ridges that were almost always highest at the southeastern portion of the bay. The professors had an explanation to account for this feature.

The two men, Frank A. Melton and William Schriever, putting together the pieces, came to a truly amazing conclusion that no one had thought of before. They visualized thousands of meteorites on a day in the dim past arriving from the northwest at an angle of thirty-five to fifty-five degrees and blasting out innumerable craters in the sandy soil of the coastal plain. Taking note of smaller craters inside big ones, they postulated that larger meteorites had fallen first and been followed by progressively smaller ones. They attributed the presence of the highest part of the sand ridges at the southeastern rim to the fact that the meteorites, as they arrived from the northwest, plowed the soil toward the southeast.

When the world received the news of the theory, there was some skepticism but also widespread applause. Melton and Schriever postulated an extraterrestrial phenomenon on a scale almost unheard of before—something that staggered the imagination. The meteorite shower, if it was one, had not only covered large portions of the Carolina coastal plain but also, as was discovered later on, had covered a huge belt from northern Florida northward into Maryland and Delaware. A few Carolina bays were discovered in the piedmont region. Recent estimates give the total number of bays at about half a million. Some four hundred thousand of them are distributed about equally between the two Carolinas.

As many times happens, when a new theory makes its appearance, there are those who support it and others who, with varying degrees of vehemence, oppose it. Within a few years, the previously unheard-of Carolina bays became widely known to the public and were the center of a raging controversy. Numerous new theories about their origin appeared. Some bordered upon the ridiculous; others were careful studies involving years of research. In a book published in 1982, Henry Savage reviewed the history of the Carolina bays and the many theories surrounding them. In looking over the evidence, he became convinced that the Carolina bays had been formed in almost a flash during an epic day when a huge meteorite shower struck the surface of the earth. Thus, he agreed with Melton and Schriever.

In spite of strong support from Savage and others, the meteorite theory has remained vulnerable on at least three counts. Critics point out that magnetic readings at many of the bays have not been backed up by the discovery of meteorite fragments and that the strata below the shallow depressions have not been altered by a major impact of any kind. Second, radiocarbon dating has not yet pinpointed any date in the past when such an event could have occurred. Estimates of the age of the bays vary widely. Finally, oriented lakes similar to Carolina bays have been found in other parts of the world. The ones on the Alaskan North Slope, at the southern tip of South America, and in northwestern Texas were obviously created by wind or water or both.

Whatever the agent may have been that formed them, the Carolina bays have, in a not insignificant way, offered added habitat for the growth of cypresses. Most of the bays have no inlet or outlet, and therefore, whatever water is in them is from the rain. When the water table fluctuates between wet and dry seasons, there are times when conditions are suitable for the establishment of cypress seedlings. The optimum time is shortly after waters recede in a year of low water levels, thus leaving behind exposed ground largely free of other vegetation. With enough flooding to suppress other competing plant life but still not enough to drown out seedlings, cypress can be expected to gain a hold and eventually become a dominant plant. Normally it is pond cypress and not bald cypress that becomes established in such shallow basins. It seems safe to say that of the thousands of Carolina bays that once existed, only about 10 percent might have had cypress growing in them. The record today is blurred by the partial or complete drainage of so many of the bays and their conversion for agricultural and other uses.

Julie Moore of the North Carolina Heritage Program tells me that two types of Carolina bays in her state contain cypress. One type is the clay-based Carolina bay. In that type the bottom stratum is composed of relatively impermeable clay, and therefore the depression holds water for long periods of time. The other type containing cypress is the bay lake, a permanently flooded body of water that is often fed by streams and that may have an outlet. The best-known example is Lake Waccamaw in the extreme southeastern part of the state. The bay lakes often have a fringing band of cypresses at the water's edge, as well as many trees standing well out into shoaler parts of the lake itself.

It seems likely that cypress originally reached the Carolina bays through dissemination by birds. As a rule, only the wetter bays, in which water is present over part of the year or throughout the year, have a sampling of cypress, as well as of such other water-loving trees as swamp tupelo, water tupelo, and red maple. Sometimes along with trees such as those, or growing in isolated stands, there will be pond pine (*Pinus serotina*) or Atlantic white cedar.

But for the most part, the Carolina bay contains plants belonging to the evergreen shrub bog community. These plants, including gallberry (*Ilex glabra*), dahoon holly, winterberry holly, titi, wax myrtle, zenobia (*Zenobia pulverulenta*), fetterbush, swamp leucothoe, sweet pepperbush, and bay trees, are characteristic of the wet, acidic peaty soils of the outer coastal plain. Sprawling all over everything is the insidious laurel greenbrier, with its sharp thorns. To complete the picture of woe for anyone trying to penetrate these tangles, there are spongy cushions of sphagnum moss that give way at each footstep. The moss is the chief ingredient of the peat that, at a rate of about one inch every fifty-five years, accumulates in the basin of the Carolina bay. If it were not for fire in dry seasons, the bay would become completely filled with peat. Frequent invasions of fire help maintain the evergreen shrub bog community, which in fact depends upon fire. Sweet bay, red bay, leucothoe, and greenbrier, for example, have the ability to sprout following a hot fire.

But with repeated burning, the shrubs may finally be replaced by a savanna-type flora. Grasses and sedges will become dominant, and generally there will be a luxuriant growth of ferns along with pitcher plants and other carnivorous plants. In a contiguous coastal area in the Carolinas, the Venus's flytrap is sometimes found in Carolina bays. This small plant, with its limited range, has leaves that close like a trap upon insect invaders. After a few years without fire, the savanna may revert into pine woods, with shrub bog plants making a reappearance.

The woody plants of Carolina bays and other southern bog regions that stood out most in the minds of early visitors were the bay trees, which, when growing in water-logged soil, often grow only to the size of shrubs. It is the bay trees, and not the water, that are responsible for the *bay* in *Carolina bay*. Bay trees have also supplied names such as *bayhead,*

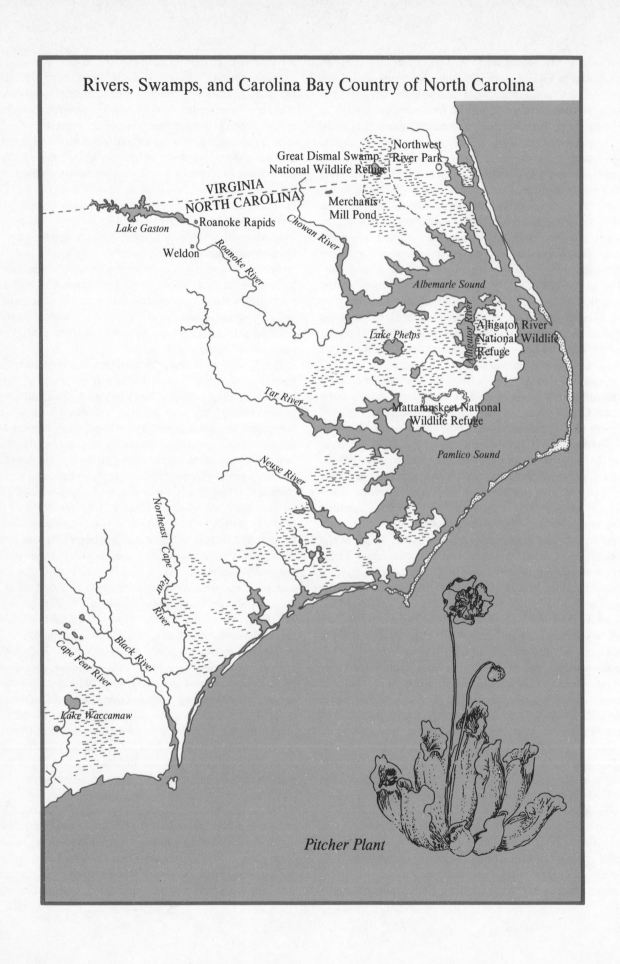

Rivers, Swamps, and Carolina Bay Country of North Carolina

Northwest
River Park

Great Dismal Swamp
National Wildlife Refuge

VIRGINIA
NORTH CAROLINA

Merchants
Mill Pond

Roanoke Rapids

Lake Gaston

Chowan River

Weldon

Roanoke River

Albemarle Sound

Lake Phelps

Alligator River

Alligator River
National Wildlife
Refuge

Tar River

Mattamuskeet National
Wildlife Refuge

Pamlico Sound

Neuse River

Northeast Cape Fear River

Black River

Cape Fear River

Lake Waccamaw

Pitcher Plant

baygall, and *bay thicket*—all terms referring to swampy terrain where bay trees are dominant. There are three bay trees, each of them belonging to a different family in the plant kingdom. Loblolly bay, a member of the tea family, is found from the Carolinas southward to Florida and Louisiana. Red bay, a member of the laurel family, ranges southward from Maryland to Florida and Texas. Sweet bay, a member of the magnolia family, ranges farther north than the other two. It is found from Massachusetts to Florida and Texas.

Some writers have characterized the Carolina bay as being relatively sterile in regard to animal life. For example, Rebecca R. Sharitz and J. Whitfield Gibbons, in a recent study of the shrub bog community, reported that there were few fish in Carolina bays and provided only short lists for reptiles, amphibians, birds, and mammals. Their appraisal does seem to fit the many Carolina bays filled with dense, tangled growth and lacking open water and zones containing a number of different plant communities. On the other hand, many of the Carolina bays are noted for their diverse plant and animal communities, as well as for the presence of rare species.

A good indicator of faunal richness in a Carolina bay is the presence of cypress trees. If cypress is present, it means that areas of open water and a number of plant communities are likely to be found. A Carolina bay with cypress and open water bears a close resemblance to the rice reserves discussed in Chapter 10. Both are potentially suitable sites for heronries and are rich in birdlife generally. The wetter Carolina bays are known for their rich herpetofaunas. The fish population, on the other hand, is likely to be limited because of the frequency with which bays, which have no permanent sources of water, dry up during very dry years.

In the past, man, through his need for a source of water for gristmills, has sometimes turned Carolina bays into permanent bodies of water. An example of a ponded Carolina bay used for milling purposes is Woods Bay in South Carolina. Now a state park, Woods Bay covers about 1,500 acres and has a variety of plant communities ranging from pond cypress to open marshland. The presence of springs within the perimeter of the bay provided an adequate source of water for milling purposes. A dam was built in 1854 to retain the water, and eventually no less than three gristmills, powered by water from the bay, were in operation at one time. To ensure an adequate water supply, a millpond was built adjacent to the bay. By the mid-1930s the mills had been abandoned, and much of the cypress had been cut. But thanks to a local conservation effort, this Carolina bay, spared the fate of so many others, was not drained.

The visitor to Woods Bay State Park has a choice of taking a nature trail leading to a boardwalk that takes him into a cypress swamp and then back via the old millpond or of renting a canoe to paddle into the heart of the Carolina bay. Some 150 acres of the cypress swamp escaped cutting and

therefore can be regarded as a virgin stand. To see this yet almost untouched Carolina bay, with its sand rim, dark waters, and varied plant and animal life, is well worth a short side trip from busy Interstate 95. Woods Bay is seven miles from the Shiloh exit and just off U.S. Highway 301 between Olanta and Turbeville. Look for a sign pointing to the park on the west side of the highway.

Visitors to the Santee Coastal Reserve, with its large bird rookeries (see Chapter 10), should watch for Carolina bays on the righthand side of the road as they drive in. The open pine woods give way to wet areas—most of them dominated by cypresses and tupelos. Some of these areas, thanks to frequent invasion by fire, have turned into grassy savannas with pitcher plants and numerous orchids. Careful examination of the ten or so low-lying areas will show that they have the typical Carolina bay elliptical shape and northwest-to-southeast alignment. However, sand ridges are barely evident or missing altogether. I would hazard the guess that these bays were invaded by the ocean at some period in the distant past, with the result that wave action has erased most of the surrounding sand ridges.

Whatever the case, these Carolina bays are rich in wildlife. During visits in April of one year, I recorded twenty-nine bird species within the bays, nearly all of them likely nesters. In the pine woods immediately adjacent to the bays were active nesting sites of the endangered red-cockaded woodpecker. But wading birds from nearby Blake's Reserve seldom visit the bays, perhaps because of the scarcity of fish in the few areas of open water. But amphibians were abundant. With the help of Dr. Julian Harrison, a well-known herpetologist, I was able to record sightings of the following amphibians: pig frog, carpenter frog, Carolina gopher frog, little grass frog, green frog, pine woods tree frog, oak toad, flatwoods salamander, broad-striped dwarf siren, and broken-striped newt. At the edges of the Carolina bays, we commonly encountered a rather large, tan-colored lizard—the brown-headed skink.

The abundant amphibian population of those Carolina bays can be duplicated in many of the others. As one moves northward, some species drop out and others take their place. The pine barrens tree frog, once listed as an endangered species, is found in large numbers in Big Collie Bay in Bladen County, North Carolina, and is present in other Carolina bays as well. A freshwater marsh Carolina bay near Laurinburg in southeastern North Carolina was reported to have had a count of twenty-five species of amphibians in two and a half acres of open water. Clay-based Carolina bays in North Carolina with grasses, herbs, and sometimes cypress trees often play host to the eastern tiger salamander, known for its spotty distribution and comparative rarity.

Beautiful Lake Waccamaw, which was visited by John and William Bartram in 1765, probably has more endemic fishes and other forms of aquatic life than any other body of water in eastern North America. The lake, some twenty miles north of the South Carolina line, is the source of the Waccamaw River and is fed by a number of small streams. Water entering the lake is highly acidic, but it is neutralized by limestone outcroppings in the lake bed. Little or no peat is evident around the shores of the lake. Instead, one is greeted by white sand and sparkling clear water. These differences seem to be responsible for the extraordinary abundance of fishes and other aquatic organisms in the lake. Of the fifty or so fish species found in the lake, somewhere between three and five, depending upon whose taxonomic study one goes by, are endemic species. The Waccamaw silverside and Waccamaw darter are limited in distribution entirely to Lake Waccamaw. On the other hand, the Waccamaw killifish has also been discovered in Lake Phelps in northeastern North Carolina. Whether these two killifish are exactly identical is open to question. Finally, according to J. R. Shute, P. W. Shute, and D. G. Lindquist, the lake has an undescribed pygmy sunfish and undescribed madtom.

Endemism is present not only in the lake's fish but also in its mollusks and crayfish. So much endemism in a body of water no more than five miles across and covering only about nine thousand acres is hard to explain. Perhaps it is best to leave this riddle, as well as the origin of the Carolina bays, in the hands of future scientists.

The lake is easy to visit. Follow U.S. Highway 74 between Wilmington and Lumberton, and look for the small town of Lake Waccamaw on the north shore of the lake and a state park on the east shore. If one explores the lake in either direction from the town, the setting becomes wilder. Cypress trees dotting the edge of the lake give way to a prominent sand ridge that separates the lake from a swamp forest.

Turtles, alligators, and the greater sirens flourish in ditches and lagoons near the lake. Whenever I visit Lake Waccamaw, I find birds that I do not see in other Carolina bays. On one visit, I saw a common loon, and on another, a double-crested cormorant. Only twenty-five miles from the ocean, the lake is often visited by sea birds. Occasionally during hurricanes, the lake plays host to birds such as sooty terns and tropic birds.

Had Smyth, whom we met at the beginning of the chapter, strayed somewhat east of his route northward to Virginia, he might have reached the largest of the bay lakes. Lake Phelps, about fifteen miles south of Albemarle Sound, closely resembles Lake Waccamaw and is thought to be a bay lake formed by two large Carolina bays lying side by side. An underwater ridge separating the suspected bay formations conforms to the typical sand ridges that surround Carolina bays. The bottom of the lake is sandy, with the only peat deposits lying at the southeast end of the lake. A narrow cypress swamp containing very big trees lines the north side of the lake. That strip and another on the south side of the lake make up Pettigrew State Park. Not only does the park preserve some of North Carolina's largest cypress trees, but within the narrow strip on the lake's north side are a state champion sugarberry and a state champion sweet gum, as well as spectacularly large sycamores and tulip poplars and laurel, overcup, and cherry bark oaks.

If one approaches Lake Phelps from the north, after taking a road from the town of Creswell on U.S. Highway 64, the country opens up into broad fields that have been cultivated almost from the time of the American Revolution. For about a mile before one reaches the lake, the road is bordered by a magnificent avenue of cypress trees that must have been planted by one of the earliest plantation owners. A likely candidate for this honor is Josiah Collins, who in 1785 joined with others to form a company to establish large rice plantations on the borders of Lake Phelps (then known as Lake Scuppernong). Rice later gave way to corn. Somerset Place, a Collins family home completed about 1830, stands on the north side of the lake and is open to the public.

The most interesting fish in Lake Phelps is the Waccamaw killifish. How this killifish reached Lake Phelps or—the other way around—how the fish might have been misnamed and reached Lake Waccamaw from Lake Phelps, is another of the unsolved mysteries associated with Carolina bays. It has been suggested that the killifish might have been introduced to Lake Phelps by man. But the two fish are not absolutely identical, and, therefore, that seems unlikely. Whatever the answer, this two- to three-inch-long fish, with dark vertical bands on its sides, is one of the most common fish in the lake.

In terms of rare or even unique forms of life, the Carolina bays, together with the evergreen shrub bogs, rate as high as any other habitats in the East. Mention has already been made of endemic aquatic forms and the pine barrens tree frog. The latter has been called by Sharitz and Gibbons "almost a pocosin endemic." *Pocosin,* as noted above, is another name for the setting of the evergreen shrub bog community and goes back to the Indian word for wetlands of that type.

The pocosin community is one of the last refuges for the black bear in the Atlantic coastal plain. With such a large portion of the uplands in cultivation or heavily settled, the black bear has had to retreat to the safest havens it can find. In the innermost depths of pocosin thickets, the black bear can find much of its food, produce its young, and safely hole up for the winter. Most of the seven hundred to a thousand black bears in eastern North Carolina are found in pocosins. Other mammal inhabitants there include the bobcat and marsh rabbit.

I was reminded by Julie Moore of the North Carolina Heritage Program of the Nature Conservancy that Carolina bays in her state contain a number of rare plants with very limited distributions. Among the plants are a laurel (*Kalmia cuneata*), a loosestrife (*Lysimachia asperulaefolia*), and a meadow beauty (*Rhexia aristosa*). Sarvis holly (*Ilex amelanchier*), rare but with a wider distribution, is also found in some of the Carolina bays. Add these plants to the many orchids, carnivorous plants, and other wildflowers found in the bays, and it can be seen what an important plant habitat exists in those shallow depressions.

Saving these rare biotic communities is an important objective of the Nature Conservancy. In South Carolina, North Carolina, and Maryland, that organization has been especially active in setting aside Carolina bays as nature preserves. Since there were once so many of them, it seems hard to believe that there is now a sense of urgency about saving them. But thousands have been drained for agriculture in a land boom that ended in the early 1980s, and the remaining ones need all the protection they can get.

References

Savage, Henry, Jr. *The Mysterious Carolina Bays*. Columbia, S.C., 1982.

Sharitz, Rebecca R. and J. Whitfield Gibbons. *The Ecology of Southeastern Shrub Bogs (Pocosins) and Carolina Bays: A Community Profile*. U.S. Fish and Wildlife Service, Division of Biological Services publication FWS/OBS-82/04. Washington, D.C., 1982.

Shute, J. R., P. W. Shute, and D. G. Lindquist. "Fishes of the Waccamaw River Drainage." *Brimleyana*, VI (December, 1981), 1–24.

Smyth, J. F. D. *A Tour of the United States of America*. 2 vols. London, 1784.

13 / The Okefenokee Swamp

Anyone who has first visited more northern swamps will be surprised at the sudden transition that takes place when he crosses into southeastern Georgia, where the Okefenokee Swamp sprawls over 430,000 acres. Eighteen miles wide from east to west and thirty-eight miles long, the Okefenokee is larger by far than any of the East Coast swamps discussed so far. It is also the most varied from a scenic standpoint. Small lakes, open marshland (called prairies), and islands covered with trees offer sharp contrasts to the other swamps. But the Okefenokee also has large stands of cypress and other water-loving trees. In that respect and also in terms of geological history, the Okefenokee Swamp closely resembles the Great Dismal Swamp.

Both the Okefenokee Swamp and the Great Dismal Swamp are situated in shallow basins that appear to have once been saltwater lagoons. The two swamps are now at higher elevations than the sea and are separated from the seacoast by sand ridges. On its east side the Okefenokee is bordered by Trail Ridge, a sand ridge that at one point reaches an elevation of 150 feet above sea level. In terms of age, as learned from their earliest peat deposits, both swamps are comparatively young. Pollen samples in the oldest peat indicate an age of 6,600 years for the Okefenokee Swamp and about 9,000 years for the Great Dismal.

There may have been earlier swamps in the basin that holds the Okefenokee Swamp. They may have dried up during periods of very dry climate. Peat in older swamps could have either blown away or been consumed by fire. With a return to a wetter regime, the shallow basin would have once again become filled with water, and new plant life would have taken hold. Early pollen samples indicate what the plant life was once like. They contain a high percentage of pollen from the water-lily (*Nymphaea odorata*), a plant of freshwater ponds and marshes. Cypress, as seen in the peat deposits, arrived about 4,500 years ago. Oaks were common trees before the advent of cypress.

The present swamp varies in elevation from between 103 and 128 feet above sea level, with the highest elevation at the northern end of the swamp. As a result, water flows southward in the swamp, slowly percolating through a maze of waterways or running in a wide sheet through and around masses of vegetation and over layers of peat during time of high water. Less than one-fourth, or about 22 percent, of the water drains out by way of the two rivers that provide the only drainage for the swamp. The rest of the water is lost through evaporation and transpiration by plants.

The St. Mary's River, which has its origin at the southeastern corner of the swamp, carries off only about 10 percent of the water. After flowing south for a few miles, the St. Mary's reverses its direction and, following a course parallel to the swamp, flows north to a point near Folkston, Georgia, and then turns east to empty into the Atlantic Ocean. The Suwannee River, which carries off the remainder of the water, leaves the swamp about midway along its western edge and, following a southwesterly direction, empties into the Gulf of Mexico.

It is safe to assume that the Okefenokee was once a freshwater marsh. Following a normal succession, the marsh became filled with decaying vegetation, which the acidic water preserved as peat. As more and more peat accumulated, the water became more shallow and, in places, dry land appeared. At that stage the marsh began to be replaced by swampland containing cypress trees and other woody plants. If nothing intervened, the swamp, gradually filling with peat, would have dried out. Pines and hardwoods would then have replaced the cypress and its associates. But fire, the great agent in preserving swamps, repeatedly invaded the swamp during dry years. Reducing the amount of peat, the fires opened up pockets that filled with water and thereby maintained the pattern of swampland, open prairie or marsh, and lakes and ponds that is seen in the Okefenokee Swamp today.

Under dry conditions, fires often began as a result of lightning strikes. The Indians, who first appeared in the swamp between four thousand and five thousand years ago, used fire as an aid to hunting game. The early white settlers used fire for much the same purpose. Until about the middle of the twentieth century, fire was an expected event and served the useful purpose of maintaining this large area as a wetland.

The wetland consists in large part of treeless areas that are either marshland or else dense thickets composed of water-loving plants. Together with waterways and small lakes, such communities make up about 55 percent of the swamp.

Another 21 percent consists of pure cypress or cypress mixed with other plants growing in flooded portions of the swamp. By far the largest proportion of the cypress is the variety known as pond cypress. Bald cypress is relatively uncommon. Swamp tupelo (black gum), together with red maple and dahoon holly, makes up about 6 percent of the swamp. Another 6 percent is made up of bay forest, primarily sweet bay, red bay, and loblolly bay. Finally, the swamp contains approximately seventy islands, which account for 12 percent of the area. Many of the islands are high ground dominated by loblolly pine, slash pine, water oak, or live oak. Billys Island, a large island on the west side of the swamp, supports pines, live oak, saw palmetto, and huckleberry.

The islands are one of the swamp's most puzzling features. What formed them? Were they a part of former karst topography (limestone formations), or were they perhaps the result of geologic faulting? C. T. Trowell, who asked these questions, left open the possibility that the islands, or some of them, were sand ridges at the southeastern edges of Carolina bays. Many of the islands, particularly in the northwestern portion of the swamp, are crescent-shaped and oriented in the same direction as Carolina bays. Unfortunately, Joseph Wadsworth, a young geomorphologist who was analyzing the surface features of the swamp with the help of aerial photographs, died before he could complete his studies.

Large open expanses known as prairies are the most distinctive parts of the swamp and remind one much more of Florida than of the heavily wooded swamps to the north. *Prairie,* however, is a misleading term. The Okefenokee's prairies are in reality marshes filled with aquatic plants, and except in very dry years, they are covered by one to three feet of water. Like most of the rest of the Okefenokee Swamp, the prairies are underlain by peat beds that average from five to ten feet in depth. The peat beds are the source of the only irregular features found on the prairies—clumps of higher ground containing a few cypress trees and other woody vegetation. These clumps are known locally as *houses* or *cypress heads,* and most of them are tiny islets hardly large enough to serve as campsites and usually too wet to be of much help to anyone unfortunate enough to be caught on one when darkness falls. On the other hand, the houses do serve very nicely as roosting and nesting sites for large wading birds and as nesting sites for the osprey and anhinga.

Prairies are of two types—those with aquatic plants, such as water-lilies, floating heart, arrow-arum, golden club, pickerelweed, and bladderwort, and those that are reedy grasslands containing panic-grasses, rushes, sedges, and Virginia chain fern. The latter are very much like the open sawgrass prairies of the Florida Everglades but are not as impenetrable. If the water is not too deep, one can wade across the Okefenokee prairies, though not without stumbling, falling, or perhaps sinking up to one's waist in water and mire. A naturalist early in this century related that he and his party, when crossing a prairie, often sank through to their waists in sphagnum mats or fell forward, cracking their ribs on cypress knees. Okefenokee "swampers" make their way across the prairies by pushing their shallow-draft boats with long poles. They often take advantage of the alligator trails that crisscross the swamp in every direction. The alligators, bears, otters, and raccoons that use the trails keep the vegetation trampled down, thereby making for easier passage by anyone following them.

About twenty of the prairies are large enough to have been given names. Chase Prairie, with 6,600 acres and described by one writer as having one of the most remarkable landscapes in the world, is the largest of the prairies and is closely followed in size by Chesser and Grand prairies. All three are in the eastern part of the swamp. On the whole the eastern part of the Okefenokee Swamp is open, whereas the western part is wooded.

Contributing to the uniqueness of the prairies are the aforementioned houses, or cypress heads, that dot them. Many of them are only a few feet across and vegetated by nothing more than a few shrubs and a single small cypress tree. Others are up to several acres in size and support a large number of cypresses as well as, in many cases, loblolly bay, titi, dahoon holly, and other shrubs. Many who have visited them have described the houses as almost impenetrable. That is because of the dense growth of trees and shrubs that covers them and, equally obstructive to one trying to get through, the thorny stems of laurel-leaved greenbrier.

As for the origin of the houses, it is generally conceded that they evolve from the underlying peat. Under some conditions, the peat floats to the surface and forms floating islands, or, in the swamper's terminology, *batteries.* The batteries are highly unstable, rising and falling with the water level and sometimes floating almost indefinitely. As described by Eugene Cypert, who has looked into their origin, the upper surface of a battery is at or slightly above the water surface. That makes for a substrate able to support much larger forms of plant life than can the open marsh. Woody plants arrive after the appearance of such herbaceous invaders as red root (*Lachnanthes*), beak rush (*Rhynchospora*), sedge (*Carex*), maidencane (*Panicum hemitomon*), and Virginia chain fern.

As woody plants send down their roots, the battery becomes better anchored and may no longer qualify as a floating island. Nevertheless, as anyone who steps on one of these platforms soon finds out, the surface is highly unstable. With each step, the platform quivers, trees sway, and the person who has dared test the footing is apt to find it difficult to stand upright. Not without good reason is the Okefenokee Swamp called the Land of the Trembling Earth.

Trembling earth is a phenomenon caused primarily by menthane gas forming in layers of peat and buoying the peat

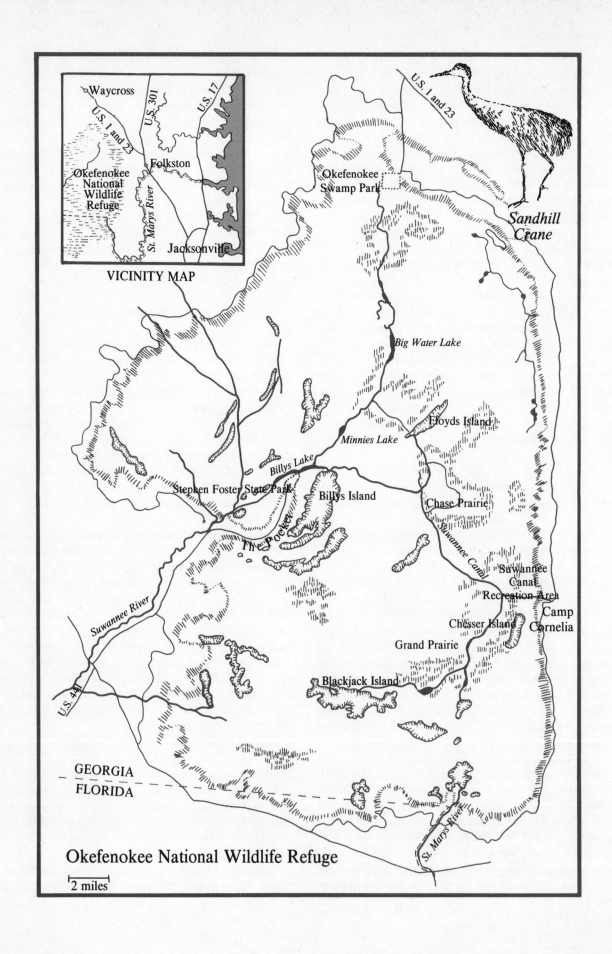

Waycross

U.S. 1 and 23

U.S. 301

U.S. 17

Folkston

Okefenokee
National
Wildlife
Refuge

St. Marys River

Jacksonville

U.S. 1 and 23

Okefenokee
Swamp Park

Sandhill
Crane

Big Water Lake

Ffoyds Island

Minnies Lake

Billys Lake

Stephen Foster State Park

Billys Island

Chase Prairie

The Pocket

Suwannee Canal

Suwannee
Canal
Recreation Area

Camp
Cornelia

Chesser Island

Suwannee River

Grand Prairie

Blackjack Island

U.S. 441

GEORGIA
FLORIDA

St. Marys River

Okefenokee National Wildlife Refuge

2 miles

Spanish moss over the Chesser Island boardwalk in the Okefenokee Swamp

The sandhill crane, represented by both a resident population and wintering migrants in the Okefenokee Swamp

A snowy egret, one of the many large wading birds of the Okefenokee

The eastern glass lizard, found in higher ground at the swamp's edge·

The barred owl, a common resident
of the Okefenokee

(right) *A raccoon family at night*

Not uncommon on trunks of cypress trees, the butterfly orchid (Epidendrum tampense) *can be seen from the boardwalk at Corkscrew Swamp.*

Photograph by Richard Kern

*The interior of a pond cypress thicket in Corkscrew Swamp.
The tree is decked with bromeliads.*

(left) *The ghost orchid* (Polyrrhiza lindenii), *with its large, white,
deeply cleft flowers, is one of the most beautiful orchids
of south Florida cypress swamps.*
Photograph by Richard Kern

White-tailed deer are plentiful in the Okefenokee Swamp.

Roseate spoonbill, a bird of shallow saltwater
lagoons in south Florida

An anhinga, or water turkey,
in the Everglades

Limpkin at Wakulla Springs

(upper left) *Eggs of an apple snail on a pickerelweed leaf*

(lower left) *Golden club* (Orontium aquaticum)

Cabbage palms, Aucilla River

(right) *Wakulla Springs*

Scene along the Wakulla River with pickerelweed in foreground

*A cypress-tupelo swamp on the edge of
the Suwannee River*

Purple gallinule

upward until it becomes a battery. Based on their origins, three types of batteries have been identified: 1) A large mat of peat may become detached and float to the surface. 2) Small, detached pieces of peat may rise to the surface of a pond or lake and collect together to form a large floating mass. 3) Gas may cause the central portion of a mat of peat to bulge to the surface while the edges remain attached to the bottom.

Although it is generally agreed that bubbles of gas are responsible for lifting the peat, it is not entirely clear why in some years no new batteries appear, whereas in other years many of them do. For example, in 1960 many batteries of the bulge type appeared in Chase Prairie. It is believed that heat generated in upper layers of peat that are exposed during times of drought causes increased bacterial activity and hence the formation of more menthane gas than usual. With reflooding upon the return of wet weather, the gas-buoyed peat either breaks away or rises to the surface in the form of a bulge. T. C. Trowell tells me of seeing a freshly risen battery covered with the tracks of birds and alligators. The newly formed islands seem to be eagerly sought out by wildlife.

Not all floating islands are formed in the same way as the ones in the Okefenokee Swamp. As Edwin Way Teale pointed out in his book *North with the Spring,* the huge roots of spatterdock, also known as yellow cow lily, sometimes break off and rise to the surface of a pond or lake, taking quantities of soil with them. The mats become floating islands made up of soil and decaying vegetation. Orange Lake in north-central Florida is well known for its many floating islands composed of the gas-filled roots of spatterdock.

Unlike the Great Dismal Swamp, which has a rich historic record going back to the earliest days of settlement, the Okefenokee has been largely overlooked until very recent times. One of the first accounts of the swamp was supplied by William Bartram, who skirted the edge of it on his way to Florida in the spring of 1773. Calling it "the Great Swamp" and its waters "Lake Oaquaphenogaw," he described a large lake that in the wet season was "near three hundred miles in circuit" and contained islands. He correctly stated that the St. Mary's and Suwannee rivers had their sources in the swamp.

But romanticism overcame accuracy when, on the basis of hearsay accounts, Bartram told of a tribe of warrior Indians with beautiful wives who lived in the swamp. When hunters from the neighboring Creek tribe became lost in the swamp, it was said, they were sometimes lucky enough to be rescued by the beautiful women. Taken in for a time and supplied with food, they would soon be urged to leave; otherwise, they were told, they would be cruelly treated by husbands about to return from the hunt. The islands where these Indians lived were called the most blissful spots on earth.

The Creek hunters were said to have made expeditions into the swamp for the express purpose of finding the islands with the beautiful women. But whenever they came near one of the islands with Indian villages, the island would disappear like a mirage. As recounted by Bartram, the image of the village seemed to fly before them, alternately appearing and disappearing.

The Okefenokee Swamp has had a long history of Indian occupancy. C. T. Trowell, writing of the Indians in the Okefenokee, stated that, beginning about 2000 B.C., Indians arrived in the swamp to live. Burial mounds, pottery, and various artifacts testify to their presence. But not until around A.D. 500 was there a sizable Indian population with a reasonably advanced culture. The Weeden Island Culture, as it is called, saw mound-building Indians settling on many of the islands and on uplands at the swamp's edge. By A.D. 1200 the Weeden Island Culture had declined, and the swamp, for a long time, was only sparsely settled by Indians. The Creek Indians, who lived in southern Georgia, largely avoided the swamp. But the Seminoles, an offshoot of the Creeks, were present in the swamp from 1750 until they were forced out by white troops. The Seminoles used the swamp both as a refuge and as a base from which to launch raids upon early white settlers. A number of white families were massacred. The most famous massacre occurred on July 22, 1838, when the Seminoles invaded a homestead, killing seven members of the Wildes family. By then calls for assistance were beginning to be heeded. In the same year as the massacre General Charles R. Floyd, with some three hundred men, entered the swamp in search of the Indians and burned their villages. But the Seminoles fled to Florida, and the tribe eventually settled in the even more inaccessible Florida Everglades or moved to Oklahoma.

One of the first serious efforts to settle any part of the swamp was made in the early 1850s by a family named Lee. Taking up residence on Billys Island in the western part of the swamp, the Lees built a dwelling and cleared some of the land. Raising a family of fourteen children and living on the bounty of the land, they seem to have led a peaceful and happy life. At about the same time, a family named Chesser settled on Chesser Island at the eastern edge of the swamp. The old Chesser homestead is still standing and has been opened to the public under the auspices of the U.S. Fish and Wildlife Service. Like most of the swamp, Chesser Island is now a part of the Okefenokee National Wildlife Refuge.

Plans to drain the swamp began to surface about the middle of the nineteenth century, when a number of surveys were undertaken for the purpose of determining how it could best be accomplished. By 1890 expeditions were traversing every part of the swamp. The men who participated told of many hardships, including near drownings and encounters with bears, alligators, and packs of wild dogs. One man described a ducking he received when he stepped on a floating battery and sank up to his chin.

Encounters with Florida cougars, sometimes called catamounts, were widely reported, and many stories were told of snakes, bears, alligators, biting flies, and mosquitoes. Writing in 1890, a member of a survey party stated that the "amount of stock that the farmers here lose annually through the depredations of bears and alligators seems almost beyond belief." On Cowhouse Island in the northeastern part of the swamp, a farmer was said to have lost over a hundred head of hogs to alligators and bears in just three months. One farmer was so furious when he discovered a bear taking one of his hogs that he went at the animal with a stout stick with a knot at one end. After a fierce struggle he finally managed to kill the animal. Hand-to-hand encounters with bears were not uncommon.

Not until 1891 did actual drainage operations get under way. Having in mind a grandiose scheme for reclaiming the swamp, Captain Harry Jackson of Atlanta purchased 389 square miles of Okefenokee swampland from the state of Georgia at a cost of 26.5 cents an acre. The plan was to construct a drainage canal that would link the swamp with the St. Mary's River at a point where the river, after turning northward, was only six miles from the swamp and at a considerably lower elevation than the swamp. A locality called Camp Cornelia, about halfway between the northern and southern limits of the swamp, was selected as the site for a labor camp and the place where digging would begin. At first everything went well. Digging began, with the help of mules and convict labor, in September of 1891. Slowly a canal sixty feet wide and thirty to thirty-five feet deep was constructed eastward toward a final but imposing barrier—Trail Ridge. As the digging progressed into Trail Ridge, landslides quickly obliterated the work. In a final effort, experienced miners and hydraulic dredging equipment were brought in for the job. But little progress was made. By the summer of 1892, realizing that the drainage project was too difficult and too costly, Captain Jackson turned his attention to recently discovered stands of cypress that lay in the swamp about twelve miles to the northwest of Camp Cornelia. Instead of continuing to dig a canal eastward, it seemed to make more sense to dig in the opposite direction and reach the cypress forest. The trees could be cut and floated out by way of the canal.

By October of 1894, the drainage project had been completely abandoned, and with the same equipment and men, a canal was being pushed to the northwest, toward the cypress. There at last might lie the means of making a profit and paying for the enormous expense incurred by Jackson and his Suwanee Canal Company, as he called it.

The cypress timbering soon got under way. The trees, after first being girdled and allowed to dry out, were cut and floated out of the swamp by way of the canal. A sawmill and lumber camp were installed at Camp Cornelia. Lumber and millions of shingles were cut from the huge logs. But poor business methods, coupled with Jackson's death in 1895, doomed the ambitious project to failure. In 1897

operations ceased entirely, and the company declared bankruptcy.

However, "Jackson's Folly," as it was called, did play a role in the next stage of the swamp's history. Profiting from past mistakes, new entrepreneurs and new methods took hold with the sole aim of exploiting the huge, almost untapped supplies of cypress and other virgin timber in the swamp. The Hebard Lumber Company of Philadelphia, having purchased the former canal company holdings, set up a subsidiary known as the Hebard Cypress Company. After five years of study and preparation, the company began timbering operations in 1909. A huge sawmill built near Waycross was linked by rail lines with large sections of the swamp. In most areas a railbed was established by driving pilings from five to fifteen feet through peat to reach solid, sandy soil. In some places track on "floating beds" that consisted of timbers placed crosswise on soggy soil was used instead of trestle.

In 1917, Billys Island, home of the Lee family and former site of Indian villages as well as of a fort built during the days of Indian uprisings, became a center for much of the lumbering activity. It was not long before a community sprang up containing as many as six hundred inhabitants, houses, stores, a hotel, and a movie theater. During the height of lumbering operations, the Hebard Cypress Company employed as many as two thousand men. Other lumber companies, including a large one called the Twin Tree Lumber Company, were also active at that time. But by 1927 the Hebard and Twin Tree companies had cut most of the profitable stands of timber and therefore ceased their operations. In a few years, other, smaller companies followed their example. Only in the most remote, hardest-to-reach parts of the swamp were there any sizable stands of uncut cypress left. Some five hundred miles of logging railroads had been built in the swamp. With only one or two exceptions, the islands with virgin pine, live oak, and southern magnolia were as thoroughly exploited as the cypress swamps. One of the islands to escape was Number One Island in the far southeastern corner of the swamp.

Long before the cutting had come to an end, local conservationists, joined by outsiders, were seeking ways to preserve the remaining timber and what was left of the swamp's beauties. A group called the Okefenokee Preservation Society, based in Waycross, was active around 1919. But the main impetus for preservation was to come from a dedicated group of scientists—most of them Cornell professors—who were studying the swamp's flora and fauna. Prominent in this group were Lucien Harris, Jr., Albert H. Wright and his wife Anna, Sherman C. Bishop, and Francis Harper. After visiting the swamp in 1912, Harper wrote a glowing account of its scenic and natural wonders. "Whoever has beheld the manifold charms of this paradise of the woods and waters," he wrote, "comes away fascinated and spellbound. Its majestic pines and cypresses, its peaceful waterways, and lily strewn prairies, together with the splendid wild creatures that inhabit them, should be safe-guarded from destruction." In 1926 a popular work entitled *History of the Okefenokee Swamp,* by two local citizens, Alex McQueen and Hamp Mizell, did much to help the cause.

Thanks to the strong support that had been building up for years, it became possible to obtain approval for the establishment of a national wildlife refuge that would take in most of the swamp. In November, 1936, land for a wildlife refuge was obtained through an executive order of President Franklin D. Roosevelt. The refuge itself was created the next year. At the present time, the refuge covers 396,000 acres, and most of it is a national wilderness area free of any type of exploitation by man.

During the years since the end of lumbering and the establishment of the refuge, the swamp has slowly returned to a more pristine condition. The wildlife returned, and soon the swamp became a major tourist attraction. About the only change in the swamp's natural makeup that old-timers like the Lees and Chessers would notice is that there are fewer cypress trees, and the ones growing today, with few exceptions, are younger and smaller than the ones they knew. In many of the heavily lumbered areas, cypresses have been replaced by trees, such as swamp tupelos and the bays, that are better able to make a quick comeback. However, as C. T. Trowell has aptly stated, "The overall character of the Okefenokee has not changed significantly during the past 7,000 years."

William C. Grimm, writing about the Okefenokee Swamp in *Bird-Lore* eight years after the creation of the refuge, found scars of earlier lumbering days, but at the same time, he told of unearthly beauty and abundant wildlife. On a boat run between Billys Island and Minnies Lake to the northeast, he reported seeing "the most beautiful swamp country to be found in the Okefenokee—or anywhere else." Actually this area happened to be one of the few parts of the swamp that was virtually untouched by earlier lumbering operations. His course, one that I followed in June of 1984, was through a flooded cypress swamp flanked by hurrah bushes, titi, dahoon holly, and other swamp shrubs. The cypresses, tall and straight, were some of the largest pond cypresses I have ever seen.

Grimm also told of traversing cut-over country "now occupied by small cypresses, sweet gums, black gums, and dense thickets." He found "numerous stumps of truly huge cypresses . . . mute reminders of the original forest which once covered the entire area." Of the former tram rail lines, he wrote: "Evidence of the days when the great cypresses were fed to voracious mills is apparent in the cypress pilings which ramify the swamp and over which the logging trams once hauled huge logs to the sawmill."

The once-thriving Billys Island was once again a wilderness. All he could find of its recent past was a few stately cabbage palms, an overgrown and forgotten cemetery plot, and a decrepit building. Nature had rapidly reclaimed her own. In June, 1986, forty-two years after Grimm's visit, I found myself, in company with Gary Williamson, exploring sites of historic interest on the island. With the mists of early morning giving way to bright sunshine as we docked our small boat, the island that lay ahead of us seemed like another world. We would be leaving the alligators and swamp behind us as we set foot on the sandy, pine-clad island. The undergrowth had recently been burned, leaving a blackened terrain devoid of signs of life. But as we made our way inland to the bed of a former logging railroad and the site of an old village, a few vultures could be seen circling overhead. Red-bellied woodpeckers, crows, tufted titmice, and crested flycatchers were the only other birds in the comparatively desolate landscape. Among the ruins of the old village we found parts of stoves, some cooking utensils, and scattered bricks. Gary's keen eye spotted two kinds of skinks, a six-lined racer, some green anoles, and a black racer.

Of greatest interest to me was a scattered growth of dwarf shrubs with creamy white blossoms. Only later did I learn that the plants were narrow-leaf pawpaws (*Asimina angustifolia*), a species with a limited range in the sandy pine woods of southern Georgia, neighboring parts of Florida, and southeastern Alabama. The flowers lent a splash of brightness to an otherwise somber scene.

Although the cabbage palms that had once shaded their residence were still standing, nothing was left of the home of the Lee family, the pioneers who had occupied and farmed the island for such a long time. Loblolly pines, now quite large, occupied their fields, and off to one side, protected by a chain link fence, was the Lee cemetery. In 1897 the Lees and members of two other families lived on the island, sharing a single dwelling that consisted of two rooms. All sixteen members slept in a single bedroom; the second room served as the dining room and kitchen. Yet the visitor who reported upon the circumstances of these backwoodsmen said that the house was surrounded by shade trees and flowers. From all evidence, the Lees loved their island home. The original couple who settled on the island were said to have avoided any travel to the outside world for a period of twenty-five years prior to their deaths. The male member of the Lee family who headed the household was always known as the King of the Okefenokee Swamp.

Whatever its taxonomic status may be, the pond cypress is the common cypress of the Okefenokee Swamp. Francis Harper wrote, "Nowhere else in the world probably does pond cypress obtain a heavier growth or finer proportions." Its comeback in some parts of the swamp can be accounted for by low water in some years, which permits the establishment of seedlings. On a visit to the swamp in 1984 I was told that pond cypress in the area of the old Suwannee Canal ranged in age between 98 and 102 years. When that part of the swamp was being lumbered, those trees were too small to be worth cutting. In "houses" around Chesser Island and some other parts of the swamp, partially blackened trunks of dead cypress trees testify to the heat generated by previous big fires. Hulks of many of them are all that is left of trees destroyed in a fire that swept through the swamp toward the end of 1954 and that was still smoldering in early 1955. Other big fires are known to have occurred around 1845 and in 1910 and 1932. Feeding upon peat dry from prolonged drought, the fires have sometimes killed the normally fire-resistant cypress.

For those who have not visited swamps as far south as southern Georgia, several additions to one's list of swamp flora are to be looked for. One of the most interesting is a woody climber belonging to the heath family. Climbing heath, as it is called, works its way up the trunks of trees by growing under the outer bark. It is most often seen on trunks of pond cypresses. Common in the Okefenokee Swamp, its branches, with leaves and flowers, can be seen every few feet protruding from the trunks of pond cypresses at the Chesser Island and Okefenokee Swamp Park boardwalks. The woody vine has a limited range in southeastern Georgia, northern Florida, and southeastern Alabama.

Another plant to look for in the swamp is Georgia fever-bark, or pinckneya. This small tree has much the same range as climbing heath but is found somewhat farther north along the coast. The flowers, which come into bloom in the spring, are highly ornamental because of the single large creamy or rose-colored sepal found with each blossom. Generally regarded as a seepage bog plant, Georgia fever-bark, according to the Wrights, is found in the Okefenokee Swamp at the edges of islands and at the margins of cypress ponds. Still another species unfamiliar to most northerners is the buck-wheat tree, which has a range rather similar to that of the other two species mentioned but reaches farther west along the Gulf Coast. The buckwheat tree can be recognized by its reddish bark and white flowers. The white flowers are followed by seeds in long, terminal racemes. Ogeechee tupelo, common along the Altamaha River to the north, is another small tree found in the Okefenokee, with a similar limited range. A small, water-loving tree, it can be recognized by its reddish fruits.

A stop at Okefenokee Swamp Park in the northern part of the swamp near Waycross will help the visitor to learn some of the local trees and shrubs. Plantings at the parking area bear labels. Besides buckwheat tree and ogeechee tupelo, the visitor will find titi, sweet bay, red bay, loblolly bay, dahoon holly, sweet pepperbush, and wax myrtle. But strangely, water tupelo, so common in coastal swamps just to the north and also in swamps to the west, is missing in the Okefenokee.

For those who want to become acquainted with the hurrah bushes, so common in the swamp, I know of no easy way to do so. The best plan is to obtain twigs from the bushes containing leaves, flowers, or fruits and key them out using one of the botanical guides on floras of the Southeast. The hurrah bushes are in the heath family and consist of two genera—*Leucothoe* and *Lyonia*. Most are evergreens and have rather wide ranges. The *hurrah* is said to come from shouts that swampers were known to give after making their way through the tangles in which the bushes grow.

The sphagnum, which covers large areas in wetter parts of the swamp, is a floating wildflower garden. To make up for lack of nutrients, some of the plants are carnivorous, preying upon insects or tiny aquatic organisms. The Okefenokee Swamp has more than its share of such plants, each with its special method of trapping live prey. A stroll along a board-walk or nature trail will lead sooner or later to the discovery of pitcher plants, with their odd funnels for capturing insects, or sundews, which capture insects in sticky traps formed by tentaclelike hairs on the leaves. The bladderworts, a group of largely aquatic plants with yellow or purple blossoms, capture small aquatic organisms with underwater traps or "bladders" attached to their finely dissected floating leaves.

Growing near or among the carnivorous plants are still other wildflowers that are not so highly specialized. Among these are the two common water-lilies—spatterdock and fragrant water-lily—iris, and several orchids. Rose pogonia, grass pink, and water-spider orchid grow in among tufts of sphagnum and Virginia chain fern. If anything, the occasional fires that sweep through the Okefenokee seem to improve the habitat for plants making up the floating wildflower garden.

With its highly acidic water (it has a pH as low as 4.2) and with few nutrients entering the swamp by way of streams, the Okefenokee Swamp at first glance may sound like it should be a biological desert. Yet the visitor is soon enthralled by the richness of both the flora and fauna. What is the explanation? The Great Dismal Swamp, which is also a highly acidic bog, has far fewer species, particularly fishes, reptiles, and amphibians—all of which are dependent upon the immediate environment for their sustenance. In both swamps whatever nutrients are present are recycled—used over and over again: Living organisms die and are eaten, and the process continues indefinitely, thereby keeping vital nutrients within the ecosystem. One can only guess that the process works more efficiently in the Okefenokee than it does in the Great Dismal.

Using faunal lists compiled in recent years, I find that in the case of every class the Okefenokee has more species than the Great Dismal Swamp. For example, the Great Dismal has somewhat fewer than thirty species of fishes, according to tabulations I have seen. On the other hand, the Okefenokee has at least forty species. Tabulations of fishes and other organisms in the Okefenokee have been made by Joshua Laerm and his coauthors, and I have discovered a few additional fishes in C. H. Wharton's *Natural Environments of Georgia.*

Many of the fishes in the Okefenokee Swamp are small species ranging from an inch to three or four inches in length. Indeed, the swamp has the distinction of having the two smallest fish in North America—the least killifish and pygmy killifish. Besides those two midgets, it can claim two pygmy sunfishes, the swamp darter, the starhead topminnow, and the mosquito fish—all under three inches in length. Of far more interest to fishermen are larger fishes suitable for the table and capable of putting up a fight. Among the choices are chain pickerel, channel catfish, largemouth bass, and a number of sunfishes. Two primitive fishes, the Florida gar and bowfin, are not in favor with fishermen but help make fishing in these waters an adventure.

During the early history of the swamp, fish were simply a source of food. In nineteenth-century correspondence unearthed by C. T. Trowell, there are frequent references to fishing and hunting but nothing about kinds of fishes caught or the pleasure of catching them. For example, a party visiting the swamp in December of 1894 took one bear, two deer, fifty-two ducks, and 125 pounds of fish. No details concerning kinds of fishes or the thrill of catching them were provided.

Today sports fishing is the major recreational activity in the swamp. Most of the many people one sees in a boat or canoe on the swamp's waterways are engaged in fishing. The many alligators and the beauty of the swamp add to the zest of such expeditions.

Recent listings show that the Okefenokee has twenty-one species of toads and frogs, sixteen species of salamanders, and fifteen species of turtles. The alligator snapping turtle, our largest freshwater turtle, is present, though it is rarely seen. A guide at Stephen Foster State Park told me that he had recently seen a large alligator snapping turtle in shallow water, with the wormlike protrusion on its tongue clearly visible inside its huge, gaping jaws.

The Okefenokee probably has more species of snakes than any other southern swamp. No fewer than thirty-eight have been recorded. It is a good idea to be aware of the poisonous ones and to watch for them. Five poisonous species, all shown in displays at the interpretative center at the Suwannee Canal Recreation Area, make up the list of venomous reptiles. Of these, only the Florida cottonmouth is likely to be encountered in wetter parts of the swamp. The eastern coral snake, eastern diamondback rattlesnake, dusky pygmy rattlesnake, and canebrake rattlesnake are residents of pine-clad islands, scrub palmetto thickets, and oak hammocks.

Water snakes are very common and can often be seen from boats and boardwalks. The most common species is the banded water snake. Also present are the Florida green, red-bellied, brown, and eastern glossy water snakes. Jimmy Spikes of Okefenokee Swamp Park tells me that snakes are as common as ever in the swamp. He is well acquainted with the swamp and the history of its wildlife. As in so many other swamps, the snakes are plentiful but largely unseen.

Represented by eleven species found in and around the swamp, lizards are also abundant. In pine woods and sandhills, one has a chance of finding as many as three kinds of glass lizards, the southern fence lizard, several skinks (including the northern mole skink), and the six-lined racer. In wetter habitats the skinks are well represented, and the ubiquitous green anole is as common as ever.

The crocodilians are represented in the Okefenokee Swamp by a large population of American alligators (at least twelve thousand) and a single specimen of the spectacled caimen. The caimen is a South American species that has become established in Florida. Except in very cool weather, alligators can be seen almost anywhere in the swamp. They are especially common in ponds, lakes, and ditches and along the entire length of the old Suwannee Canal. In lagoons at the Okefenokee Swamp Park, Oskar, a fourteen-foot specimen, holds sway. He chases off male intruders and sports a harem of females. Alligator holes, water-filled depressions in the peat bed, are kept free of vegetation by the one or two alligators that live in them. As in Florida, the Okefenokee's alligator holes are oases for fish and other forms of aquatic life during dry weather.

Along the East Coast, the Okefenokee probably ranks second only to Florida's wetlands in number and variety of large wading birds. I had my first taste of this profusion when on a November day I took a guided boat trip from the Suwannee Canal Recreation Area to Chesser Prairie. The first part of the trip, which was on the old Suwannee Canal, was somewhat monotonous. A wall of pond cypresses on both sides of the canal meant that there was little to see. But after we left the canal and turned into Chesser Prairie, I was treated to a magnificent panorama of open marshland dotted with wading birds. Among the great egrets, great blue herons, and white ibis, I picked out a small group of wood storks. Larger than any of the others, they were easy to distinguish. This endangered wading bird once nested in the swamp in small numbers.

I could have spent all day there watching birds and enjoying the landscape. But Eddie, my guide, was having trouble with water weed fouling the propeller. So we reluctantly turned around and retraced our course. The decision was all the more painful when he added that if the water had been higher, he could have taken me to Grand Prairie to the southwest, where there were even more birds.

Depending to some extent upon such factors as the time of year and the depth of the water, the prairies—their waters or the sky over them—offer a surprising variety of birdlife. Among the more interesting birds of these wetlands are the pied-billed grebe, anhinga, wood stork, swallow-tailed kite, bald eagle, osprey, sandhill crane, king rail, and a variety of herons, egrets, ibis, waterfowl, and birds of prey. Prairies conveniently close to the Suwannee Canal Recreation Area are some of the largest and best suited for seeing waterbirds. Chase Prairie is immediately north of the old canal; to the south is Chesser Prairie, which can be viewed from the canal and also the Chesser Island boardwalk and lookout tower. The tower, which is at the end of a mile-long boardwalk, offers a magnificent view of prairies, cypress thickets, and wooded islands. It is one of the best places to see and hear sandhill cranes. The swamp has a resident population of sandhill cranes that belong to the Florida race, as well as migrant cranes that arrive in the fall from the North. The year-round local population consists of between 250 and 300 birds.

During some years the swamp contains a thriving breeding colony of herons and egrets. But the colony's success depends a great deal upon water conditions. If the water is too high, the small fish the birds feed upon are widely scattered and hard to obtain. In very dry years, ponds, where wading birds fish, may become so low that, again, there is insufficient food. In 1979, a good year, five thousand nesting wading birds were present at Macks Island, a rookery immediately to the west of Stephen Foster State Park. About three-fourths of the birds that year were white ibis, and the remainder were cattle egrets, great egrets, and little blue herons. Visiting the Stephen Foster State Park area in May, 1986, I saw an almost constant stream of white ibis flying over. Nesting was probably under way at the Macks Island rookery.

Vultures and hawks are well represented. It would be unusual not to see the dark forms of black or turkey vultures perched in dead trees or not to see one or both species circling overhead. The red-shouldered hawk, as is true in other southern swamps, is the common hawk. But in winter the northern harriers (marsh hawks) arrive, and they become the common raptor out over the prairies. Unlike the osprey, which is a common nesting bird, the bald eagle is only a winter visitor. Wild turkeys, often in sizable flocks, can sometimes be seen when one takes the "wildlife drive" to Chesser Island.

Any large owl sleepily perched in a tree at the edge of a pond or waterway will almost certainly be a barred owl. In spite of heavy boat traffic on some days, there are always a few in trees at the edge of the Suwannee Canal. But one should take a second look at any bird that seems somewhat unfamiliar. For example, limpkins have been recorded a few times in the swamp. The swamp, however, seems not to offer them the kinds or amounts of snails that are such important items in their diets. There have also been sightings of such unexpected species as the white pelican and roseate spoonbill.

Smaller birds are much the same as those seen in the Great Dismal Swamp. Prothonotary warblers obligingly appear at edges of waterways, and northern parula warblers frequent wooded areas where Spanish moss festoons the trees. But the Swainson's warbler, one of the rarer species of southern swamps, is, according to Albert Wright and Francis Harper, an elusive resident of the Okefenokee's cypress bays and small patches of cane. The writers have told of finding it in "some of the wildest and densest cypress woods of the swamp." In the remote Minnies Lake region, the two scientists once became hopelessly lost for part of a day and had to camp that night on one of the tiny batteries that dot the prairies.

Chances of seeing either the ivory-billed woodpecker or the Bachman's warbler in the Okefenokee Swamp seem extremely remote. The last ivorybill sighting, according to the literature, was in 1948, and the last Bachman's warbler sighting in 1933. One cannot, I am afraid, put much confidence in two reports in 1985 of birds thought to have been ivorybills in the southeastern part of the swamp. C. T. Trowell has told me that no tradition or folklore exists among old-timers of there ever having been either passenger pigeons or Carolina parakeets in the swamp. In 1937, however, motion pictures were taken of parrotlike birds in or near the Okefenokee Swamp (see Chapter 7).

Although there are no endemic mammalian forms in the Okefenokee, a number of small mammals seem to reach peak numbers here. One is the round-tailed muskrat, sometimes called the Florida water rat. Replacing the muskrat, which is not found in extreme southeastern United States, this small mammal is much like the muskrat in habits and appearance. It is smaller and somewhat less aquatic in its habits. It is primarily a marsh dweller and builds a dome-shaped house of plant fibers. Its houses and nearby feeding platforms are a common sight in the Okefenokee prairies. The feeding platforms, about five or six inches in diameter, are floating rafts made of marsh vegetation. They contain one or two openings through which the animals can dive in case of emergency. Primarily a nocturnal species, the round-tail rarely shows itself in daylight. Francis Harper, in his article "Mammals of the Okefenokee Swamp Region," stated that the round-tailed muskrat was a "prairie species, with one of the most restricted habitat ranges of any Okefenokee mammal." The Okefenokee Swamp and the Florida Everglades seem to be centers of abundance for this queer little mammal that not many people have ever heard of.

The cotton mouse, a close relative of the white-footed mouse, is abundant in the prairies and wooded islands of the Okefenokee Swamp. A good climber and swimmer, it nimbly makes its way about in wet or thickly grown habitat throughout the swamp. Harper told of a trapper taking twenty-two of the mice in one night at a site in the swamp. Another small mouse shares some of the same habitat with the cotton mouse, though it is more of a cypress bay species. This is the golden mouse, a handsome swampland dweller with reddish-gold fur and good climbing and swimming ability. Edwin

Way Teale told of one that was seen entering the Suwannee Canal and emerging on the other side after having swum the distance underwater. After leaving the water, the small animal dried off almost instantly and went its way.

That the shrews, North America's smallest mammals, should be represented in swamp habitats may seem surprising. But the Great Dismal Swamp has an endemic shrew, and several species, including the water shrew of more northern districts, are accomplished swimmers and divers. The Okefenokee can claim the southeastern and least shrews, both of which seem more at home in aquatic habitats in the Deep South than elsewhere.

Probably the only small mammal in the swamp that is more secretive than the shrew is the star-nosed mole. According to C. H. Wharton, this mole is one of the rarest of the swamp's mammals. But its supposed rarity may be due partly to its underground and underwater way of life. It is an expert swimmer and diver, even preying upon small fishes and other aquatic organisms. Wharton suggests that the star-nosed mole, which is unrecorded over most of the southeastern coastal plain, has either been overlooked or else the Okefenokee Swamp contains a disjunct population.

The southern mink is another of the Okefenokee's mystery animals. What its numbers are, or if it is even present, is not known for certain. But in a Florida publication on rare and endangered species, it is stated that a remnant population of the mammal does occur in the Okefenokee Swamp.

Fortunately, not all of the mammal inhabitants of the Okefenokee Swamp are as rare or well-hidden as those mentioned so far. The marsh rabbit is often abroad in bright sunlight and sometimes allows a close approach. With luck the observer may see a family of river otters or even a bobcat. At Stephen Foster State Park, the white-tailed deer are so tame that they simply stand their ground and stare at you when you pass them. It is not unusual to see cattle egrets settle on the backs of the deer and pick off ticks and flies.

As for the raccoon, many tales have been told about its boldness and clever methods wherever it is found. When I was camping in the Congaree Swamp, a raccoon, under cover of darkness, once opened my ice chest, removed an opened quart of milk, and, without spilling a drop, set it down on the ground nearby. My guest was more interested in the bacon and ate its fill of that delicacy. However, an Okefenokee raccoon, if I can believe the story, was even more "considerate." An employee at Stephen Foster State Park told me about a raccoon that robbed an ice chest of a bottle of beer and, sitting on its haunches and holding the bottle between its hind legs, unscrewed the cap, drank for a while, and then screwed the cap back on and returned the bottle to the chest.

The large mammal that everyone who visits the swamp wants to see is the black bear. From the days of great bear hunts until the present, the black bear has been as much of a symbol of this great swamp as the alligator. From being a marauder that made heavy inroads upon domestic stock, the black bear in more recent years has become respectable and is now in demand mostly for the photographic opportunities it offers. During the fall of 1983, many visitors to the swamp had an opportunity to see and photograph the black bear. At Chesser Island and throughout the perimeter of the swamp, black bears appeared in live oaks, harvesting an unusually good crop of acorns. Climbing the trees, the bears even broke off top limbs and stripped them of their acorns. Although the black bear population in the swamp is said to number around 150 individuals, that is only an estimate. It could be considerably larger.

Toward dusk, bats that have roosted during the day in hollow trees or in clusters of Spanish moss come out to feed. Of the seven or so species known to be present in the swamp, the Seminole bat is the most common and the most easily seen. A mahogany-colored bat, it leaves its roosting sites in Spanish moss at dusk, and, according to Harper, forages over watercourses, pine barrens, clearings, and, to a lesser extent, over prairies and hammocks. Unlike most other bats, which hibernate in winter, this species is out foraging on warmer days in mid-winter and may appear in broad daylight. A second common bat, the eastern pipistrelle, is one of our smallest bats and, like the Seminole bat, may be seen out over watercourses toward dusk. It can be recognized by its mothlike flight. Another species, the evening bat, common both in the Okefenokee and in other large swamps, roosts in hollow cypress trees. A reddish-brown bat, the evening bat has a slow, deliberate flight.

Like so many other southern swamps, the Okefenokee has its share of purported cougar sightings. But the catamount of earlier times has not been reliably reported since about 1906. The extinct Florida red wolf was reliably reported in 1908 and may have still been present until 1918.

The Okefenokee Swamp, a refuge for a wide variety of wildlife, is full of paradoxes. Floating islands may not be floating islands at all but are probably houses, or, as they are sometimes called, *tree houses*. Fire, instead of harming the ecosystem, assists by burning away the peat, thereby creating basins that become filled with water. Past lumbering destroyed the virgin timber but paved the way for the regeneration of new growth. And in spite of its highly acidic water, the swamp has an abundant fish population and a large number of reptiles and amphibians dependent upon an aquatic environment. The same abundance and diversity extends to birds and mammals as well.

There are three major points of access to the swamp. Okefenokee Swamp Park, in the northern corner of the swamp, is about eight miles south of the city of Waycross, just off State Highways 1 and 23. It is managed by the Okefenokee Swamp Park Association, a nonprofit organization that operates under an agreement with the United States

Fish and Wildlife Service. The park is therefore distinct from the national refuge, and most of it is located outside the refuge boundary, though some of its tours extend into the refuge. At the Okefenokee Swamp Park the visitor can take guided tours by boat along a winding watercourse through part of the swamp's beautiful cypress forest and into a typical Okefenokee wet prairie. There are museum and wildlife exhibits that give the visitor a good picture of the swamp.

The eastern entrance to the swamp is at Camp Cornelia, site of Jackson's Folly and now a part of the refuge called the Suwannee Canal Recreation Area. That historic area, which offers a visitors' center, boat rentals, guided tours, a wildlife drive, and a mile-long boardwalk into the swamp at nearby Chesser Island, can be reached by turning west from State Highway 23, about seven miles southeast of Folkston. A four-mile-long paved road leads to Camp Cornelia.

The western entrance to the swamp is reached by going to Fargo on U.S. Route 441 and then eastward to Stephen Foster State Park. The park, with its concessions and camping grounds, is at the eastern tip of a seven-mile-long tongue of land bordered on both sides by the swamp and known as the Pocket. The park, managed by the Georgia Department of Parks, affords easy access by boat or canoe to Billys Lake, Billys Island, and other well-known sections of the swamp.

Information concerning the Okefenokee Swamp National Wildlife Refuge—hours to visit, what to see, reservations for using canoe trails, and the like—can be obtained by writing the refuge office, P.O. Box 338, Folkston, Georgia 31517. The phone number is (912) 496-3331.

References

Cohen, Arthur D., *et al.*, eds. *The Okefenokee Swamp*. Los Alamos, N.M., 1984.

Cypert, Eugene. "The Origin of Houses in the Okefenokee Prairies." *American Midland Naturalist*, LXXXVII (1972), 448–58.

Grimm, William C. "Marvelous Okefenokee." *Bird-Lore*, XLVII (1945), 333–42.

Harper, Francis. "The Mammals of the Okefenokee Swamp Region of Georgia." *Proceedings of the Boston Society of Natural History*, XXXVIII (1927), 191–96.

Laerm, Joshua, *et al.* "Vertebrates of the Okefenokee Swamp." *Brimleyana*, IV (Fall, 1980), 47–73.

Layne, James N., ed. *Mammals*. Gainesville, Fla., 1979. Vol. I of Peter C. Pritchard, ed., *Rare and Endangered Biota of Florida*. 6 vols. to date.

Teale, Edwin Way. *North with the Spring*. New York, 1963.

Trowell, C. T. *The Suwanee Canal Company in the Okefenokee Swamp*. Douglas, Ga., 1984.

Wharton, Charles H. *The Natural Environments of Georgia*. Atlanta, 1978.

Wright, Albert H., and Francis Harper. "A Biological Reconnaissance of the Okefenokee Swamp in Georgia: The Birds." *Auk*, XXX (1913), 477–505.

Wright, Albert H., and Anna A. Wright. "The Habitats and Composition of the Vegetation of Okefenokee Swamp, Georgia." *Ecological Monographs*, II (1932), 111–32.

14 / South Florida Swamps

fter visiting the Okefenokee Swamp, the swamp enthusiast from the North faces a choice of whether to continue south to visit the south Florida swamps or to drive west to the many river swamps along the Gulf Coast. Either trip will provide all the natural wonders one could ask for. In south Florida the visitor reaches the subtropics and finds marked differences in the plant life, though cypress trees are still present and there are open prairies much like those in the Okefenokee Swamp, but stretching as far as the eye can see.

Two great ecosystems dominate the swamps of south Florida. One is the Everglades, east and south of Lake Okeechobee and covering some 4 million acres. Vastly altered by drainage and agriculture, the Everglades is no longer a pristine wilderness. But Everglades National Park, established in 1947 and containing 1.4 million acres of land and water, preserves some of the best samples of the River of Grass, as it is sometimes called. The other great ecosystem is the Big Cypress Swamp, lying to the west of the Everglades and covering about 1.5 million acres. Less changed than the Everglades, the Big Cypress Swamp is far from being a solid forest of cypress trees. In fact, only about a third of the region is clothed in cypress; the rest consists of pine woods, wet prairies, dry prairies, hardwood hammocks, and mangrove swamps. In 1974 Congress set aside 570,000 acres in the Big Cypress Swamp as a national preserve. Acting as a buffer to protect the Everglades National Park and saving large tracts of vital wetland, the Big Cypress National Preserve was a welcome addition to the south Florida system of parks and preserves.

The *big* in "Big Cypress" does not refer to the size of the trees but to the vastness of the area. At one time "big" would have been an appropriate term to describe the trees in some parts of the swamp, but the bigger trees have largely been logged off. Both in the Everglades and in the Big Cypress Swamp, however, there are thousands of acres of pygmy cypress—trees that are often a hundred or more years old but that are stunted because of poor growing conditions.

Within the bounds of the Big Cypress Swamp and immediately west of the Big Cypress preserve is the Fakahatchee Strand, a junglelike area of a hundred thousand acres. Most of this area is a state wildlife preserve established largely for

the protection of the endangered Florida cougar, or panther. To the northwest is Corkscrew Swamp, an eleven-thousand-acre National Audubon Society sanctuary. The sanctuary is noted for its large wood stork nesting colony and the largest remaining stand of virgin bald cypress in Florida.

The most difficult part of becoming acquainted with this watery domain at the southernmost part of the Florida peninsula has to do with the plants. A bewildering variety of tropical plants replaces the common species seen in more northern swamps. One has no trouble finding bald cypress and pond cypress. Both are common trees in the wetlands, and both are at their southernmost range limits in south Florida. But almost lost among the tropical plants will be temperate ones such as red maple, sugarberry, and dahoon holly, which recall swamps to the north.

For the visitor trying to understand this often baffling and sometimes contradictory part of Florida, there is one fact to bear in mind: Lower Florida emerged from the sea less than ten thousand years ago. As a consequence, there has not been time enough for the development of many endemic species. Plants and animals present are primarily pioneers—ones that are readily conveyed to new places by the wind or ocean currents. Some, including birds and mammals, traveled to the area on their own, using their special forms of locomotion. West Indian plants arrived with hurricanes or rode northbound ocean currents. Many plants were bird-borne, the seeds arriving in the digestive systems or feathers of birds.

During the several hundred years that the white man has been upon the scene, south Florida has been inundated with plants and animals from all over the world. Presently, exotic species often overshadow native ones by sheer weight of numbers and the amount of space they take up. Of particular concern in saving the Everglades and associated wetlands is the weedlike spread of the Brazilian pepper tree (*Schinus*), the Australian pine (*Casuarina*), and the cajeput tree (*Melaleuca*). The latter in particular is well adapted to growing in swampy soil and has invaded thousands of acres along the fringes of the Everglades.

South Florida's emergence has been so recent that there has not been sufficient time for the development of well-defined drainage systems. The bed of Lake Okeechobee is believed to have been a sea-bottom depression that, after the land rose, became a freshwater lake. Several other large lakes to the north of Lake Okeechobee are believed to have had a similar origin, among them Lake Istokpoga, Lake Kissimmee, and Lake George. However, the largest number of lakes scattered through the Florida peninsula originated as solution holes in the underlying limestone. But from Lake Okeechobee southward, no more large lakes appear on the map. Limestone rock is present, yet there has not been time enough in this recently emerged part of Florida for large water-holding basins to dissolve out the rock and form lakes. On the other hand, there has been enough time for the development of countless small solution holes. Some small solution holes might be called lakes, whereas others are more appropriately called ponds or potholes.

Small solution holes in the limestone often become homes for snails, turtles, fish, and alligators. The latter not only use existing holes but construct their own. They do so by tearing away vegetation and muck with their teeth and using their tails to sweep the debris to one side. Gator holes, as they are called, become especially important to wildlife during times of drought. Aquatic forms of life live in them, and thirsty birds and mammals use them as drinking places. The most common plant growing in the gator holes is spatterdock. Two other water-lilies, floating heart and fragrant water-lily, share these small oases with spatterdock and the many wildlife inhabitants.

At the mercy of the elements, the Everglades, like the river swamps, have had to adjust to periods of water abundance and water scarcity. During the wet season, from June through November, rain falls down on the once-parched peatlands. Water, spilling over at the southern rim of Lake Okeechobee, adds to the flood. Slowly, in what is known as sheet flow, the water trickles on a broad front through the sawgrass and inches past cypresses and mangroves, eventually making its way to Florida Bay and the Gulf Coast. Even after the dry season returns, there will be another two or three months during which water is still flowing. Fish-eating birds time their nesting seasons to coincide with optimal water levels. Indeed, most living organisms in this land of changing water levels time their life functions to coincide with dry and wet seasons rather than cool and warm seasons. If there is too much water, as during hurricanes, or too little, the population levels of many species decline. If, as is so true today, man aggravates the situation by siphoning off water when it is needed and releasing it when it is not needed, the ecology of the whole region suffers.

Peat, like the largely undissolved limestone, is another indicator of how recently this part of Florida has emerged from the sea. The oldest peat in the Great Dismal Swamp was formed about 9,000 years ago, and that in the Okefenokee Swamp, about 6,600 years ago. In south Florida the oldest peat dates back to only about 5,000 years ago. The peat in the Everglades is largely derived from the native sawgrass.

Not a grass but a sedge, sawgrass is the dominant form of vegetation in the Everglades, making up approximately 65 to 70 percent of the plant cover. Reaching a height of about ten feet, sawgrass has blades with three sharp, serrated edges. The blades present a formidable barrier to anyone who would attempt to strike out over a sawgrass paririe on foot. Sawgrass has wildlife value, in that ducks eat the seeds and many birds use it as nesting sites and protective cover. But other aquatic plants rate much better in the benefits they provide wildlife. Because it takes up space and draws upon the often limited water supply, sawgrass, like the newly arrived exotic plants, is to be regarded with suspicion.

Moundlike clumps of vegetation exist in the Everglades. Some have palm trees, some cypresses, and some still other plants. They rise above the featureless sawgrass and, like small islands everywhere, are an invitation to the naturalist to visit them and explore their interiors. What is their origin? How do they differ from one another? What kinds of plants and animals are found on them?

The somewhat similar islands of vegetation in the Okefenokee Swamp provide a clue to the origin of those in the Everglades. It is thought that some of the tree islands in the Everglades were at one time floating masses of peat, which, like the Okefenokee islands, became anchored and covered with trees. Both in the Okefenokee and in portions of the northern Everglades, the tree islands are circular in shape. But southward in the Everglades and in the neighboring Big Cypress Swamp, the tree islands take on an oval or even elongate shape. They are oriented parallel to the direction of the water flow, with their blunt end pointed upstream. The upper end is the highest part of the island, rising as much as three or four feet above the surrounding terrain. The remaining 95 percent of the island is likely to be only inches higher than the surrounding terrain.

Floridians, unlike the swampers of the Okefenokee Swamp, do not call the tree islands houses. Instead, without bothering about the origins of the strange formations, they call them *hammocks* or *heads*. If cypress is the dominant tree, the tree island is called a *cypress hammock* or *cypress head*. On the other hand, if the two bay trees found in south Florida—sweet bay and red bay—are dominant, the tree island is called a *bay tree hammock* or *bayhead*. Depending upon the dominant growth, other hammocks in south Florida are given other names—*mahogany hammock, palm hammock,* or simply *hardwood hammock.*

The origin of the word *hammock* is obscure. But as applied to south Florida, the word, according to a recent edition of *Webster's International Dictionary,* means "an island of dense tropical undergrowth in the Everglades." A second definition in the same edition is "a fertile area in the southern U.S. (as Florida) that is often somewhat higher than its sur-

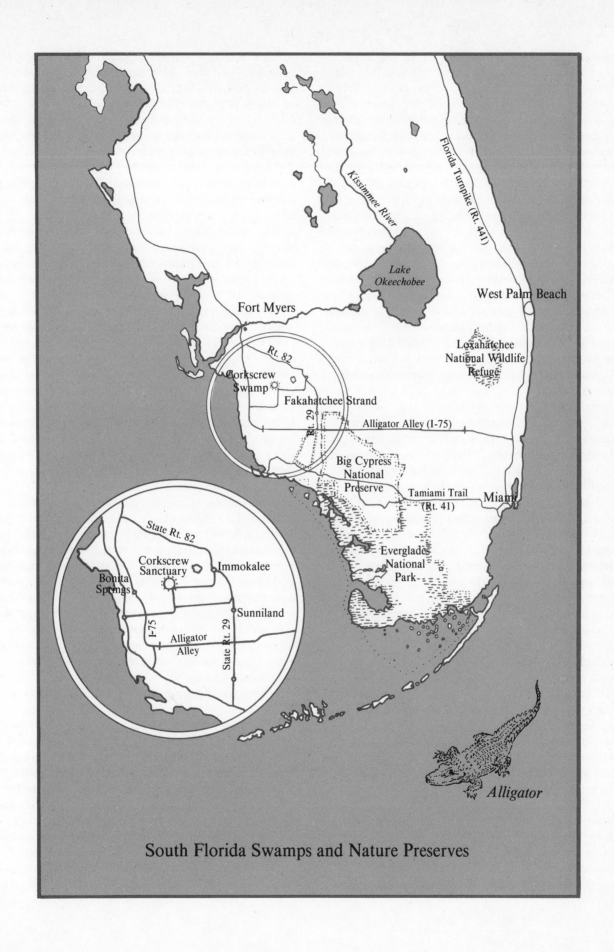

Florida Turnpike (Rt. 441)

Kissimmee River

Lake Okeechobee

Fort Myers

West Palm Beach

Rt. 82

Corkscrew Swamp

Loxahatchee National Wildlife Refuge

Fakahatchee Strand

Rt. 29

Alligator Alley (I-75)

Big Cypress National Preserve

Tamiami Trail (Rt. 41)

Miami

Everglades National Park

State Rt. 82

Corkscrew Sanctuary

Immokalee

Bonita Springs

I-75

Sunniland

Alligator Alley

State Rt. 29

Alligator

South Florida Swamps and Nature Preserves

roundings and is characterized by hardwood vegetation and soil of greater depth and containing more humus than that of the flatwoods or pinelands."

Deeper soil and higher elevation best describe most of the south Florida hammocks. But such a statement reveals little about their appearance and structure. William Spackman and his fellow researchers, who have studied these topographical features in both the Okefenokee Swamp and the Everglades, admit that they are unable to explain the origin of the hammocks in Florida. In a paper written in 1976, they stated that some of the Everglades hammocks appear where bedrock is high, others where the bedrock is low; still others have no relation to bedrock. They add that the hammocks seem to develop where there is little or no competition with sawgrass. Chances of hammock development are furthered if fire kills the sawgrass or if the terrain is too high or too low for sawgrass. In very low sites where water is present, the hammock may become colonized by cypress. Under these circumstances, the stand cannot correctly be called a hammock, since the ground on which the trees grow is lower than the surrounding terrain. It is more appropriate to call such a stand a *cypress dome*.

Much larger stands of cypress, as a rule, are found in strands. *Strands* are low-lying drainage systems in which the limestone bedrock has been eroded away and replaced by peat. Sometimes described as shallow, forested rivers, the strands are an important feature of the Big Cypress Swamp and may run for miles. Typically the larger bald cypress trees occupy the center of the strand, whereas pond cypresses occupy the outer edge, where the soil is shallower. Inasmuch as the smaller trees are at the edge, cypresses growing in strands have the same domelike outline as those growing in cypress domes. Wherever cypress stands are growing in solution holes or strands, they have the shape of a dome. Although the trees in such cypress stands may all be approximately the same age, those toward the center grow taller because of the deeper, richer soil. Some of the cypress domes have a small lake or pond at the center.

A third type of cypress forest occurs widely in the Big Cypress Swamp and is also represented in the Everglades. This is the dwarf, or hatrack, cypress forest, in which the trees are seldom over thirty feet tall and have a diameter at breast height of nine inches or less. The trees grow on shallow marl or sandy soil underlain by limestone bedrock. Although the trees are small, they may range in age from sixty to three hundred years. By far the largest part of south Florida's cypress is made up of dwarf cypress.

An extreme example of a dwarf cypress forest may be seen in the southern part of the Everglades National Park along the road to Flamingo. Near the Mahogany Hammock, the motorist will see, off to the left, a pygmy forest of tiny cypress trees ranging in height from two or three feet to six or seven. They grow in marl-filled pockets in the limestone bedrock, which is almost at the surface. Under the harsh conditions—the trees have almost no soil and experience long dry periods—cypresses over a hundred years old may be only head high. Botanist John K. Small, writing of this forest in 1933, stated that he had noticed no changes in the aspect or size of the trees during the course of the thirty years since he had first observed them.

Oddly enough, to the south the pygmy cypresses give way to another dwarf forest—the diminutive red mangrove forest. The presence of dwarf red mangroves indicates a zone where salt water is beginning to replace fresh water. Closer to Flamingo, white and red mangroves and buttonwoods line saltwater lagoons. The trees are quite large. The belt of mangrove forest that hugs the south and southwest coasts of south Florida constitutes one of the world's largest mangrove swamps.

Of as much interest as the origin and development of tree islands in this flat, often infertile part of Florida is the occurrence of animal life. Thanks to wildlife films, nearly everyone has seen the birds and other wildlife forms of south Florida. From colonies of roseate spoonbills nesting in mangroves, the scene changes swiftly to clouds of white ibis and other large wading birds filling the skies over the Everglades. Usually the film will show American alligators (in freshwater habitat), American crocodiles (in saltwater habitat), raccoons (almost anywhere), and, if the photographer had extremely good luck, a Florida cougar stalking its prey in dense, junglelike growth.

There will almost certainly be a few shots taken from the Anhinga Trail boardwalk in Everglades National Park, where there will be many more people than birds. Nevertheless, the photographer will have a hard time *not* finding a few purple gallinules there—gorgeous birds that flaunt their bright colors and act as though they have been trained to be tourist attractions. Equally obliging will be the anhingas, or water turkeys, which, in keeping with the name of the trail, are always on hand. After diving below the surface to obtain fish, an anhinga soon finds a place to perch and, with wings outstretched and tail spread, remains motionless sunning itself. Lacking the water-repellent feathers of most other birds, anhingas must spend inordinate amounts of time drying themselves.

In recent years far fewer birds are seen at the Anhinga Trail and in the Everglades generally. What has happened? Florida's larger, more spectacular forms of birdlife have always been subject to heavy losses as a result of various factors. Whether the losses came from hurricanes, drought, fire, or some other natural factor, numbers usually rebounded quickly enough once there was a return to normal conditions. The arrival of the American Indian in south Florida about two thousand years ago probably had little impact upon the birdlife. The Tequestas and Calusas, the original Indian inhabitants, were nonagricultural peoples who relied upon fishes, shellfish, game, and wild plants for food. Some idea of their diet has been gained by sifting through the debris they left behind at the many mounds they constructed. For example, an Indian mound near Shark River, on the southwest coast, yielded remains of small mammals, deer, birds, alligators, fishes, crabs, and possibly manatees.

By the middle of the eighteenth century, the early Indian inhabitants were being replaced by raiding bands of Creeks from the north, who were later known as Seminoles. By 1820 the Calusa and Tequesta Indians of south Florida had disappeared completely and been replaced by the Seminoles. Although more agrarian than their predecessors, the Seminoles were also hunters and were soon supplying white traders with hides, furs, and feathers. Prior to 1837, according to Charlton W. Tebeau in his book *Man in the Everglades,* the interior of south Florida was almost completely unknown to the white man. It was the realm of the Florida cougar, the black bear, the alligator, limitless numbers of birds, and small bands of Seminoles.

In 1850, the first date for which we have an educated guess, there may have been a total population of 2.5 million large wading birds in south Florida. But it was not long before the Seminoles and white hunters were taking an increasingly heavy toll of the plume birds. In greatest demand were the feathers of roseate spoonbills, white ibis, egrets, herons, gulls, and terns. They were used to decorate women's hats. At the same time, game of all kinds was being shot for food and sport. The havoc had reached such proportions that by 1900 hunters and trappers were complaining about the comparative scarcity of wildlife. And that was before agriculture, settlement, and diversion of the region's water had significantly harmed the environment. But even in 1900 it appeared that many species would be driven to extinction.

The National Association of Audubon Societies (now the National Audubon Society) met the challenge in 1905 by securing the passage in Florida of a model protection law for nongame species and by employing four wardens to protect the dwindling populations of plume birds. The murder of two wardens—Guy Bradley in 1905 and one C. McLeod in 1908—by plume hunters aroused public condemnation of the feather trade as nothing else had done. Before long the ravages of the plume hunters were a thing of the past. But there was no quick rebound in numbers of wading birds. Not until about 1920 did their numbers begin to increase significantly. Between 1920 and 1950, there seems to have been a rapid increase followed by a leveling off in numbers. In his book *In Lower Florida Wilds,* published in 1920, Charles Torrey Simpson, well-known Florida botanist, was gloomy about the outlook. "The heyday of bird life has passed and is passing," he wrote. He noted the near disappearance of several groups, including egrets, gulls, and terns. He went on to say that raccoons and otters were fairly abundant and that bobcats and deer were occasionally seen.

Although the outlook for large wading birds began to improve soon after Simpson wrote his book, new threats, not only to birds but to wildlife generally, were appearing on the horizon. With the spread of roads, collectors of rare fauna and flora were penetrating every part of south Florida. A road to Paradise Key (in what is now Everglades National Park), completed in 1915 and extended to Flamingo on Florida Bay by 1922, gave collectors easy access to the riches of Royal Palm Hammock and other hammocks lying to the south and west. The completion of the Tamiami Trail in 1928 hastened the exploitation of the eastern portions of the Everglades as well as the Big Cypress Swamp.

One of the most eagerly sought prizes during this period was tree snails of the genus *Liguus.* Exceptionally beautiful, the snails inhabit the hammocks of the Everglades as well as tropical growth in the Florida Keys. Between fifty-two and sixty color forms, all belonging to one species, were present originally. Collectors, ransacking every hammock and sometimes setting fire to them so that no one else would have the opportunity of competing with them, reduced the number of forms to fifteen or twenty.

Rare orchids and air plants are trophies eagerly sought by the plant collector. Hammocks in the Everglades and especially those in the Fakahatchee Strand abound in epiphytic orchids. No fewer than forty-four species of orchids grow in and around the Fakahatchee Strand, and of those, six are listed as endangered by the state of Florida. Nodding catopsis is an endangered air plant (bromeliad) discovered in the Fakahatchee Strand in 1959 and to date found nowhere else.

According to Tebeau, "By the early 1920s the curious and adventurous as well as profiteers and vandals roamed almost at will throughout the Everglades." So far the cypress trees had escaped. But the opening of the Tamiami Trail made the Big Cypress Swamp easily accessible to lumbering interests. During the 1930s and 1940s the lumber industry moved into that part of Florida. From Monroe Station and Ochopee on the Tamiami Trail to the Fakahatchee Strand, the sounds of lumbering filled the air, and huge cypress trees, some of them as much as six hundred to seven hundred years old, crashed to the ground. Fortunately, a few escaped the lumberman's ax and saw.

After the cutting came to an end, many of the men stayed on to make their living as hunters, fishermen, guides, plant collectors, and cattlemen. According to a brochure on the Big Cypress National Preserve, "They were latter day frontiersmen fleeing urban restraints." Oil drilling, drainage for land development, and plans for a huge jetport for Miami in 1968 were some of the new threats to the region that quickly followed timbering for cypress.

How were the large wading birds bearing up under the new pressures? For a time they did surprisingly well. Estimates of their total numbers in 1947, when Everglades National Park was established, vary from 1.5 million to 2 million, which indicates that the birds had indeed made a good comeback after the days of the plume hunters. Had the park lived up to the expectations of Ernest F. Coe and others who were instrumental in getting it established, the large waders and other wildlife in the park would be more abundant today than when the park first opened. But today, according to some estimates, there are only one-tenth as many large wading birds in south Florida as when the park was established. Why?

As the population of south Florida grew apace and more and more Everglades muck was turned into agricultural land and residential property (presently about 45 percent of the Everglades is agricultural and residential), there developed an acute shortage of fresh water for wildlife. More and more of it was diverted for human use, and Lake Okeechobee, which had a tendency to spill over badly during hurricanes and drown nearby residents, was kept at a permanently low level, much of its water being wastefully drained off by canals emptying into the ocean. Everglades National Park, having the lowest priority rating in the eyes of the U.S. Army Corps of Engineers, who controlled the floodgates, either suffered from lack of water or was flooded at the wrong time of year.

According to Charlotte Orr Gantz in her book *A Naturalist in Florida,* a more or less normal amount of water was allowed to flow through the undrained, "unmanaged" section of the Everglades until 1962. At the end of that year the water was cut off, as the last of the retaining basins, or conservation areas, were completed. The conservation areas were huge, diked impoundments to the east and southeast of the lake where excess water could be held until needed. In 1965, during a severe drought, the Everglades National Park was given only 140 acre-feet of water in the month of April, whereas 280,000 acre-feet was released directly into the sea as "unneeded excess." As Gantz noted, there was an enormous loss of wildlife as a result of that shortsighted policy.

After 1965 the populations of large wading birds plummeted because of insufficient water in the Everglades and because the water was released at the wrong times. At least that explanation for the decline was the one most generally accepted. But according to Gary Hendrix, chief ranger-naturalist at Everglades National Park, with whom I discussed the question, loss of feeding habitat outside the park might have had almost as much of a negative effect upon wading bird populations as did curtailment of the water supply. Among habitat losses he listed were first, freshwater areas to the east of the park lost to urbanization, and second, feeding grounds on shoals in Lake Okeechobee destroyed by higher water after the dike around the lake was raised by a height of five feet.

To those factors, one other should perhaps be added. Hurricanes, though highly destructive to birdlife and other wildlife as well, may release nutrients that in the long run make them more helpful than otherwise to the wildlife that lie in their paths. Hurricanes, as Hendrix pointed out to me, churn up the soil and water, thereby releasing untold amounts of nutrients and bringing them into the food chain that ultimately supplies higher forms such as the large waders. South Florida has not had a big hurricane since Donna in 1960. That might be one of the reasons that the large wading birds are faring so poorly.

Not all of the large waders are in trouble. Hendrix was quick to point out that some of the park's more spectacular bird species are doing well. For example, roseate spoonbills and reddish egrets, nearly wiped out by the plume hunters, are now common residents of the keys and saltwater lagoons of the park. The great white heron, now regarded as only a form of the great blue heron, has also made a comeback. It, too, largely occupies saltwater portions of the park. Finally, the snail kite, another nearly vanished species, can be seen in some numbers in the park today and is nesting in the park for the first time.

According to Hendrix, the most productive part of the park for large waders is behind the mangroves on its far western side, a part of the park that the tourists do not see. However, reasonably good birding can be obtained at saltwater lagoons in the vicinity of the Flamingo Visitor Center, where State Route 27, which takes the visitor through the southeastern portion of the park, comes to an end. The egrets and ibis can be seen there in good numbers, as well as the great white heron, roseate spoonbill, brown pelican, and many other birds.

There are signs that a new day is dawning for the Everglades and its wildlife. The Corps of Engineers, in a reversal of policy, is now dechannelizing the Kissimmee River—letting the river revert to its former winding course to Lake Okeechobee instead of making it take the fifty-mile straight channel dug for it. It was by way of the Kissimmee River and small streams reaching Lake Okeechobee from the north that the Everglades once received much of its water. When the lake was high, it overflowed, and the water worked its way southward. A gradual drop in elevation from north to south, averaging less than three inches to a mile, aided the process. But highways and canals constructed over the years have diverted or impeded much of this flow.

In a move to overcome the problem in part, more culverts and bridges have been constructed on Alligator Alley, the highway that crosses the Everglades and the Big Cypress Swamp to the north of the Tamiami Trail. The new culverts enable the seasonal flow of water to move south more easily, as in former times. In addition, undercrossings are being built, so that Florida cougars and other wildlife can get to one side or the other of the highway without exposure to the dangers of traffic. These and other measures may do much to restore the Everglades to a more natural and pristine state. But they do not necessarily ensure a return of the large wading birds to anything approaching their former numbers.

Usually my first stop on a visit to south Florida is the Loxahatchee National Wildlife Refuge. Taking U.S. Highway 441 south from West Palm Beach, one reaches the refuge entrance on the right after driving about fifteen miles. For those primarily interested in birds, the 145,635-acre refuge should receive high priority. Among birds of special interest usually found there are the snail kite, fulvous whistling duck, and smooth-billed ani. However, I tend to spend most of my time looking at the plants.

By the time one reaches the latitude of Lake Okeechobee, the plant life is quite different from that farther north. I am obliged to put aside my northern botanical guides and rely upon Robert W. Long and Olga Lakela's *A Flora of Tropical Florida* and special guides to the tropical plants of the region. One of the best ways to become acquainted with plants growing in the cypress swamps of south Florida is to visit the Loxahatchee Refuge. A short distance inside the refuge is a cypress dome, only a few acres in extent, with a quarter-mile-long boardwalk leading to its interior. A visitors' center conveniently located nearby contains helpful exhibits, and there is always someone on duty who is glad to answer questions and help with identifications.

Although cypress domes are scattered over much of Florida, it is normally difficult to visit one of them. If the dome is in a cattle pasture—and most of them seem to be—the visitor must approach his objective cautiously, keeping an eye out for snakes and cattle, remaining alert in case the latter stampede in his direction. To get to the edge of the cypress dome, it is necessary to make ever so many detours around clumps of saw palmetto, with its sawlike petioles. Then one must push through dense stands of small cypress, their trunks no more than an inch or two in diameter. The trees get bigger and the water deeper as one nears the interior. Once, when visiting a cypress dome in northern Florida, I tripped and half fell into the water. As I fell, the binoculars I was carrying slipped out of their case and disappeared forever in the murky depths of this beautiful but seemingly treacherous cypress dome.

On my visits to the Loxahatchee Refuge there has usually been a foot or two of water below the boardwalk. Conditions, therefore, are much like those in the Okefenokee and other swamps to the north: There is standing water except during dry periods of the year. It is no wonder, then, that cypress (in this case pond cypress) is the dominant tree. That far south, one no longer finds water tupelo, swamp tupelo, or any close relatives of these trees. Free of competition from these other water-loving trees, cypress grows in pure stands throughout much of south Florida. But smaller trees can be found growing in the understory. At Loxahatchee I was surprised to find small guava trees blending in well with the other growth and apparently thriving in this wet habitat. Other exotics, including Brazilian pepper tree and the cajeput tree, grow at the edges of the dome. Although the list of "newer," more unfamiliar species is long, there are also some "old-timers" that the south Florida swamps share with cypress swamps to the north. They include such woody plants as red bay, buttonbush, red maple, wax myrtle, groundselbush, Virginia creeper, waterwillow (*Itea*), peppervine, muscadine grape, Virginia creeper, and dahoon holly. The willow is coastal plain willow; black willow, the common species in more northern swamps, does not grow this far south.

Having noted familiar shrubs, trees, and vines, the visitor can then peer over the edge of the boardwalk rail and pick out familiar aquatic plants growing among a profusion of ferns. Not until entering a cypress dome does one realize that it is also a fern garden. Ferns grow in every imaginable kind of site. But at Loxahatchee there are arrowheads, pickerelweed, lizard's-tail, and water arum competing for space in the overcrowded waters of the small wetland. Although the visitor from points north will recognize royal fern and a few others, most of the ferns are new to him. The leather fern, with fronds ten to twelve feet long, is one of the most spectacular of these ferns. Reminiscent of exhibits in florist's shops are the many Boston ferns growing everywhere in the dark shade of this typical cypress dome. An escape from cultivation, the Boston fern (*Nephrolepsis exaltata*) has become one of south Florida's ubiquitous ferns. Another species, strap fern, grows among the fronds of the cabbage palm. Strap fern is easily recognized. It grows in clumps on fallen logs and in pockets in trees and has long, swordlike fronds. A companion species, swamp fern, grows both in the cypress domes and in open wetlands throughout the Florida peninsula. Growing in the water and scarcely recognizable as ferns are tiny plants with floating leaves no more than half an inch in diameter. The plant is water fern (*Salvinia rotundifolia*).

I have been told at the Loxahatchee visitors' center that eleven species of ferns have been identified along the boardwalk and that still more need to be keyed out in order to determine their identity. As if this is not enough of a challenge, the cypress dome has five species of bromeliads, or air plants, including Spanish moss. The most common species is stiff-leaved wild pine (*Tillandsia fasciculata*), which grows abundantly on the trunks and branches of the cypress trees. In the fall it produces small blue flowers that are almost hidden in red bracts.

The most common shrub or small tree in the understory is pond apple (*Annona glabra*), which has many of the same growth characteristics as cypress. In the same family as pawpaw, pond apple grows in the cypress and mangrove swamps of south Florida and also in solid stands by itself. Formerly, there was a dense forest of pond apples at the southern end of Lake Okeechobee. Like cypress, pond apple also grows well in water and typically has a broad, buttressed base from which a short trunk rises. The crown consists of ungainly branches holding large leathery leaves. The fruit is greenish yellow and insipid, though favored by raccoons. Like those of cypress in south Florida, the trunks and branches of pond apple are often heavily decked with air plants and frequently with epiphytic orchids.

Another unfamiliar small tree of cypress domes is coco plum (*Chrysobalanus icaco*), which, if anything, is even more widespread in the region than pond apple. It has reddish brown bark, leathery evergreen leaves, and edible white to purple fruits ranging from one to two inches in diameter. At Shark Valley in Everglades National Park a trail leads into a hammock filled with coco plums.

Quite different is another small tree I saw from the board-walk at Loxahatchee. It has lustrous green leaves and, depending upon the season, small white flowers or blue-black berries arranged along the twigs. The tree reminds me of bayberry because of the way the fruits grow on twigs that, toward their tips, hold leaves. This small tree is myrsine, or guiana rapania (*Myrsine guianensis*), a hammock species that ranges quite far north in the Florida peninsula.

A few strangler figs (*Ficus aurea*) were present—a tree noted for the way it smothers and eventually kills other trees in its embrace. Gaining its start as a seedling in upper portions of a host tree, strangler fig sends down aerial roots that grow around the trunk of the host. Eventually the roots reach the ground. There are spectacular examples of strangler fig embracing the huge trunks of bald cypresses in Corkscrew Swamp and the Fakahatchee Strand. The big trees seem to withstand the embrace without ill effect.

Although the plant life takes first priority when I visit the cypress dome of the Loxahatchee Refuge, I also watch for birds and other wildlife. On most visits I am struck by the scarcity of birdlife. On one visit the only bird I saw was a yellow-bellied sapsucker. Gradually, on my boardwalk tours I have added a few others, including the green-backed heron, mourning dove, red-bellied woodpecker, Carolina wren, and cardinal. Others have told me of seeing the limpkin, barred owl, and pileated woodpecker. Even river otters and bobcats have been seen from the boardwalk. Not far from the cypress dome a round-tailed muskrat (Florida water rat) was seen crossing the road. That small mammal—listed as a species of special concern by the state of Florida—appears to have its centers of abundance in the Okefenokee Swamp and the Everglades.

I regard the Loxahatchee Refuge as an introduction to south Florida. After reestablishing contact there with the flora and fauna, I am usually ready to move on and seek out broader horizons. I know of no better way to begin than to continue south on U.S. Highway 441. After driving about thirty miles, I turn right onto U.S. Highway 75 at Fort Lauderdale. Better known as Alligator Alley, this heavily traveled highway crosses portions of the Everglades, as well as sections of the Big Cypress Swamp. Fortunately, there are frequent turnoffs where one can park to watch birds or get out to look for alligators in roadside ditches. Along the way, Seminole Indians will be seen engaged in their time-honored pursuits—fishing, paddling dugout canoes, weaving blankets, and practicing other traditional crafts.

Going this way in May of 1983, I was pleasantly surprised to see wading birds—solitary ones and others in large flocks—along the entire route. If I stopped my car after pulling off to the side, there would almost invariably be a rush of wings as a group of waders took flight. After moving off a short distance, they would begin feeding again. As I reached the Big Cypress Swamp, large stands of cypress appeared on each side of the highway. Their branches often held egrets and ibis and, making for a sharp contrast, dark-plumaged birds such as crows, cormorants, vultures, and anhingas. The most common of the dark birds were anhingas. They seemed as much a part of the trees as the air plants.

Thanks to having taken a dirt road into the Big Cypress Preserve, I saw rarer species. A pair of swallow-tailed kites appeared overhead, and a short-tailed hawk (dark phase) momentarily appeared above the tree line. A flock of about fifty wood storks, taking advantage of a thermal, circled slowly, high in the sky, and finally disappeared from view.

Nearly every pond and ditch had its quota of alligators. Some of them scarcely moved as I stood still observing them; others would quickly disappear under the water, leaving a trail of bubbles behind them as they swam away. Often a pair of common moorhens would be feeding, ever so complacently, near the alligators. I wondered what the relationship was between those birds and the alligators. I also wondered about the presence of pig frogs—close relatives of the bullfrog—in water frequented by alligators. It would take time to sort out the many predator-and-prey relationships that exist in these waters.

To the south, where the Tamiami Trail crosses south Florida, there are much the same wildlife and wildlife spectacles. The older highway borders Everglades National Park for about ten miles and then enters the Big Cypress National Preserve. When making that crossing, one should allow time for making frequent stops. The Shark Valley area in the park and the nearby Miccosukee Restaurant, on the trail, are good places to see the endangered snail kite. According to James A. Lane's *Birder's Guide to Florida,* airboats operated by the Indians along the trail keep down the marsh vegetation, and that aids the kites in finding apple snails (*Pomacea* spp.), which are virtually their only source of food. Lane states that snail kites are most active in the early morning and late afternoon. The Tamiami Trail is also a good place to see limpkins, which are also snail eaters. Limpkins are most likely to be seen at the same times and in the same places as the snail kites.

In comparison with states to the north, the Everglades and nearby parts of south Florida may seem like a paradise for large wading birds. That will seem particularly true if the visitor sees the large flocks that collect at roadside ditches to feed when water is low in the Everglades. So why all the fuss over the decline of wading birds?

Actually, there are still plenty of large wading birds in south Florida, but there are not the numbers that once existed. Only one species, the wood stork, has declined to an alarming degree. Others, though no longer as plentiful in south Florida as they were, still have populations elsewhere. For example, the glossy ibis, Louisiana heron (tricolored heron), and snowy egret are presently expanding their ranges northward along the Atlantic Coast. For someone who never witnessed the fabulous flocks of wading birds of south Florida around midcentury, the numbers today may seem more than adequate. It is all a matter of perspective. But I miss the big flocks I used to see around Lake Okeechobee and the busy throngs of feeding birds I used to see at the Anhinga Trail.

To see fish, the food the large wading birds are most dependent upon, one needs only to peer into the waters of a roadside ditch. I parked my car at the edge of Alligator Alley and got out to see what it was that was attracting so many egrets and other large waders. Darting about close to the surface were schools of mosquito fish. Those small fish are attracted to any disturbance in the water—a characteristic taken advantage of by the wading birds that feed upon them. Although I could not be sure of my identifications, two other very small fishes swimming about in the same water may have been Everglades pygmy sunfish and sheepshead minnows. Both are important items in the diets of fish-eating birds. Size is not important if the birds can catch enough of any one species to satisfy their appetites. The smallest of the small fishes here and in other waters of south Florida is, of course, the least killifish. Scarcely reaching an inch in length, they are also present in the Okefenokee Swamp and are sometimes extremely abundant in both fresh and brackish waters.

At another roadside ditch I observed large fish that appeared at the surface as soon as three or four alligators had swum away. They had wide, grinning mouths that stretched from one side of their heads to the other. I soon recognized them as bowfins, primitive fish that I had already met in other southern swamps. Well adapted to south Florida's changing water levels, they have the ability to stay alive by burrowing into the mud as ponds and ditches dry up. The Florida gar, another common fish, and also several of the sunfishes and catfishes are equally well attuned to dry and wet seasons. With the help of alligator holes and the ability to live in poorly oxygenated water, they survive when other fishes die.

The walking catfish, accidently introduced from Thailand in 1966, is abundant in many canals and ditches but is not found everywhere. A predator, it takes other fish and almost any freshwater organism within its capacity. At one of my stops, I observed several walking catfish herding small fish into shallow water where they would be easier to catch. Able to walk with the aid of its pectoral fins and adapted to air breathing, it has an advantage over native fishes during south Florida's dry seasons. When one body of water dries up, it simply moves to another. These strange catfish are often seen crossing roads and highways after a rain. So far, there seems to be no indication that the walking catfish is having a serious impact upon native species of fishes. In fact, smaller walking catfish are well liked by large wading birds, and whether they are having a positive or negative impact upon the ecology of south Florida remains to be seen.

The Anhinga Trail boardwalk is sometimes as good a place as any for fish watching. Both Florida gars and largemouth bass collect in places where there is motion in the water. The gars lie almost motionless near the surface; the largemouth, the delight of fishermen all over the South, is more restive and every ready to make a dash somewhere. Bluegill, common in these waters, are often seen fearlessly following alligators.

Much more visible, and as interesting to me as the fishes of the region, are the butterflies. Many are West Indian species that have established breeding populations or that appear as strays. On June 4, 1984, I was fortunate enough to see a mimic near the Shark River visitors' center in the park. Listed as a rare casual in south Florida, this strikingly marked butterfly is an Old World species that might have reached the West Indies on board slave ships. Many of the other butterflies I have seen in the Everglades and the Big Cypress Swamp are *specialties*—ones that belong there and seem out of place any great distance to the north. Butterflies in this category in south Florida include the queen, zebra, Gulf fritillary, white peacock, polydamas swallowtail, giant swallowtail, and cloudless sulphur. Also present is the palamedes swallowtail, the most characteristic butterfly of cypress swamps. The viceroy, present in good numbers, is such a dark chestnut color that I hardly recognized it. In this part of its range it mimics the queen instead of the monarch. The queen is a close relative of the monarch in the Deep South and has the same taste-repellent properties that make many monarch populations so distasteful to birds.

Beggar ticks (*Bidens* spp.) are the favorite plants of the butterflies in the region. Lowly members of the composite family and viewed as weeds, the beggar ticks have white blossoms the year round, which furnish butterflies with a sweet elixir. Buttonbush and pickerelweed are other common plants of the region often visited by butterflies. Firebush (*Hamelia patens*), a native shrub with tubular red blossoms, is also well patronized.

The hardwood hammocks are among the best places to find butterflies in south Florida. Barbara Lenczewski, author of *Butterflies of Everglades National Park,* lists ninety-nine butterfly species in the park. Many of the butterflies are found in hammock habitat. During the course of her research, she was struck by the ever-changing composition of the butterfly fauna of the region. Species formerly known as common had declined greatly in numbers; others previously unknown in the region were becoming established. In the foreword to her book, Dennis Leston invoked the same theme. Nowhere else in the world is there such a rapid turnover of species as in south Florida. He stated that this phenomenon cannot be explicable solely in terms of man and his works.

Lying at the western edge of the Big Cypress Swamp is the Fakahatchee Strand, a lesser-known wilderness area that contains all of the plant communities discussed so far in this chapter. Of special significance is the Fakahatchee's stand of virgin bald cypress and the sizable number of royal palms both within the cypress stand and within other parts of the wilderness. The virgin cypress can be viewed from a boardwalk immediately to the north of a Seminole Indian village at Big Cypress Bend on the Tamiami Trail. Look for the village and the foot path to the cypress stand on the north side of the highway about twenty-five miles to the southeast of Naples. Many of the huge bald cypress trees there, as at Corkscrew Swamp, are partly engulfed in the folds of strangler figs. Ferns and bromeliads are everywhere, and the bananalike leaves of fire flag (*Thalia geniculata*), rising from the wet ground, add still another dimension to this lush tropical setting.

A second point of entry to the Fakahatchee Strand is at the tiny community of Copeland, located on State Route 29, three miles north of this route's junction with the Tamiami Trail. After turning left at Copeland, look for an unpaved road leading in a northwesterly direction into the heart of the Fakahatchee Strand. This unpaved road is the W. J. Janes Scenic Drive. From the scenic drive one can view a good cross-section of the plant communities found within the twenty-five-mile-long and seven-mile-wide state preserve that includes most of the Fakahatchee Strand. Midway through the twenty-mile drive, towering royal palms appear on both sides of the road. Since that part of the Strand was logged for cypress prior to 1950, some of the palms growing there are much taller than the second-growth cypress. In places along old logging railroad embankments thousands of royal palm seedlings have taken root—a cheerful note for a native tree that has rarity status in Florida and that has disappeared from many of the sites where it was formerly found.

There is always the faint hope of seeing a Florida cougar when taking the scenic drive. Only thirty or so of the large cats still roam the wilds of south Florida. Although the Fakahatchee Strand is regarded as their stronghold, it takes long and patient observation to see one. A ranger at the preserve told me that he had only seen one in a full year of working there. The footprints of the cat are often found in soft earth, but seeing the animal is another matter.

The grand finale of the tour of south Florida is Corkscrew Swamp, which lies northwest of the Fakahatchee Strand at the very outer fringes of the Big Cypress Swamp. As early as 1912, the National Audubon Society employed a seasonal warden to protect the large colony of wood storks and great egrets that nested in big cypress trees in Corkscrew Swamp. In the 1950s this was the last large remaining stand of virgin bald cypress in the state. To save the stand, the birdlife, and the many rare plants, the Corkscrew Cypress Rookery Association was formed in 1954 and, in the same year, obtained title to much of the land contained in the present sanctuary. The National Audubon Society, which accepted the responsibility for managing the area, has built a boardwalk over a mile long into the swamp and has acted in many ways to ensure the sanctity of this unique area.

To reach the sanctuary by way of State Highway 29 from Copeland, continue north to Immokalee and then turn left to follow State Road 846, as it twists to the south and west, for sixteen miles, at which point there is an entrance sign to the sanctuary.

Entering this magnificent swamp after driving through mile after mile of citrus and cattle country to the north is like stepping into another world. But if the visitor has first explored the Loxahatchee Refuge, Everglades National Park, the Big Cypress National Preserve, and the state preserve at the Fakahatchee Strand, the transition will not be so overwhelming. He will already be familiar with many of the plants and animals at Corkscrew. Corkscrew Swamp is another large strand dominated by cypress trees. This strand differs from the one at Big Cypress Bend by having many more very large bald cypress trees and, in my experience at least, by being somewhat wetter.

At Corkscrew one sees a profusion of floating and emergent aquatic plants. Water lettuce (*Pistia stratiotes*) covers the entire surface of many ponds. Floating fern and other aquatic plants in evidence in the cypress dome at Loxahatchee are also present in Corkscrew Swamp. Ferns, bromeliads, and orchids are as numerous as in any of the other parts of south Florida discussed above. Before one starts out on the foot trail, which leads to the 5,800-foot boardwalk, it is advisable to look at the exhibits at the visitors' center and to obtain a brochure that provides directions for a self-guided tour of the boardwalk. The brochure is well illustrated and contains a wealth of information on what there is to see.

Comparing these bald cypress trees with large ones I have seen to the north, I was impressed, first, by the way the giants of Corkscrew rise straight up from the forest floor with almost no basal swelling. The lack of basal swelling, as well as the smallness of the knees, is an indication that water levels are typically low. At Corkscrew Swamp the knees are rarely more than two or three feet in height. Second, I was impressed by the way the trees—many of them dating back to the time of Columbus or earlier—have been able to withstand the devastating hurricanes that have struck the area again and again over the years. Although there are many broken branches and broken-off tops, the trees remain solidly upright, uncowed by the strong winds—a tribute to the cypress tree's root system.

I was also struck by the wide spacing between individual trees. At Corkscrew Swamp the cypress trees are far enough apart to allow sunlight to reach the ground below. As a consequence, there is a thriving understory containing such woody plants as Carolina ash, red maple, wax myrtle, pond apple, and dahoon holly. Fire flag, which was also present at Big Cypress Bend, is abundant in the understory. Its large, handsome leaves often contain small holes, which indicate insect damage.

The wood stork nesting colony at Corkscrew is a sight that attracts visitors from far and wide. The nests of these endangered birds are in colonies at or close to the tops of large bald cypresses. Easily visible from the boardwalk, the wood storks and their nests with eggs or young can usually be seen to good advantage during the winter and spring months. I have seen wood stork nesting activity at Corkscrew as early as November and as late as June. If the first nesting is unsuccessful, the birds will sometimes nest a second time.

Limpkins are common at the sanctuary. I once saw one walking along the top railing at the edge of the boardwalk as unconcernedly as if the railing were a floating log. At least two pairs of swallow-tailed kites nest in tops of cypress trees bordering the boardwalk. Barred owls are so tame that they perch on limbs over the boardwalk and stare down at visitors. February and March are regarded as the best months to visit the sanctuary to see birds. It is not unusual to see as many as sixty-five species from the boardwalk during either of those two months.

In my experience each tour of the boardwalk offers something new in a person's wildlife experiences, and this statement applies to mammals as well as birds. On one occasion a family of river otters, half swimming and half leaping, approached to within a few feet of the spot on the boardwalk where I was standing. They may have been hunting, playing, or doing both. Sanctuary personnel tell of seeing both the Florida cougar and the black bear at Corkscrew. Unseen by anyone, a black bear prowling through the swamp once

slightly damaged the boardwalk. Still another rarity, the mangrove fox squirrel (listed as endangered by the state of Florida), is present in small numbers at the sanctuary. I was lucky enough to see this handsome squirrel farther south in the Big Cypress Swamp. Chances of seeing the Everglades mink, listed as threatened, are remote both at Corkscrew and elsewhere in south Florida. Much the same is true of the Florida black bear, which also has a threatened status.

One can find many unusual plants and spectacular forms of wildlife on a single visit to south Florida. But it takes a number of visits spread over different seasons to become familiar with so much that is unique to the region or new to the traveler from farther north. Thanks to persons with vision and dedication, large portions of this part of Florida have been saved for future generations. Yet there is still much to do—lands to acquire, plants to control, species to save, and water to regulate better.

References

Douglas, Marjorie S. *The Everglades, River of Grass.* Miami, 1978.

Gantz, Charlotte Orr. *A Naturalist in Southern Florida.* Coral Gables, 1971.

Lane, James A. *A Birder's Guide to Florida.* Denver, 1981.

Lenczewski, Barbara. *Butterflies of Everglades National Park.* Homestead, Fla., 1980.

Loftus, William F., and James A. Kushlan. *Freshwater Fishes of Southern Florida.* Bulletin of the Florida State Museum of Biological Sciences, XXXI. Gainesville, Fla., 1987.

Long, Robert W., and Olga Lakela. *A Flora of Tropical Florida.* Coral Gables, 1971.

Loveless, Charles M. "A Study of the Vegetation in the Florida Everglades." *Ecology,* XL (Winter, 1959), 1–9.

Simpson, Charles Torrey. *In Lower Florida Wilds.* New York, 1920.

Small, John Kunkel. "An Everglade Cypress Swamp." *Journal of the New York Botanical Garden,* XXXIV (1933), 261–67.

Spackman, William, *et al.* "A Field Guidebook to Aid in the Comparative Study of the Okefenokee Swamp and the Everglades–Mangrove Swamp–Marsh Complex of Southern Florida." Unpublished paper, 1976. Copy in author's possession.

Tebeau, Charlton W. *Man in the Everglades.* Coral Gables, 1968.

In 1980 the Nature Conservancy, after a string of successes in procuring and safeguarding swampland in the South, initiated one of its most ambitious programs in saving natural habitat. The goal was to save the fast-disappearing swampland along major rivers flowing into the Gulf of Mexico. The Conservancy had already won a big victory, and had gained valuable experience, along the Pascagoula River in Mississippi. In 1976, after complex negotiations lasting about three years, the Conservancy announced that thirty-two thousand acres of matchless bottomland hardwood forests and wetlands along the Pascagoula had been acquired and transferred to the state's Wildlife Heritage Committee for management. Another three thousand acres was added in 1979, and still more after that.

The new initiative, called the Rivers of the Deep South Program, got off to a good start in 1980 with the help of a $15 million grant from the Richard K. Mellon Foundation. Major attention was to be focused upon seven large river systems—the Suwannee, Apalachicola, Choctawhatchee, and Escambia rivers in Florida, the Tensaw-Mobile Delta in Alabama, the Pascagoula River in Mississippi, and the Pearl River, lying between Mississippi and Louisiana.

Of these rivers, only the Suwannee is at all well known. Thanks to Stephen Foster, who never visited the river, the Suwannee is one Florida river that perhaps everyone has heard of. Comparatively few people, however, know of its beauty and natural treasures. If there was to be a song extolling a southern river, a better river than the Suwannee could not have been chosen. It is one of the most beautiful of our rivers and also one where cypress, against a background of sparkling white sand and swiftly flowing water, adds to the beauty. Although other rivers covered by the Conservancy's program have much to offer, the Suwannee is worth describing in greater detail. In contrast to most other scenic rivers, it can easily be visited by the public. The river and its tributaries can be viewed from state and county parks and from a national wildlife refuge at its mouth. Those who have the best view of all are the many canoeists who test its swift current.

Hard to classify and differing in many respects from rivers treated so far, the Suwannee has its origin in the Okefenokee Swamp of Georgia. Instead of taking a short cut to the Atlantic Ocean, the Suwannee flows for 265 miles across a portion of southern Georgia and diagonally across the top of Florida to reach the Gulf of Mexico. Along the way, it is fed by no less than seventy-one large springs and three major tributaries. The springs, which include a number of well-known ones, furnish much of the water that enters the Suwannee. Nine of the springs are large enough to be classified as first-magnitude springs. Some of the springs gush from fissures in limestone rock; others bubble up from the bottoms of rock-rimmed pools and flow out to the river by way of short runs. The water in these springs has a bluish cast and is so clear that fish and objects on the bottom are easily visible. Some of the pools are as much as fifty feet deep; others connect with underwater caves and grottoes. To the north of the town of Mayo, in the Peacock Springs area, explored portions of an underwater cave system extend for a distance of twenty-eight thousand feet, making it one of the longest of such cave systems in the United States.

William Bartram, visiting the Suwannee River in 1774, was enthralled by the sight of "the clearest and purest river he ever saw." At Manatee Springs on the lower Suwannee, he observed large numbers of fishes swimming about in clear water and wrote: "It is amazing and almost incredible, what troops and bands of fish, and other watery inhabitants are now in sight, all peaceable, and in what variety of gay colours and forms, continually ascending and descending, roving and figuring amongst one another, yet every tribe associating separately."

Today the springs and much of the river are still clear and, thanks to the almost complete lack of industrial pollution in the region, as clean as any of Florida's waters. But on leaving its headwaters in the Okefenokee Swamp, the Suwannee has the same dark, tea-colored water that is found in swamps everywhere. Downstream the acidic swamp water is neutralized by hard water from springs and limestone in the riverbed. After traveling less than a third of its course, the Suwannee, as a result, becomes a calcareous stream with relatively clear water.

Two of the river's larger tributaries flow south from Georgia to meet the Suwannee. The Alapaha and Withlacoochee rivers, whose drainages lie partially in agricultural regions of Georgia, take silt into the Suwannee's otherwise unmuddied water. The Alapaha, which flows through a region of karst topography in northern Florida, has a habit of disappearing and flowing underground. Much of the Alapaha's underground flow reaches the Suwannee by way of two first-magnitude springs. Gushing forth dark tannin-stained water, instead of clear crystalline water, like other springs, Holton and Alapaha Rise springs pour into the Suwannee below the town of White Springs. The Alapaha River, or what is left of it, joins the Suwannee just below the two springs.

The third large tributary, the Santa Fe River, also disappears underground, but well before reaching the Suwannee. The Santa Fe lies wholly within Florida and meets the Suwannee downstream from the other two tributaries. Thanks to its tributaries and many springs, the Suwannee is the second-largest river in Florida in terms of water flow. It is surpassed only by the Apalachicola, the next large river to the west targeted by the Nature Conservancy.

On leaving the Okefenokee Swamp, the Suwannee River is at an elevation of 107 feet above sea level, which accounts for the relatively swift current along portions of its length. Above White Springs, two stretches of the Suwannee have the only significant white-water rapids in Florida. The rapids, along with the springs and the river's wild beauty, is just another reason why the river is becoming ever more popular with canoeists.

Along its upper reaches, the Suwannee is lined by small cypress trees and equally small ogeechee tupelos. Both trees have swollen bases, which tell of marked fluctuations in water level. The swollen, fluted bases of the cypress look like ornamental vases designed to hold the top of the tree and its branches. Another indication of how high the water reaches during flood stages is that some of the cypress knees rise to heights of eight and nine feet.

Cypress takes on a different appearance in sinkholes near the Suwannee in Florida and neighboring Georgia. There are cypress domes similar to those of south Florida, with taller trees growing in deep peat deposits at the center and the trees becoming ever smaller toward the periphery. Pond cypress is the dominant tree in these depressions, and red maple, swamp tupelo, sweet bay, and wax myrtle are also likely to be present. Ferns are plentiful in the sinkholes and around spring openings, but they do not attain the overpowering luxuriance at this latitude that they do in south Florida.

The Suwannee is hemmed in by high banks along most of its length and therefore differs from most other southern rivers, which have wide floodplains. Yet cypress and tupelo do occur in sloughs and backwaters along almost the river's entire length. One of the largest stands of bald cypress is at the confluence of the Suwannee and Santa Fe rivers. There bald cypress, along with water tupelo, water elm, swamp privet, and Carolina ash, extends along both banks of the Santa Fe and along sloughs flowing into the Suwannee. Higher slopes in the same area are clothed with live oak, southern magnolia, pignut hickory, and spruce pine.

Not every elm tree along the Suwannee can be dismissed as merely another American elm. The only sizable populations of cedar elm (*Ulmus crassifolia*) east of the Mississippi are found along the Suwannee. Recently a few cedar elms have been found along the Crystal River in west-central Florida. Small leaves, twigs with corky wings, and fall flowering are aids in identifying this tree. Another rarity is corkwood (*Leitneria floridana*), a small tree with very light wood and a spotty distribution in swamp habitat in this part of Florida, neighboring Georgia, and a few places in the Mississippi Valley and eastern Texas. Two other trees worth noting are the American beech and the water tupelo, both of which are at their southern range limits in the East in the Suwannee drainage.

In terms of fauna, the Suwannee can claim a number of endemic species as well as others that are listed as endangered or threatened. Several endemic crustaceans are found in springs and sinkholes along the Suwannee. For example, in the Peacock Springs area near the town of Mayo are such rarities as the pallid cave crayfish, the Florida cave amphipod, and the Hobbs' cave amphipod—all of which are known to exist only as a result of their presence at a few sites in Florida.

The clear waters of springs and spring runs provide a home for two vertebrate species with limited ranges—the Suwannee bass and the Suwannee cooter. The first is a smaller species of black bass measuring not over one foot in length. It occurs in the lowermost 130 miles of the Suwannee drainage and also in the Ochlockonee River System to the west. It appears to be most abundant in the lower thirty miles of the Santa Fe River. There it is found in springs and spring runs as well as in the river itself. The second species, the Suwannee cooter, is found in a few western Florida rivers, including the Suwannee, and seems to seek out springs and spring runs. An excellent swimmer, this turtle is known to venture well out into the Gulf of Mexico. It is one of the few almost purely grazing turtles in the world. The state of Florida lists it as threatened.

The Atlantic sturgeon, listed by Florida as a species of special concern, is more plentiful in the Suwannee than in any other Florida or Gulf Coast river. The lower Suwannee supports one of the last commercial fisheries for this species in the South. Like the striped bass, the Atlantic sturgeon is an anadromous fish, migrating between fresh water and salt water. Counting saltwater fish that enter its lower reaches, the Suwannee can claim a total of eighty-nine species, which is more than twice the number of fishes found in the Okefenokee Swamp. In terms of total catch taken by sportsmen, the redbreast sunfish takes first place, followed by the catfishes. The not highly esteemed bowfin also looms large in the fisherman's catch.

Like the Okefenokee Swamp, the Suwannee has its rare mammals. They include the threatened Florida black bear and two endangered species—the Florida cougar and the

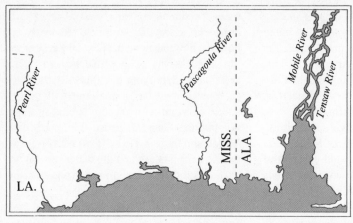

MISSISSIPPI AND ALABAMA GULF RIVERS

Pearl River

LA.

Pascagoula River

MISS. | ALA.

Mobile River

Tensaw River

WEST FLORIDA PANHANDLE RIVERS

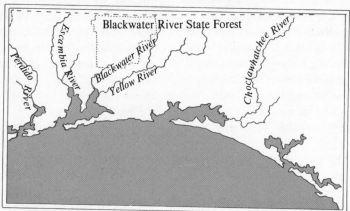

Blackwater River State Forest

Perdido River

Escambia River

Blackwater River

Yellow River

Choctawhatchee River

EAST FLORIDA PANHANDLE RIVERS

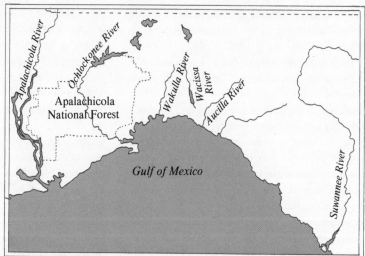

Apalachicola River

Ochlockonee River

Apalachicola National Forest

Wakulla River

Wacissa River

Aucilla River

Gulf of Mexico

Suwannee River

Sawback Turtle

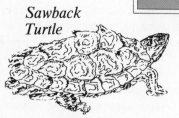

Rivers of the Florida Panhandle and the Alabama and Mississippi Gulf Coast

West Indian manatee. The latter appears in small numbers in summer in lower reaches of the river. At one time manatees were common at Manatee Springs, fifteen miles upstream from the river's mouth. But the "sea cows" are rarely seen in that large spring at the present time.

The Suwannee is famed for its birdlife. As noted in Chapter 7, the Suwannee's rich forests were one of the last retreats of the ivory-billed woodpecker and the Carolina parakeet. It was also one of the few places where the Bachman's warbler appeared in numbers during its brief resurgence in the 1880s. Today, thanks to the Suwannee's varied habitat and its position along the Atlantic Flyway, bird watchers can enjoy the same opportunities there as in south Florida. Coastal marshes and waterways at the Suwannee's mouth offer excellent opportunities to see brown pelicans, shorebirds, gulls, terns, bald eagles, and ospreys. About a dozen active osprey nests are present in or near the Lower Suwannee National Wildlife Refuge. This comparatively new refuge is also a good place to see Atlantic bottle-nosed dolphins and manatees.

Although the lower Suwannee manatee population is small—about 65 individuals—that is a significant number, considering that only about 750 to 850 manatees are left in the United States, all of them in Florida, though occasionally a few may wander northward along the Atlantic coast. Manatees use the lower Suwannee as feeding and nursery grounds during spring and summer. During the fall the Suwannee manatees perform a short migration southward to the warm-water springs of Kings Bay in the Crystal River—a coastal movement involving a swim of only about forty miles.

The stretch from the Suwannee's mouth to its confluence with the Santa Fe River is nesting habitat for Mississippi and swallow-tailed kites. Both are notably common in that part of the river's drainage. The rare short-tailed hawk nests in the extensive swamps and marshes at the river's mouth.

With seven active rookeries along its course, the Suwannee offers the bird watcher good opportunities to see most of Florida's large wading birds. The largest rookery—one patronized by white ibis, cattle egrets, little blue herons, and great blue herons, as well as anhingas—is on a cypress slough near the confluence of the Suwannee and the Santa Fe. Somewhere between five hundred and a thousand pairs of waders have been nesting there in recent years. The number of white ibis seen in flocks at the mouth of the Suwannee, however, has decreased from sixty thousand or more birds ten years ago to only about eight thousand at the present time. No reason has been given for the decrease.

The lower Suwannee represents the northern range limits of the Florida scrub jay on Florida's west coast. This colorful bird is listed as threatened by the state of Florida. The limpkin, a species of special concern, is a bird to look for at springs and spring runs along the Suwannee. In addition to rarities, the Suwannee offers a good cross section of birds from all major groups and families. One can do as well with small landbirds as with wading birds, waterfowl, and raptors.

Of the state parks, two, Ichetucknee Springs and O'Leno, are in the Santa Fe watershed, and two others, Manatee Springs and Suwannee River, are on the Suwannee. For the Suwannee's high bluffs, white sands, springs, and special plants, including the cedar elm, I would recommend the Suwannee River State Park. It is located thirteen miles west of Live Oak on U.S. Highway 90. The Nature Conservancy, in connection with its Rivers of the Deep South Program, has conducted an ecological study of the river basin and acquired acreage that has gone into public ownership and helped in establishing the 56,866-acre Lower Suwannee National Wildlife Refuge. The Conservancy is working hard to acquire other vital areas. Riverside vacation homes and clear-cutting lumbering operations seem to be the major threats to this largely unspoiled river.

Although not a part of the Suwannee drainage, a 64,631-acre tract called Big Bend Coast, to the north of the Lower Suwannee refuge, helps preserve marshes, cypress swamps, and rare species along this strip of the Gulf Coast. The tract was acquired by the Nature Conservancy in 1986.

Rivers to the west of the Suwannee are in the Panhandle—the part of Florida that stretches for over two hundred miles along the north shore of the Gulf of Mexico. The first three of these rivers are small by Suwannee standards but nevertheless are fully as scenic and have much the same geological history. The Aucilla, which flows into the Gulf to the southeast of Tallahassee, disappears underground along one stage of its course. In spite of the limestone karst topography through which it flows, the river is somewhat acidic. In a day spent hiking and boating on its lower reaches, I noted outcrops of limestone rock and an imposing forest consisting chiefly of live oaks and cabbage palms. Both large hollow bald cypresses and much smaller ones are present.

In 1987 the Nature Conservancy secured title to 14,149 acres along the Aucilla and its tributary, the Wacissa. Within this largely swampy area are springs, sinkholes, and aquatic caves. The caves are the only known home of the rare Horst's cave crayfish.

West of the Aucilla, two other rivers—the St. Marks and the Wakulla—like the preceding relatively short spring-fed rivers, join and flow for a short distance through the St. Marks National Wildlife Refuge. Like the Suwannee, the two are hard-water, calcareous streams. The Wakulla River issues from famous Wakulla Springs, a tourist mecca with glass-bottomed boats and guided tours. According to Edwin Way Teale, "The springs are a drowned circular chasm of greenish-white limestone dropping away for 185 feet straight down into the earth." The springs' stupendous outpouring consists of over six hundred thousand gallons per minute.

Alligators (including very big ones) on every log, fishes clearly visible in the transparent water, turtles, and abundant birdlife contribute to one's enjoyment of this unique area. In 1987, with the assistance of the Nature Conservancy, the springs, along with three thousand acres containing pristine swamp forest, aquatic caves, another rare crayfish, and such other rarities as the alligator snapping turtle, gopher tortoise, and Suwannee cooter, were turned over to the state of Florida as a state park.

The limpkin, near the western limits of its range on the Wakulla River, is so tame that it hardly notices persons with cameras and binoculars. On a short canoe trip in March on the river, fellow canoeists and I saw forty double-crested cormorants, numerous little blue herons and egrets, seven ospreys (several on nests), twenty wood ducks, fifty lesser scaup, and ten prothonotary warblers. These and other birds made this trip one of the best birding expeditions I have ever had in the Florida Panhandle.

The Ochlockonee, the next river to the west, is a larger stream with a sand bottom and somewhat acidic water. The Ochlockonee shares fifty-three species of fishes with the Suwannee, including the Suwannee bass. The fish fauna of the Ochlockonee, like that of other rivers in this part of Florida, can be divided into three groups—a limited number that live only in waters of springs, others that are adapted to acidic water and avoid springs, and, finally, a large number that enter water of both types. The lower Ochlockonee is a valuable breeding ground for many marine fishes.

Crossing the Ochlockonee heading west, the traveler leaves behind some of Florida's most beautiful spring-fed streams and encounters large rivers with winding courses and wide floodplains. These rivers are brownwater streams having their origins in the highlands of Georgia and Alabama. The first, the Apalachicola, with its high bluffs and muddy water, reminds me of lower tributaries of the Mississippi. Two branches, the Chattahoochee and Flint rivers, join at the Georgia line to form the Apalachicola. A large dam with an impoundment behind it has been built at this point.

To view the Apalachicola's forested floodplain and high bluffs merely from a highway crossing is to forgo great opportunities to observe its rich wildlife and rare plants. Reptiles and amphibians alone account for 108 species, making the Apalachicola system the richest area in North America in terms of species diversity for these two classes. The plant life is especially diversified and includes both endemic species and northern species that have entered Florida by way of the river. No less than 24 species of plants are known to occur in Florida only because they are present on the river's bluffs and, to a lesser extent, its floodplain. In addition, another 16 species of plants occur in Florida only in the Apalachicola floodplain.

Daniel B. Ward, in a publication on rare and endangered plants of Florida, has stated that the botanical wonders of the Apalachicola were discovered in the early 1830s by a botanist named Hardy Bryan Croom. A herb, croomia (*Croomia pauciflora*), in a family not otherwise found outside of Asia, was discovered by him in bluffs on the east side of the Apalachicola. An equally rare plant, Florida torreya (*Torreya taxifolia*), was another of his discoveries. Also known by the uncomplimentary name of stinking cedar, Florida torreya is an endemic Florida species whose nearest relative is in California. According to Ward, the flora of the Apalachicola bluffs is rather well known today and is "usually interpreted as a relic flora persisting from the Tertiary, a time when a widespread mesic vegetation extended from Asia across North America and southward into what is now northern Florida." He continued, "The Apalachicola bluffs, with their cool and moist lateral ravines, have functioned as a refugium for these ancient species."

Torreya State Park, on the east side of the river, contains many of the Apalachicola's rare plants. The 1,063-acre park can be reached by leaving Interstate 10 at Exit 24 west of Tallahassee and driving fifteen miles to the south, keeping a careful watch for signs pointing to the park. The park, with bluffs rising 150 feet above the river, ravines, and floodplain, contains the two species already mentioned, as well as such rarities as needle palm (*Rhapidophyllum hystrix*), Florida yew (*Taxus floridana*), and Ashe's magnolia (*Magnolia ashei*). Although the Florida torreya was nearly destroyed throughout its small range by a disease prevalent during the late 1950s and early 1960s, the plant, represented by stump sprouts, can still be found today. Its future remains precarious, however.

Below the bluffs and throughout much of the river's wide floodplain is bald cypress, a tree that almost certainly has an ancestry as old as that of any of the other plants. But it is still widespread because of its remarkable adaptability. Near the river's mouth, corkwood grows plentifully on muddy riverbanks and in sawgrass marshes. Almost like the Altamaha River's Lost Franklinia is a shrub called Chapman's rhododendron in the Apalachicola valley. Found at the edge of titi swamps in pinewood areas near the river, this small rhododendron is extremely limited in its distribution. It has been found only on the Apalachicola and in one other small area in Florida.

As for rare reptiles, forms of the eastern kingsnake known as the "Apalachicola populations" occur in the lower Apalachicola region. These snakes have distinctive color patterns. The Barbour's map turtle, a species in which the female is much larger than the male and has a disproportionately large head, is found only in the Apalachicola drainage system. Gary Williamson and I observed a number of them on logs in the Dead Lake section of the Chipola River. A tributary of the Apalachicola, the Chipola is a calcareous river originating in cave-limestone country in northern Florida. Like several other such rivers, the Chipola disappears underground at some points.

Like the Suwannee, the Ochlockonee, and other large

Gulf Coast rivers, the Apalachicola is an important spawning ground for marine and freshwater fishes. No fewer than 128 species, including marine forms from the lower river, have been recorded from the Apalachicola and its tributaries. Three fishes, including a freshwater bass and a shiner, are endemic to these waters. Along with the Suwannee and the Choctawhatchee, the Apalachicola is one of the few Florida rivers where the Atlantic sturgeon seems to be holding its own. The Apalachicola leads all other Florida rivers in number of species of freshwater fishes. The Escambia River, to the west, is the second-richest Florida river in freshwater species.

The Nature Conservancy has its own rare plant preserve on the eastern bluffs of the river not far from Torreya State Park. Known as the Apalachicola Bluffs and Ravines Preserve, the 4,430-acre tract is not presently open to the public. In addition, the Conservancy has been acquiring land in the river's floodplain. So far some 35,000 acres (now under the Northwest Florida Water Management District) has been set aside.

Fifty miles to the west of the Apalachicola is the next big river of the Florida Panhandle. Not many people have heard of the Choctawhatchee, and even to Florida naturalists and nature lovers the river is relatively unknown. Yet the Choctawhatchee is the third-largest river in Florida in terms of the amount of water it discharges, and of Florida Gulf Coast rivers, only the Apalachicola has a larger river-bottom swamp. These facts were enough to spur me to see something of the Choctawhatchee.

In early May of 1986, after poor weather conditions had prevented an earlier visit, Gary Williamson and I explored a small portion of the river's swamp near the highway crossing at Ebro, Florida. We were astonished to see some of the biggest cypress trees we had seen in Florida outside of Corkscrew Swamp. The knees, rising to heights of nine and ten feet, were as imposing as the trees from whose root systems they had sprung. The tall knees and debris lodged high up in trees told of the high water that invaded the bottomlands during times of flooding. The Choctawhatchee is known to be a river that floods easily. It receives much of its water in the form of runoff from agricultural lands in Alabama. As might be expected, the river carries a heavy load of silt, which is obvious in the way mud clings to the lower trunks and branches of trees. But at the time of our visit the river was low and the water so clear that we could easily see fishes, snails, and other forms of aquatic life. Gary, entranced by the many small fishes swimming about in a slough that had been partially dammed by beavers, described seeing a species that had a brilliant blue snout. The fish was about two inches long, had a dark lateral stripe on each side, and was very colorful. There is no question but that they were specimens of the bluenose shiner, a rare species found in a few Gulf Coast rivers and the St. Johns River in eastern Florida. This small fish is regarded as one of the most attractive and color-

ful of all our native freshwater fishes. Also clearly visible in shallow water were catfishes, largemouth bass, pickerels, spotted gar, and needlefishes. The river has 118 fish species, freshwater and marine, and therefore is not far behind the Apalachicola.

The Nature Conservancy has assisted the Northwest Florida Water Management District in obtaining acreage along the lower Choctawhatchee. So far, no less than thirty-eight thousand acres has been set aside as a nature preserve.

The Escambia, the last of the Florida Gulf Coast rivers receiving special attention in this chapter, flows into Pensacola Bay near the city of Pensacola. Its drainage basin lies in northwestern Florida and southern Alabama. In spite of the close proximity of the lower river to a large urban center, the Escambia is surprisingly wild. On a boat trip by way of the river's east channel to a point about ten miles upstream, the only signs I saw of man or his works were a few vacant cabins used by hunters or fishermen. But on my return trip by way of another channel, I did see a large industrial plant.

For many years the Escambia had a serious pollution problem from industrial wastes. The focal point of the problem was in Escambia Bay, at the river's mouth. Numerous fish kills occurred during the 1960s and early 1970s. One investigator reported a tremendous decline in fish populations between 1957 and 1967. However, thanks to pollution-abatement efforts, the Escambia is well on its way toward becoming a moderately clean river. The river and bay are now considered to be in an intermediate stage of recovery from past pollution. Signs of improvement include shrimp and blue crabs in the lower estuary and spawning by the Atlantic sturgeon for the first time in many years.

As the fishing has improved, more and more anglers can be seen in small boats on the Escambia. Their take includes such species as the redear sunfish (known as the stumpknocker), bluegill, warmouth, largemouth bass, chain pickerel, and striped bass. A number of fishes found in the Escambia, including the cypress darter and cypress minnow, are western species that barely cross the line into western Florida.

A few large "cull" bald cypresses were the only sizable trees in evidence that I could see along the lower Escambia. But a second-growth forest, containing cypress, water tupelo, water hickory, water locust, red maple, and sweet gum, is rapidly maturing and will someday look like the original forest of prelumbering days. If it were not for the presence of dwarf palmetto in the understory, I could easily have pictured myself in a river swamp in Virginia. The only exceptional plant I found along the river was buckthorn bumelia (*Bumelia lycioides*), a shrub with more northern affinities that barely crosses the line into Florida.

Spring comes early to the river swamps of northern Florida. In late March, the somewhat somber-looking swamp forest along the Escambia was decked with pink, yellow, and orange from early blooming azaleas, swamp yellow jessamine, and crossvine. The most striking blossoms of all were those of an orange azalea (*Rhododendron austrinum*), whose colorful flowers stood out even more than those of nearby bushes with pink blossoms. To witness this display, and also see a swallow-tailed kite appear from nowhere and swoop low over the water, were unforgettable experiences.

As was the case with the Apalachicola and the Choctawhatchee, the Nature Conservancy has assisted the Northwest Florida Water Management District in obtaining portions of the Escambia's floodplain. An eighteen-mile stretch of the river, embracing seventeen thousand acres, has been set aside as a preserve. This part of the Escambia was considered critical to the continued vitality of the fisheries of the lower river and bay.

In Alabama, only forty-five miles west of Pensacola Bay, there appears another large indentation in the coastline. It is Mobile Bay, a large expanse of water bounded on the northwest by the city of Mobile and immediately to the east by a delta formed by the Mobile and Tensaw rivers. It differs from Pensacola Bay in several ways. It has larger marshes around its rim and receives a much greater flow of fresh water. Since the Mobile and Tombigbee rivers join about twenty-five miles above the bay, flow together for a short distance, and then divide into the Mobile and Tensaw, the latter two might be said to constitute a single river. If one considers the Mobile-Tensaw a single river, there are only two other rivers in the United States that exceed it in the amount of water discharged. The two are the Columbia and Mississippi.

The Mobile and the Tensaw are responsible for building up a large delta at the head of Mobile Bay. To find one's way about in this watery maze by boat is difficult enough; by foot it is impossible. Seldom in my explorations of southern swamps have I encountered more unstable ground. With each step one sinks knee-deep in mud, if not deeper. Gary Williamson and I, boating on one of the swamp's waterways with two employees of the United States Fish and Wildlife Service, on several occasions tried to reach points of interest by foot. We had to give up after going only a few yards. Perhaps there has not been time enough for the silt brought down by the rivers to solidify and build firm ground.

The Mobile-Tensaw Delta is the largest Gulf Coast bottomland east of the Mississippi. Its 250,000 acres are roughly one-fourth marshland, one-fourth bay forest (made up largely of sweet bay and red bay), and one-half hardwood forest with large stands of bald cypress. Little known except to hunters and fishermen, this watery wilderness has been extensively logged but otherwise has remained much as it was during the days of William Bartram. Visiting the Mobile Bay area in July and August of 1778, Bartram traveled as far upstream as the Tombigbee River and along the way noted ruins of plantations once owned by the French. He told of

"canes and cypress trees of an astonishing magnitude" and of huge alligators basking on the shores. He attributed the size of the trees to excellent soil conditions.

Although a wilderness half as large as the Okefenokee Swamp, the Mobile Delta region has escaped the publicity and cries of protest that have accompanied the development of so many other swamp areas. Perhaps that is because it has not been subjected to drainage schemes and attempts at agriculture. But today portions of the hardwood forests are being completely leveled by pulpwood operators who see a chance of harvesting the stump sprouts as sources of raw material. So far these operations have made only a dent upon the landscape. But almost certainly the time will come when a campaign will need to be waged to save this swamp.

In October, 1985, Gary Williamson and I made our first foray into the upper delta. We walked across a railroad trestle over the Tensaw River and then followed the rail line as far as the Mobile River. Not a recommended way of seeing the swamp, the tour nevertheless allowed us to observe a good cross section of the swamp and its watercourses. Although we saw no very large trees, the swamp, with its hardwoods and cypress, seemed to be recuperating well from past lumbering operations. We saw a mink, a fair sampling of large wading birds, seven or eight pileated woodpeckers, and ever so many catbirds and warblers.

Our next trip—this one by boat the following May with C. Dwight Cooley and Daniel J. Dunn of the Fish and Wildlife Service as our guides—took us much deeper into the wooded bottomlands and endless waterways that make up such a large part of the delta region. We confirmed what we had suspected earlier, namely that one part of the delta woodland looks very much like every other part. There is not the contrasting habitat and varied scenery that is found, for example, in the south Florida swamps or the Okefenokee. There is beauty in seeing wide stretches of bottomland forest broken only by the winding river channel and small patches of sawgrass marsh along the edges. But some people, I daresay, would find this kind of terrain too much alike everywhere, if not oppressive.

Part of our mission that day was to get some idea of the numbers and whereabouts of the several species of rare or endemic turtles that inhabit the delta. Although we searched for the Alabama red-bellied turtle in its known haunts, we failed to sight a single specimen. This species is restricted to the delta region and has only one nesting area known to receive annual usage. The primary nesting area is a sand bank consisting of spoil dredged from the river. It is located on a partially wooded island in the Tensaw River. The turtles also lay their egg clutches in alligator nests. The decaying vegetation in the nests provides enough heat to incubate both the alligator and turtle eggs. The Alabama red-bellied turtle is presently a candidate for federal listing as threatened. We did better with two other rarities—the black-knobbed sawback, found only in the delta and rivers emptying into it, and the wider-ranging Alabama map turtle. We saw several sawbacks during the day and numerous map turtles.

The birds proved to be more accommodating than the turtles. Unaccustomed to gulls and terns following rivers into bottomland swamps, Gary and I looked up every time a gull-like bird flew over. We lost count of the laughing gulls, the most numerous species, but noted anywhere from one or two to five or six herring gulls, royal terns, least terns, and Caspian terns. Of the many landbirds, the American redstart was the one that most caught our attention. Absent as a breeding bird in most of the Atlantic coastal plain, the redstart appears as a summer resident in extreme northwestern Florida, and in the delta, as we discovered, it is a common nesting species.

We learned from our Fish and Wildlife Service hosts that of an estimated thirty-five thousand alligators in Alabama, most were residents of delta swamps and marshes. The alligator snapping turtle, we were told, is an inhabitant of delta rivers, oxbows, and sloughs, and sometimes reaches a weight of two hundred pounds and over. We learned that the primitive paddlefish is also found in delta waterways. Of far more interest to sportsmen are the many game fish found in delta waters. They include the bluegill, redear sunfish, spotted sunfish, warmouth, green sunfish, largemouth bass, black crappie, white crappie, chain pickerel, channel catfish, blue catfish, and mullet. We were told that no fewer than 114 freshwater and marine fishes are found in the delta area—a number comparable with that in nearby Florida rivers.

Our hosts, both of them eager bird watchers, told us that an up-to-date census of wading-bird rookeries in the delta area was badly needed. Most nesting areas were in and around marshy areas of Mobile Bay, and only a few—perhaps only three—were in the wooded bottomlands. The little blue heron was said to be the most common nesting species. We learned that the mallard, the pintail and the blue-winged and green-winged teal were common waterfowl species in winter and that the wood duck is a common year-round resident. Very few geese winter in the area, but the American coot is abundant in winter. Being particularly interested in the status of the two kites found in southern Alabama, we were surprised to hear that as many as a hundred Mississippi kites can sometimes be seen on a single day in late April in the delta area and that swallow-tailed kites are also common. Few figures, however, seem to be available regarding nesting populations of the two species.

Our hosts supplied us with equally interesting information about the mammals. We learned that a major effort is under way to preserve the Florida black bear. Present in small numbers, the bear was once a common resident of the bottomland forests. Although the Florida cougar is reported from time to time, we were told, no one should place much confidence in the reports. As in so many southern swamps, the common bat is the evening bat. Muskrats, we learned, are

common, and for those who may wish to look for them, both the cotton mouse and golden mouse occur in the river swamps. Among the other mammals of the swamp are beavers, minks, bobcats, and river otter.

The Nature Conservancy, through its Rivers of the Deep South Program, has made a good start toward saving delta marshes and bottomland swamps. The Conservancy presently holds title to seventeen thousand acres and hopes eventually to procure a much larger portion of this threatened wilderness that somehow has survived for so many years within the shadow of a big city.

The Pascagoula River, the next river westward in the Conservancy's program, is more like the Escambia than the Tensaw-Mobile. It is a medium-sized river lying almost wholly in Mississippi. As the river flows toward the coast, it begins to meander, thereby over the years leaving behind numerous oxbow lakes, as well as high ground in the form of ancient levees. If one tries to chart a course in any direction in the Pascagoula bottomlands, he finds himself forced to make a detour around one oxbow lake after another.

There is a plant community for every level of elevation. Bald cypress and water tupelo are the common trees at edges of lakes; on slightly higher ground one finds oaks and sweet gum. Possum haw holly, ironwood, swamp dogwood, and titi are common in the understory. The plants found along the Pascagoula are little different from those of more northern river swamps. An exception is spruce pine, common here but not found north of South Carolina.

The Pascagoula was one of the few river bottomland forests in Mississippi that were not drained during the 1950s and 1960s or earlier. The procedure was almost always the same: channelize the streams, cut the trees, remove the stumps, and plant soybeans. An alternative, usually reserved for higher ground, was to plant row after row of young pine trees that in as short a period of time as twenty years would be harvested for pulpwood. The pine plantations, seen all over the South, are grazed by white-tailed deer when the trees are young, but otherwise are nearly devoid of wildlife. By 1973 whatever was left of wild beauty and former wildlife abundance in Mississippi was in the Pascagoula bottomlands and a few other river swamps. But that year a crucial turning point was reached. Some forty-four thousand acres along the Pascagoula was up for sale, and unless there was almost a miracle, these lands would meet the same fate that had overtaken so many other pristine river bottoms. Would most of Mississippi become pinelands and cropland, or would some of the state remain as wild land—a place for hard-pressed forms of wildlife and a retreat for man himself, so badly in need of peace and outdoor recreation?

The fight to save the Pascagoula has been vividly told by Donald G. Schueler in his book *Preserving the Pascagoula*. In a story filled with suspense, Schueler tells how the Nature Conservancy, represented by David Morine, together with a few other dedicated persons, fought a determined battle for three years and finally won.

The victory in Mississippi provided all the impetus that was needed to initiate new programs to save vital swamp and river-bottom habitat. The instrument that the Nature Conservancy uses to attain its ends is the state natural heritage program. As described in the *Nature Conservancy News* of November–December, 1985, state natural heritage programs are innovative biological inventory and data-management efforts that have been developed through a unique partnership between the states and the Nature Conservancy. In most cases the Conservancy is contracted by state governments to create, to train, and initially to supervise a staff of biologists and others who will eventually serve as a unit of state government. The heritage programs undertake such chores as making inventories of plant and animal species within the state, seeing which ones need protection, and helping to identify tracts that need to be protected. The Conservancy, with national offices in Arlington, Virginia, provides technical assistance and financial support. Lands that are set aside are either handed over to federal, state, or private agencies (with strings attached) or are managed solely by the Nature Conservancy. Only rarely are heritage programs involved with managing land. From a single program in South Carolina, initiated in 1974, natural heritage programs by 1985 had expanded to the extent that they were functioning in thirty-eight states and Puerto Rico and in the holdings of the Tennessee Valley Authority and the Navajo Nation.

The thirty-seven-thousand-acre preserve on the Pascagoula River established by the Nature Conservancy with the help of a Mississippi natural heritage program is presently a wildlife management area under the Mississippi Department of Wildlife and Conservation. But the preserve is owned by the Nature Conservancy and could be placed under other management if the preservation goals of the Conservancy were not being met.

The wildlife found in the Pascagoula preserve is much like that along the Mobile and Tensaw rivers except for its endemic turtles. The Pascagoula has its own endemic species—the yellow-blotched sawback. On a visit to the Pascagoula in late October, 1985, Gary Williamson and I counted twenty of these sawbacks on a single oxbow lake. With that many present on one small body of water, the swamp, with its hundreds of sloughs and oxbow lakes, must hold a sizable population of yellow-blotched sawbacks.

The next river to the west under the Conservancy's program to save Gulf Coast rivers is the Pearl River. The east branch of the Pearl River forms the boundary between Mississippi and Louisiana. Swamps along the Pearl River constitute a wilderness area that has largely escaped the evils of drainage, channelization, and conversion to agriculture. As in the case of the Pascagoula, the Nature Conservancy and its friends arrived in the nick of time.

Long before I had visited Gulf Coast swamps, I had heard of Honey Island in Louisiana on the lower Pearl River. Several persons had spoken of it with awe. An ill-defined tract of bottomland timber lying between the East Pearl and West Pearl rivers, Honey Island is between three and seven miles wide and from fifteen to twenty miles long. It is (or once was) the home of the ivory-billed woodpecker, red wolf, black bear, and Florida cougar. Small numbers of black bear are still present, and as in so many other swamps, there are recent unconfirmed reports of the cougar. The name Honey Island comes from the swarms of honey bees seen there during earlier days.

Honey Island has achieved fame of sorts because of the real or imagined presence of a creature that fits the description of the Big Foot of movie renown. Known as the Thing, the creature is sometimes seen by fishermen. Paul R. Wagner, a biologist who lives at the edge of the swamp and conducts guided tours, provided me with details of a recent sighting. A fisherman told him that he had encountered a creature six and a half feet tall, weighing somewhere between three hundred and four hundred pounds, and having long hair, large teeth, and white eyes. The odor of the unknown creature permeated the air. When the creature saw the fisherman, it let out a loud shriek and disappeared into the underbrush. Since then, whenever Wagner visits the remote part of the swamp where the sighting was made, he has an uncomfortable feeling verging upon fear.

In many cases, sightings such as this one are inspired by traditions that go back as far as Indian days. If a region is wild and inaccessible and has a history of encounters with strange forms of life, chances are that similar encounters will occur again—or at least be reported. For my part, let me say that in my many years of visiting swamps, many of them as wild or wilder than Honey Island, I have never obtained a glimpse of anything vaguely resembling Big Foot, nor have I ever seen suspicious-looking footprints. I have, however, heard sounds that I could not identify. On one occasion, returning from visiting an Indian mound deep within a swamp in South Carolina, I had barely reached the edge of the woods when I heard a piercing, unearthly scream that lasted several seconds. My dog pricked up its ears, and I felt a chill down my spine. No one was in sight, and the nearest house was over a mile away.

But Honey Island, in my experience, does not live up to its reputation as a scary place. Launching our canoe at the Wagners' cottage, Gary and I have paddled for miles through a labyrinth of waterways. We have seen nothing more disturbing than the shadows of something large stirring in the water near our canoe. Whether it was a very large alligator garfish, an Atlantic sturgeon, a paddlefish, or an alligator snapping turtle we had no way of knowing. Alligator gars up to ten feet in length and paddlefish up to seven feet have been seen. We have yet to see an alligator snapping turtle. Ugly and secretive, they spend almost their entire life on the bottom. But alligator snappers are known to occur in most Gulf Coast rivers, and shells we saw exhibited at homes of local residents provided evidence of their presence in the Pearl River.

The fishes in the Pearl River system are largely Mississippi valley species, which is to be expected, since the mouth of the Pearl lies only twenty-five miles in a straight line from the lower Mississippi. Therefore, such fishes as the alligator gar, the flathead catfish, the freshwater drum, and suckers (known as buffalo fish) make their appearance. But the local catch seems to consist largely of such familiar species as bluegill, warmouth, redear sunfish, largemouth bass, and crappies. It would have been exciting to have tried one's luck in those waters. But our quest was for plants and animals that would help us set the Pearl apart from other Gulf Coast rivers.

We had already noted sourwood (*Oxydendrum arboreum*), a tree more often associated with mountain terrain than swamps, growing only a few feet above the swamp. It was surprising to find it there, at the southwestern edge of its range, within sight of bald cypresses and swamp tupelos. We had not seen the greenfly orchid since leaving the Choctawatchee River in Florida. Yet this small epiphytic species, a disjunct far outside its normal range in eastern Louisiana, was not uncommon on trunks of water tupelo. If we had gone farther upstream, we would have seen spruce pine—a species that seems to be most common along river banks in Georgia and northern Florida. Eastern Louisiana is the western edge of its range. The same is true of Florida anise (*Illicium floridanum*), an evergreen shrub of swamps and riverbanks that ranges eastward from the Pearl into northern Florida. Therefore, the Pearl River, from the standpoint of plants and animals, is an outpost for eastern species and, at the same time, well within the range of midwestern ones.

The birdlife of the Pearl River is as exciting as that of any of the Gulf Coast rivers. Not only are ospreys and the two kites common nesting species, but an active bald eagle nest, which we viewed after canoeing downstream from the Wagners' place, has a history of occupancy dating back to about 1910.

On a return trip to the Pearl River in October, 1985, Gary and I noticed large numbers of birds streaming into a swamp tupelo laden with fruits. Feasting upon the fruits were one or more of the following species: northern flicker, hairy woodpecker, red-bellied woodpecker, hermit thrush, wood thrush, mockingbird, rose-breasted grosbeak, and scarlet tanager. It was a treat to be watching that many landbirds in the same habitat in which we had been observing waterfowl and large wading birds. In Chapter 6 I told of another visit to the Pearl River on which Gary and I were surprised at the great number of small landbirds we saw. A ratio of four species of landbirds to one of other, larger species is about what one expects in a southern swamp.

The Pearl River is a Louisiana scenic river. From the marshes at its mouth to a point about forty-five miles upstream, the Pearl contains a wilderness of about 185,000 acres. Much of that wilderness is either part of a state wildlife management area or within the limits of the Bogue Chitto National Wildlife Refuge. With about 60,000 acres under protection at the present time and prospects of additional acreage to come, the swamplands along the Pearl River, including Honey Island Swamp, seem reasonably secure from destruction.

By taking advantage of the Wagners' wildlife tours, some of the richest wildlife stretches of the river, as well as portions of Honey Island, can be viewed from the comfort of a tour boat. Arrangements should be made with Paul R. Wagner of Slidell, Louisiana.

References

Schueler, Donald G. *Preserving the Pascagoula*. Jackson, Miss., 1980.

Teale, Edwin Way. *North with the Spring*. New York, 1963.

Ward, Daniel B., ed. *Plants*. Gainesville, Fla., 1980. Vol. V of Peter C. Pritchard, ed., *Rare and Endangered Biota of Florida*. 6 vols. to date.

The name of John James Audubon is closely associated with the bald cypress as the tree nears its northern limits along the Ohio River. At Henderson, Kentucky, where the famous bird painter lived between 1810 and 1819 and where his business enterprises eventually ended in bankruptcy, bald cypress still occurs in old oxbows along the Ohio. In 1985 I observed scraggly specimens below the state park established at Henderson in Audubon's honor. The museum at the park houses a large collection of Audubon memorabilia. One can picture Audubon, leaving his business in the hands of his partner and strolling off for the whole day to roam the banks of the Ohio. He would have certainly found many wood ducks. In their volume on Audubon, Mary Durant and Michael Harwood state that ponds with cypress trees near Henderson are gathering points for hundreds of wood ducks in the fall as they prepare for their flight southward.

Another site associated with Audubon and cypress trees is downstream on the Kentucky side of the river not far from where the Ohio joins the Mississippi. This is Swan Lake, a seven-hundred-acre body of water surrounded by venerable cypress trees. Audubon and his wife Lucy had hardly settled in Henderson before he was off with his partner, Ferdinand Rozier, to see if business opportunities might be better in Missouri. Finding new birds to paint may have been the real reason that spurred Audubon to set out on this expedition just as winter was closing in. With a cargo of whiskey and other goods, Audubon and his party floated by barge to a point where the Ohio is joined by a small river of southern Illinois, the Cache. They stopped for a few days on the banks of the Cache because of ice floes that blocked the lower reaches of the Ohio.

Early one morning during this interlude, Audubon joined a band of Shawnee Indians who were crossing the river to hunt swans on what is now called Swan Lake. They were not the well-known tundra (whistling) swans, but rather the larger trumpeter swans now restricted to the Far West and once on the verge of extinction. In Audubon's day trumpeter swans wintered in good numbers in the Mississippi Valley.

The Indians found hundreds of swans on the lake and immediately set about killing them. Over fifty were taken. Even at this early date, the feathers of the trumpeter swan were shipped to Europe to adorn ladies' dressing apparel. When Swan Lake was visited by Durant and Harwood on their tour of places in North America associated with Audubon, the lake and surrounding land was a private hunting preserve. Swans had last been seen on the lake in the 1880s, but chances are that they were tundra and not trumpeter swans.

In 1985, with help from the Nature Conservancy, the Kentucky Department of Fish and Wildlife Resources received title to a tract of 2,500 acres along the Ohio that included Swan Lake and ten smaller lakes. According to some accounts, the lakes were among those that were formed by the great New Madrid earthquakes of 1811–1812. But since Audubon visited Swan Lake in December, 1810, this explanation seems unlikely. A far more plausible one is that the lakes lie in a former channel of the Ohio River. When the river changed course, the lakes were left behind. Like hundreds of other oxbow lakes along the Ohio, they were the product of a shift in the river's course.

Metropolis Lake, about twenty-five miles upstream from Swan Lake, is another of Kentucky's cypress-lined oxbow lakes that has been preserved with the help of the Nature Conservancy. The oxbows are known not only for good fishing but also for their reptiles, amphibians, and water birds. Besides ducks and geese, the lakes in winter are visited by bald eagles.

Bald cypress in Indiana, across the Ohio River from Kentucky, has fared poorly since the time of Audubon. Formerly extensive stands existed in the southwestern part of the state, a section bordered on the south by the Ohio River and on the west by the Wabash River. A stand of cypresses in Knox County, higher up the Wabash, competes with one in Sussex County, Delaware, for the distinction of being the farthest-north naturally growing cypress in existence. This means cypress within the tree's natural range and not the occasional tree or stand that owes its presence to birds or man. In terms of naturally growing northernmost cypress, Delaware seems to have a slight edge over Indiana.

To find naturally growing cypress at all in Indiana at the present time is difficult. However, in company with Mike Homoya of the Nature Conservancy, I viewed several cypress sloughs and ponds in Posey County in the extreme southwestern portion of the state. Two of the sites were so degraded by the works of man—flooding from an impoundment in one case and oil wells in another—that most of the trees were dead or dying. But Twin Swamp, a 480-acre tract acquired by the Conservancy in 1986, contains some of the best remaining cypress in the state. The swamp contains a wet portion where swamp cottonwood and some of the last remaining overcup oaks in the state grow; a second wet portion has the cypress. The two different wet portions are the reason for the name Twin Swamp.

Another large stand of bald cypress in Posey County extends for three miles along a body of water called Goose Pond. More like a cypress swamp of the Deep South than Twin Swamp, Goose Pond has the look of a Louisiana bayou. Many of the birds and plants that one would see in Louisiana, however, are missing. But prothonotary and yellow-throated warblers are abundant during the nesting season, and providing a contrast, a more northern bird, the brown creeper, is also present. Goose Pond is largely in the hands of private owners, but thanks to agreements with the Nature Conservancy, the area is reasonably well protected.

To return to Audubon and his trip down the Ohio, we will recall that he camped at the mouth of the Cache River. Calling the river Cash Creek, he noted that it was a small stream and that the alluvial soil at its mouth was extremely rich. He saw black walnut, ash, pecan, "closely tangled cane," and "nettles that are in summer at least six feet high." By nettles he probably meant cockleburs, the fruits of which were eaten by Carolina parakeets. He spoke of seeing "thousands of parroquets" that came each evening to roost in hollow trunks of sycamore trees at the mouth of the Cache River.

Today the area where he camped is so changed that he would not recognize it. The river has been diverted so that most of its flow empties into the Mississippi above the town of Cairo. Yet in spite of drainage and stream channelization, there are sections of the Cache River that are almost as wild and unchanged as when Audubon visited the area. A portion of the river known as the Lower Cache has some of the oldest and largest cypress trees in the Mississippi Valley. This tract, which lies along the river just west of the small town of Karnak, also has many of the same species that flourish in swamps farther south. Examples among fishes are the cypress darter, cypress minnow, and banded pygmy sunfish; among amphibians, the mole salamander, green tree frog, and western bird-voiced tree frog; among snakes, the western cottonmouth and western mud snake. That so many southern reptiles and amphibians are at or almost at their northern range limits along the Cache reminded me of the situation in southeastern Virginia.

In October, 1984, Gary Williamson and I were shown the Lower Cache tract under the able guidance of Max Hutchison, an ardent conservationist who lives in the area and knows its natural history as well as anyone else does. We were fortunate to make our visit at a dry time of the year; otherwise a large portion of the swamp would have been underwater. Dry conditions and open, parklike terrain under the big trees allowed us to wander wherever we liked. Thanks to our guide, we saw a national champion water locust and several of the twelve state champion trees that grow in the swamp. Among them were a water tupelo, a water elm, and a pumpkin ash. Gary and I felt as though we were back in the Congaree Swamp.

As is so often true, many of the old cypresses and water tupelos were hollow inside and could be entered by openings at ground level. Once inside a hollow tree, a person can often look upward and see the sky above. Max informed us of the uses that the wildlife make of these hollows. Sometimes hundreds of bats could be found taking shelter within the cavernous hollows of giant cypress trees. He said that both barn owls and chimney swifts nest in hollow cypresses. As sometimes happened in drought years, the inside of hollow trees would catch on fire as a result of lightning strike. The hollow would then become a caldron, with flames shooting hundreds of feet up into the air. In the old days, according to Max, lumbermen used to stable their horses in hollow cypresses or water tupelos. A large cavity might hold two or three horses.

Although marred to some extent by cutting, fire, and vandalism, the Lower Cache has many of the same aspects as a virgin forest—lack of undergrowth, for example, and a cathedral-like atmosphere with tall trunks of trees and sunlight filtering down through the lacy foliage high above. Only too often, however, we came to stumps of sawed-off cypress knees. Inevitably, there are people who think nothing of cutting cypress knees and hauling them off for whatever selfish use they have in mind. Such acts mar the beauty of the trees and may impair the ability of the tree to "breathe" through its root system. Large knees that had been spared gave us an indication of how high the average water level was during the flood season. One of the taller knees was seven feet nine inches in height and had a circumference at its base of nine feet.

In the face of discouragement and setbacks, local citizens, including Max Hutchison, have been waging a fight to save the Lower Cache. So far, about one-third of the swamp forest has been acquired for preservation through a cooperative effort by the state of Illinois and the Nature Conservancy. It is hoped that the remainder of the swamp can be saved and that the entire tract will become a national wildlife refuge.

In a lengthy report on the Cache River that Max submitted to the Nature Conservancy in 1984, he told of both the natural and human history of this nearly northernmost outpost of the bald cypress. Parts of the report read like early accounts of the Great Dismal Swamp. For example, Max wrote that early hunters were attracted by the abundance of game along

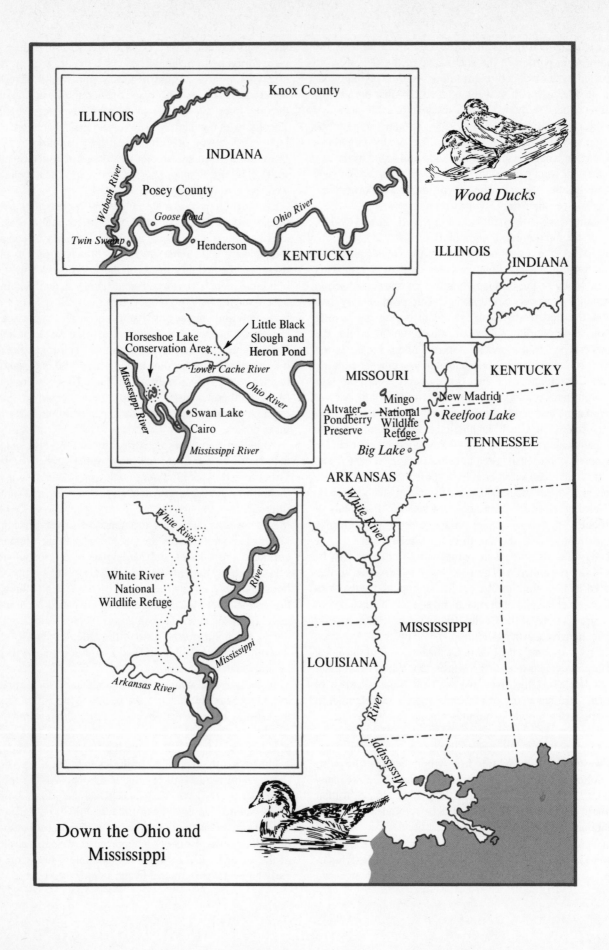

Knox County

ILLINOIS

INDIANA

Posey County

Wabash River

Goose Pond

Twin Swamp

Ohio River

Henderson

KENTUCKY

Wood Ducks

ILLINOIS

INDIANA

Horseshoe Lake
Conservation Area

Little Black
Slough and
Heron Pond

Lower Cache River

Mississippi River

Ohio River

Swan Lake
Cairo

Mississippi River

MISSOURI

Altvater
Pondberry
Preserve

Mingo
National
Wildlife
Refuge

New Madrid

KENTUCKY

Reelfoot Lake

Big Lake

TENNESSEE

ARKANSAS

White River

White River

White River
National
Wildlife Refuge

River

Mississippi

Arkansas River

MISSISSIPPI

LOUISIANA

Mississippi River

Mississippi River

Down the Ohio and
Mississippi

Fishing in Horseshoe Lake in southern Illinois

*A typical cabin on a
river backwater*

*A waterfowl impoundment at Mingo
National Wildlife Refuge provides
good fishing.*

Huge sycamore trees along the Ohio
are perches for ospreys.

Cypress trees dating back to the New Madrid earthquake line Reelfoot Lake.

Beavers are plentiful at Reelfoot Lake.

The green tree frog is closely associated with cypress swamps from southern Illinois southward.

Cypress trees at sunrise on Reelfoot Lake

Waterweed, in this case duckweed, is a problem at Reelfoot Lake, where it sometimes leads to depletion of oxygen in the water.

The swamp rabbit, the common rabbit of Mississippi Valley swamps

A flock of cattle egrets over the Atchafalaya Swamp

White-eyed vireo, a common nesting species in the Atchafalaya Swamp

A great egret fishing

*The little blue heron, the common large
wading bird of the Atchafalaya Swamp*

*Crayfish support a
burgeoning food chain in
the rich bottomlands
of the Atchafalaya.*

Miles of levees hold back the floodwaters.

Aerial view of the Atchafalaya Swamp

*A red-cockaded woodpecker near the resin-coated
entrance to its nesthole*

Sunset over the Neches River

The Big Thicket contains the westernmost of the large cypress swamps.

the Cache River but that the first settlers disliked and avoided the swamp because of the swarms of mosquitoes, the supposed danger of disease, the lack of healthy drinking water, and the abundance of snakes. Almost all the residents had malaria, and the typical early logger carried "a bottle of chill tonic" in one back pocket and a bottle of whiskey in the other. The mosquitoes were so bad that loggers often worked in the hot summer wearing coats buttoned up to their necks.

Although a dislike for swamps is seen in almost all early accounts of them, it should be pointed out that the big swamps in the East did not have the same reputation that the Cache River did as a breeding ground for malaria. Convinced that the swamps were to blame for the prevalence of malaria, the settlers in southern Illinois began small-scale drainage efforts as early as 1870. In one instance a ditch cut to drain a swamp had the opposite effect. Water from a nearby creek drained into the swamp through the ditch.

A second tract, about ten miles upstream on the Cache River, has already been saved. This is the four-thousand-acre, state-owned Little Black Slough and Heron Pond Nature Preserve. Many of its lakes, ponds, and sloughs support healthy stands of bald cypress, together with much the same flora and fauna as are found on the Lower Cache. According to Max, who was also our guide on this part of our tour, there is some question about how the lakes and ponds in the preserve were formed. They are circular in shape and therefore do not conform to the half-moon shape of the typical oxbow lake. One theory is that these bodies of water owe their origin to beavers that existed in the region several hundred years ago. After the beavers were eradicated by heavy trapping around 1800, their ponds remained behind.

We did see some differences between this tract and the one downstream. The trees were smaller but, for the most part, sounder and more vigorous. Oaks were more in evidence, whereas there were fewer water locusts and water tupelos. The fact that large cypress trees were missing could be explained by heavy timbering that took place there toward the end of the last century. Many of the cypresses had been cut for use as pilings on the Chicago lakefront.

Max told us that along a railroad line running through a corner of the preserve there were so many snakes that the railroad company at one time periodically employed armed guards to accompany the track section crews solely for the purpose of killing the snakes. The cottonmouth and the diamondback water snake were the two common species. Great blue herons nest in rookeries in the preserve. Black vultures also nest and maintain a roost.

Besides the cypress along the Cache River, southern Illinois has other stands, including some in wet areas at elevations as high as five hundred feet above sea level. A visit to Horseshoe Lake, about ten miles northwest of Cairo, will reward the swamp enthusiast with the spectacle of cypress in typical bottomland habitat and also a perfect example of an oxbow or horseshoe lake. A former loop in the Mississippi River, the lake almost doubles back upon itself and, like the Cache River, contains a good sample of southern flora and fauna. Worth visiting at any season, Horseshoe Lake is a famous wintering ground for Canada geese, and there are always a few bald eagles present with them. The lake is within a nine-thousand-acre conservation area.

In Missouri, across the Mississippi, bald cypress reaches the northwestern limits of its range. One of the best stands is at the Mingo National Wildlife Refuge near Puxico, in the southeastern corner of the state. At the refuge headquarters area, one is treated to a spectacular view of rolling wooded country with a deep valley below, through which the Mississippi River once flowed. The old riverbed is now lined with cypress. A former state champion bald cypress (killed by lightning a few years ago) once grew there. The tree had a breast-high circumference of thirty-five feet.

Missouri offers another surprise. In Ripley County, in a sandy, swampy area about sixty miles due west of New Madrid of earthquake fame, is perhaps the only place where bald cypress can be found growing with two rare shrubs. One of them is corkwood, which is present in Florida swamps, and the other is pondberry (*Lindera melissaefolium*). The latter is in the same genus as spicebush and is known only as a result of its presence in a few widely scattered sites in the South. Bald cypress and its two rare companions receive protection at a 120-acre tract called the Altvater Pondberry Preserve.

On a second float trip, Audubon and a group of frontiersmen left Henderson in November, 1820, and slowly worked their way downriver to Louisiana. Impoverished and at the lowest point in his career, Audubon was looking for greener fields. The only thing that lifted his spirits on the long trip was the many birds he saw. Some of them were new to him, and thus, he had never painted them. Soon after entering the Mississippi, they came to a dismal, half-ruined town on the west side of the river—New Madrid, a town whose name was immortalized as a result of its location at the epicenter of the famous New Madrid earthquakes of 1811–1812. Audubon, on visiting the town, was aghast at the poverty he saw. "This almost deserted village," he wrote, "is one of the poorest that is seen on this river." He said the Indians were a thousand times better off than the ragged, ill-clothed inhabitants.

When on December 10 Audubon and his party reached the mouth of the White River, they stopped to reconnoiter. The White River, which has its source in southern Missouri and northern Arkansas, flows to the southeast and meets the Mississippi about halfway between Memphis and the Arkansas-Louisiana state line. Audubon wanted to reach a community named Arkansas Post some miles away on the Arkansas River. Once a prosperous settlement, Arkansas Post, like New Madrid, had fallen on hard times.

Taking two other men with him, he set off in a skiff, hoping to travel seven miles up the White River and then, by way of a water route, reach the Arkansas River. But the current was so strong in the White River that they had to pull their small craft upstream as they walked along the shore. They left their skiff at the water cutoff and set off on "a narrow path often so thickly beset with green briers that we would be forced to give back and go around—this followed through cypress swamps and round ponds and cane brakes until we reached the first settlement."

On the trip down the Mississippi, Audubon often complained of the dense canebrakes and tangles of greenbrier that grew luxuriantly on the riverbanks. Like Thomas Nuttall, who was visiting that part of America at about the same time, Audubon had little enthusiasm for the endless canebrakes and hardwood forests that stretched as far as the eye could see. In describing the swamps where the ivory-billed woodpecker was found, he used such adjectives as *gloomy, pestilential, suffocating,* and *horrible.* It would be almost another hundred years before many people would begin to appreciate the true beauty and value of the southern swamp.

I can sympathize with Audubon as he made his way through the overgrown river bottoms of southeastern Arkansas. At the White River National Wildlife Refuge, a short distance upstream from where Audubon and his companions left the White River, I have found the going as difficult as it probably was for him.

When Gary Williamson and I visited the 113,380-acre refuge in mid-October, 1984, we encountered rainy weather and gummy mud that stuck to the bottoms of our boots with every step we took. If we left dirt roads, we would find ourselves in poison ivy that reached as high as our waists and engulfed trunks of trees. I thought of Florence Page Jaques, wife of the bird painter, who found this swamp hostile and terrifying. We shared her feelings to some extent, but it may have been at least partly because of the weather.

White River is the largest federal wildlife refuge in the Mississippi Valley. From three to ten miles in width and thirty-two miles long, the refuge covers a wide expanse of bottomland forest filled with sloughs, lakes, and bayous. Only about a hundred of the lakes are well known enough to have names. The frequent changes the White River has made in its course account for the many oxbow lakes. In Arkansas the lakes and interconnecting waterways are often called bayous.

Willows and cottonwoods grow on newly deposited soil, whereas cypresses and water tupelos line the edges of lakes and sloughs. The hardpan clay soil of the White River bottoms is not particularly well suited to the bald cypress, with its long taproot. The term *cypress swamp* does not fit. Rather the forest is made up largely of such trees as the pecan, green ash, sycamore, overcup oak, water hickory, persimmon, and Nuttall oak (*Quercus nuttallii*).

The Nuttall oak, with a limited range in the central states, makes a prominent appearance in the White River bottoms. The wood of the tree, and, to a lesser extent, that of other members of the red oak group, sometimes undergoes a process known as *choctawing.* As described by Brooke Meanley in his book on swamps, in this process the wood, after lying on the ground, becomes thoroughly glazed, trapping air in its porous interior. Wood in this condition, according to Meanley, looks like an empty honeycomb. The wood varies in color from light brown to dark brown or almost black. Logs that have become choctawed are buoyant enough to serve as floats or even as pontoons to support houseboats. But if cut, the logs lose their buoyancy. I used to find these logs in the Big Thicket in Texas, which is also within the range of the Nuttall oak. In the White River bottoms choctawed logs are commonly seen piled up in flood debris.

The White River bottoms are subject to as much as six months of continual flooding. High water usually appears in December and may not recede until the end of June or July. In some years there is an early flood season beginning in December and lasting through the winter, followed by a second flood season beginning in May.

As the swirling waters climb ever higher, some forms of animal life retreat; others, well adapted to this condition, stay where they are. The American alligator, formerly at its northern range limit in the Mississippi Valley at the White River, once thrived in the area. No longer present, the alligator now extends only to the southernmost part of Arkansas. The 100,000 to 300,000 ducks present each winter at the White River refuge are particularly well adapted to flood conditions. The mallard, which makes up 90 percent of the winter duck population, has a way of "tipping up" to feed on food in shallow water.

Thanks to protection, the black bear has climbed from a population of only a few individuals in 1935, when the refuge was established, to one of 180 to 200 individuals today. When high water inundates the swamp in early winter, the black bears climb trees. Perched high in treetops with water all around them, they live on nuts, acorns, and whatever is edible in the floodwaters. They forage by swimming from tree to tree and occasionally moving to high ground. Young are raised in tree cavities that may be as high as sixty feet from the ground.

Gary and I, on our visit, were impressed by the large numbers of red-headed woodpeckers we saw. Busy storing acorns and pecans in cavities in trees, they, like the black bears, would have food supplies to fall back on when the floodwaters came. The calls of woodpeckers resounded from every part of the forest. Their lively movements and cheerful notes did much to lift our spirits during our first day in the swamp. We were also buoyed by a short period of sunshine that dispelled some of the gloom.

Audubon, with his distaste for swamps, certainly would

have found good reason not to ascend the White River any farther than he did. He was doubtless relieved to be back on the Mississippi in a couple of days and once again floating downstream. On December 14, somewhere below the confluence of the Mississippi and Arkansas rivers, he saw five ivory-billed woodpeckers feeding on the berries of a creeper. They kept up a gentle cry of "pet, pet, pet." Without elaboration, Audubon tells of an ivorybill shot on December 20. He had, however, seen and heard ivorybills shortly after he and his party had entered the Mississippi during the early stages of the trip. He described the bird's tin-trumpet call notes and observed that this largest woodpecker was closely associated with bottomland timber.

Audubon frequently saw flocks of Carolina parakeets on his trip down the Mississippi. He noted accurately that the species was becoming rare. Nevertheless, he had no qualms about shooting them. He told of boiling ten parakeets. The flesh of one or more of these birds was used to test a theory that went back to early pioneer days. It was believed that the meat of the parakeet was toxic to cats and other animals. He offered the test meat to his dog, Dash, "who has had 10 Welps," to see what effect it would have. Apparently the dog was not harmed by the meal.

It is known that cocklebur (*Xanthium* sp.), a favorite food of the Carolina parakeet, has toxic properties. Although the parakeets are immune to the poison, animals eating their flesh may be susceptible to poisoning. That seems to have been particularly true of house cats, which, according to old accounts, were frequent victims.

Almost any bird species was shot for food by Audubon and his friends as they traveled the river. The birds served Audubon in two ways—some of them were painted, and virtually all were eaten. Wild turkeys and waterfowl were in greatest demand, but even grackles were eaten. Large flocks of birds were often seen overhead. One day he might see several hundred purple finches in a single flock, and two days later hundreds of mallards flying south. Audubon also once saw hundreds of gulls and, another time, "four white-headed eagles regaling themselves on a deer carcase." He noted sandhill cranes in good numbers and on another occasion claimed to have seen "probably millions of cormorants flying over."

During most of his trip down the Mississippi, Audubon passed through a region of hardwood forest little altered by man. Even today there are few dramatic changes in scenery as one follows the Mississippi toward its mouth. The river's banks are lined with endless rows of willows, and behind them, cottonwoods. One difference, since Audubon's day, is the levees, which confine the river to a narrow floodplain. The towns and fields behind the levees are another significant contrast. Land clearing, which by Audubon's time had already begun on a large scale in Louisiana, has continued with little letup ever since. Figures reveal that since 1937, bot-

tomland forests in the floodplain have been reduced in area by 60 percent.

Audubon wrote very little about the landscape as he made his way down the Mississippi. It seems safe to assume that he saw a monotonous repetition of sandbars, wooded islands, and wooded shorelines rarely broken by signs of human habitation. But the country opened up when he and his party reached the sugar and cotton plantations of Louisiana. Instead of endless forests, there were large plantations worked by slaves. Many of the plantations had magnificent mansions, Audubon said. The croplands stretched away like vast prairies, he wrote, and "scarce a tree was to be seen."

After experiencing numerous difficulties in New Orleans, the farthest point he reached downstream, Audubon traveled upriver to St. Francisville. That was in June, 1821, when he was still penniless and discouraged. St. Francisville offered him new hope. He had received a welcome assignment to teach art to a fifteen-year-old daughter of wealthy plantation owners. During the three months that Audubon spent with the family at Oakley plantation near St. Francisville, he was able to pursue painting and ornithology to his heart's content. But because of tensions aroused by his fondness for his pupil and hers for him, he was dismissed from his duties. This episode in Audubon's career occurred amid a setting of live oaks, Spanish moss, and wooded bluffs in West Feliciana Parish. After an absence, Audubon again returned to West Feliciana, this time in company with his wife, who had received an assignment as a governess at another plantation. By now Audubon was busier than ever with his bird painting.

When Gary Williamson and I visited St. Francisville in early May, 1986, we were mainly interested in finding the national champion bald cypress. Nevertheless, we did take out time to visit Oakley plantation, now an Audubon shrine. But first we drove northward and then took a circuitous route that brought us to the Mississippi River. Following a dirt road southward along the edge of the river, we came to what is known as the Cat Island Swamp. An uninhabited area of many square miles belonging to a big lumber company, the swamp, except for lumbering operations, has probably changed little since the time of Audubon. Following a compass bearing that took us perhaps two to three miles inland from the river, we came to some of the largest cypress trees we had ever seen. Almost any of the first dozen we saw would have qualified as state champion in any state other than Louisiana. The trees had enormously swollen bases, and many of them appeared to be hollow. After crawling through an opening into the dark interior of one of the trees, Gary reported that he could distinguish bats clinging to the inside walls of the hollow trunk. Judging from his description, the bats were almost certainly evening bats—the species that often roosts in hollow cypress trees.

We gasped in amazement when, from a distance, we could make out the national champion looming ahead of us. We easily recognized the tree from photographs we had seen of it. The tree was not particularly tall, having a height of eighty-three feet. Moreover the tree was somewhat mis-shapen, probably as a result of past hurricanes that snapped off branches. The tree's spread, the distance from the outer tips of branches on one side to the outer tips of branches on the other side, was eighty-five feet, or approximately the same as its height. But what stood out and gave the tree its title was its enormous girth. At breast height, the trunk's circumference was an awe-inspiring fifty-three feet eight inches. To find a tree in North America with a larger girth, one would have to travel to California and view the giant sequoias. The General Sherman Tree in Sequoia National Park has a girth of eighty-three feet two inches.

One other detail caught our eye. The tree had only one large knee and a few small ones. Other cypress trees in this frequently flooded swamp had many more knees and taller ones. Why the paucity of knees at the base of the giant? We had no explanation.

Near absence of knees and the tree's shorn look did not lessen our admiration for it. The tree has withstood the vicissitudes of a thousand, or perhaps even two thousand, years. It has weathered the great floods and hurricanes and been spared by the timber cutters. And now, though perhaps with part of its top missing, as well as many limbs, it stood before us, a majestic relict that testified to the passage of the centuries.

The surrounding forest was almost as inspiring. We esti-mated that there were at least fifty bald cypresses in the near vicinity of the champion that had a breast-high circum-ference of over thirty feet. Most of them were hollow, which was probably why they had been spared by lumbermen.

Along with the cypresses were large trees of other kinds. Chief among them were sugarberries, water hickories, over-cup oaks, and pecans.

We did not allow the big trees to absorb our whole atten-tion. Whenever we looked up, we saw birds flying over. In small, fast-flying flocks were white ibis and other large wad-ing birds heading in set directions. Mississippi kites were constantly circling in the sky above us. Leaving Gary to search for more big cypress trees, I set off in the direction the large wading birds were taking. I soon came to an opening containing a nearly dried-up pond. Surrounding the opening were dense stands of water elm and swamp privet. Cocklebur stalks almost head high filled an expanse of about ten acres. On the far side of the opening was a flourishing wading bird rookery in tops of trees and shrubs. Small flights of white ibis were arriving or departing every few minutes. Along with them were great egrets, great blue herons, and little blue herons.

Our final ornithological treat of the day was a pair of swallow-tailed kites that appeared overhead as we returned to our car. During Audubon's sojourn in West Feliciana Parish, he had painted a swallow-tailed kite in flight with a snake in its talons. Had he visited Cat Island Swamp and taken in the sights that we found so thrilling?

References

Durant, Mary, and Michael Harwood. *On the Road with John James Audubon*. New York, 1980.

Meanley, Brooke. *Swamps, River Bottoms, and Canebrakes*. Barre, Mass., 1972.

Peattie, Donald Culross. *Audubon's America*. Boston, 1940.

17 / Reelfoot and Other Earthquake Lakes

On December 16, 1811, the inhabitants of the small Mississippi River town of New Madrid in southeastern Missouri were suddenly awakened from their sleep. Terrifying noises, the earth giving way, and clouds of sulphurous gases rising from the ground were early manifestations of a series of earthquakes that rocked the region for over a year. The first tremor was one of the most violent.

According to one witness, the river ran upstream for a period of forty-eight hours. Islands in the river disappeared, new ones formed, thousands of trees were broken off by the force of the onrushing water, and many boats on their way downstream were totally wrecked. In spite of the destruction, there was little loss of human life. The earthquake vented its fury chiefly upon the wilderness. The region was sparsely settled, and the few towns, with their one-story houses, were not death traps. Yet the first earthquake was so powerful that its shocks were felt as far away as Louisiana, South Carolina, and Massachusetts. John James Audubon, on horseback in Kentucky, one hundred miles away, told of his horse groaning and spreading out its forelegs to keep from falling. He stated that "the ground rose in successive furrows like the ruffled waters of a lake." He said he was "bewildered in all my senses."

Describing the earthquake in a letter to her pastor, Eliza Bryan of New Madrid wrote: "About 2 o'clock a.m., a violent earthquake shock was accompanied by a very awful noise, resembling loud but distant thunder, but hoarse and vibrating, followed by complete saturation of the atmosphere with sulphurous vapor, causing total darkness. The screams of the inhabitants, the cries of the fowls and beasts of every species, the falling trees, and the roaring of the Mississippi formed a scene truly horrible."

After the inhabitants of New Madrid had recovered enough from the first few shocks to look around, they began to take note of what they saw. One observer reported, "Lately it has been discovered that a lake was formed on the opposite side of the Mississippi, in Indian country, upwards of 100 miles long and from one to six miles wide, of a depth of from ten to fifty feet." That first description of Reelfoot Lake, though not entirely accurate, does correctly state that a large lake was suddenly formed by the earthquake. As is now known from existing lakes and ones that have been drained, it is likely that the earthquake did create, on the east side of the Mississippi, a series of lakes that extended for a distance of one hundred miles. Located in western Kentucky and western Tennessee, some of these lakes are now nature preserves and national wildlife refuges.

The Chickasaw Indians, who lived in the area, did not leave a scientific account of the birth of Reelfoot Lake. But they did leave a legend still remembered in western Tennessee. They placed the blame for the earthquake upon a young chieftain of their tribe who had just taken power. His name was Reelfoot, or, in their language, Kalopin, and he had been given that name because of a deformed foot that caused him to reel from side to side when he walked. One of the first tasks of the new chieftain was to find a bride suitable to his tastes and high office. Dreaming of finding a beautiful princess in a tribe to the south, Reelfoot with his warriors set forth. Among the Choctaw, he found exactly the princess he had been looking for. Her name was Laughing Eyes, and she was the daughter of a prominent chief. All might have gone well except for the fact that her father would not agree to the match, because of Reelfoot's deformity. Not even the offer of rich booty in the form of skins and pearls would move him. Reelfoot was obliged to return empty-handed and dispirited to his tribe. Moreover, the Great Spirit, to whom he took his troubles, warned him not to steal the beautiful princess. If he disobeyed, he and his people would be swallowed up by the waters of the great river on the banks of which they lived. But Reelfoot was determined to have his chosen bride, regardless of the consequences. He would steal Laughing Eyes and carry her off under the cover of darkness. His mission was successful. To the great rejoicing of his people, he brought her back to his tribe. But no sooner had his people gathered to celebrate the event than the earth began to rock to the beat of tom-toms. The waters of the great river rushed in to swallow up Reelfoot and his people. That was the origin of Reelfoot Lake.

For many years the heavily wooded country around Reelfoot Lake remained empty and unclaimed. Not until 1852 was a small settlement established on the lake's shores. As word spread about the great abundance of fish and game in the area, more and more people drifted in. The inhabitants were self-sufficient pioneers who made good use of the bounty all around them. But toward the end of the last century there came a threat to their way of life. As had been the case with the Great Dismal Swamp and so many other of America's great swamps, the one thought in the minds of entrepreneurs who knew Reelfoot Lake was to drain it and turn the land into cropland. The schemers were a group who called themselves the West Tennessee Land Company. As word got around of the company's plans, the settlers banded together to resist a takeover. The result was the Night Riders' War. The culmination of the trouble came one day in 1908 when two agents of the land company were kidnapped by Night Riders. One of them, Captain Quentin Rankin, was lynched. The other man, Colonel R. Z. Taylor, somehow escaped by swimming across a bayou amid a hail of bullets. No one was ever convicted for having taken part in the lynching.

No more was heard of drainage plans after the unhappy fate of Captain Rankin. In 1925 the Tennessee State Game and Fish Commission began purchasing land around the lake for a game preserve. Further protection for the lake was afforded by the establishment of a national wildlife refuge in 1941. The Reelfoot and Lake Isom national wildlife refuges contain a total of about 13,500 acres. Except for 1,850 acres at Lake Isom, five miles south of Reelfoot Lake, the refuge is at the northern end of Reelfoot Lake and extends a short way across the state line into Kentucky. State ownership in the form of a wildlife management area and state park account for another 16,000 acres.

In spite of these acquisitions, the future of the lake is not altogether bright. Most of the forested land beyond the borders of state and federal properties has been cut and converted into cropland. The clearing was largely the result of demand for fresh land following World War II. Two lakes that once lay between Reelfoot Lake and Lake Isom have been drained and are now soybean fields. As a result of so much land clearing, silt from highly erodible loess in the hill country to the east of the lake has been pouring down into the lake at an ever accelerating rate. The consequences of siltation were described in an article in *Nature Magazine* in 1955 by C. Van Dresser entitled "Reelfoot: A Dying Lake." He stated that erosion from nearby cropland had reduced the size of the lake from forty-three thousand acres at the time of its formation to twenty-three thousand acres. The size of the lake has recently been given as twenty thousand acres. Not only is the lake much smaller, but it is also far shallower, than it used to be. Instead of ten feet deep, and in some places a maximum of thirty feet deep, most of the lake is now between four and five feet deep. Although efforts are being made to check the rate of siltation, the lake is still filling in at an alarming rate.

Well into this century, Reelfoot Lake was a forest of gray and broken trunks of dead trees—remnants of the forest that grew there before the great earthquake. In 1949, when I first visited the lake, dead snags dotted the surface of the water. They provided perches for kingfishers, cormorants, and other water birds. Holes in the snags were used as nesting sites by wood ducks, tree swallows, crested flycatchers, and prothonotary warblers. But today the main body of water making up the lake is largely free of snags. Nearly all of them have fallen over. But submerged stumps, along with countless logs, remain in the mud at the bottom of the lake. That many of them are only a few inches beneath the surface became apparent to me when I visited the lake in October, 1984, and saw dozens of great blue herons perched singly as far as the eye could see on submerged snags.

The lake is filled largely by rainwater and runoff from nearby slopes. During times of flood, the Mississippi River backs up into the lake. Overflow from the lake, in turn, reaches the Mississippi by way of a spillway. When I visited the lake in May, 1983, the Mississippi was in flood. Reddish, silt-laden waters were flowing through a portion of the swamp near Bayou du Chien within the national wildlife refuge. To reach a dirt road leading into the swamp, I was obliged to wade some distance through the swirling, muddy water. Sharing my passage were a number of water snakes far more at home in the environment than I was. Other snakes were stretched out on the road basking in the warmth of the sun.

The fishes, reptiles, birds, and mammals of Reelfoot Lake have made the region famous in the eyes of sportsmen and naturalists. The lake has been called one of the richest fishing grounds in the interior of North America. Its birdlife is so outstanding that the lake is a mecca for large numbers of bird watchers and photographers. When "Cranetown," a large water-bird rookery on the west side of Reelfoot Lake, was in its prime, it was frequently visited by bird photographers. In the *Migrant* in 1937, Karl Maslowski spoke of large numbers of nesting great egrets, great blue herons, cormorants, and anhingas at the rookery. He estimated that there were three thousand pairs of nesting birds using the rookery. The most common species was the great egret. Above the din of Cranetown, he could hear the songs of prothonotary and parula warblers. Overhead, black vultures cruised ceaselessly, ever on the lookout for offal and dead birds.

In 1938 an ornithologist named Eva Gersbacher spent eight weeks studying the rookery. She estimated that over 5,000 birds nested in the thirteen-acre site. Nesting in the many cypress trees in Cranetown were 3,500 great egrets, 1,000 double-crested cormorants, 350 great blue herons, 225 black-crowned herons, and 200 anhingas. But beginning in 1957, in a debacle reminiscent of Chief Reelfoot's ill-fated attempt to possess the beautiful Laughing Eyes, Cranetown, because of the ill-conceived ambitions of men, was nearly destroyed. The trouble started with the filming of a portion of

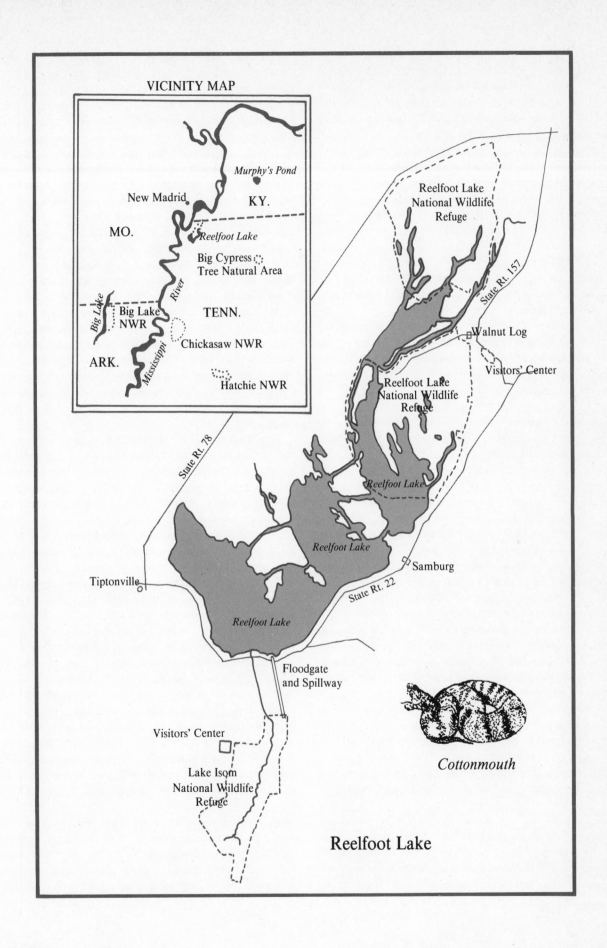

VICINITY MAP

Murphy's Pond

New Madrid

KY.

MO.

Reelfoot Lake

Big Cypress
Tree Natural Area

Big Lake

Mississippi River

Big Lake
NWR

TENN.

ARK.

Chickasaw NWR

Hatchie NWR

Reelfoot Lake
National Wildlife
Refuge

State Rt. 157

Walnut Log

Visitors' Center

Reelfoot Lake
National Wildlife
Refuge

State Rt. 78

Reelfoot Lake

Reelfoot Lake

Reelfoot Lake

Samburg

Tiptonville

State Rt. 22

Reelfoot Lake

Floodgate
and Spillway

Visitors' Center

Lake Isom
National Wildlife
Refuge

Cottonmouth

Reelfoot Lake

a movie called *Raintree County,* starring Elizabeth Taylor and Montgomery Clift, at Reelfoot Lake. Although the novel *Raintree County,* by Ross Lockridge, was set in Indiana and had little to do with birds or other wildlife, MGM in Hollywood decided that a teeming bird rookery was just the place to do some of the filming. What better place was there than Cranetown, with its lofty cypress trees and many egrets?

Guides at Reelfoot Lake who remember the filming recall that dynamiters opened up a ditch to the rookery to allow passage into its midst of eighteen boatloads of people and equipment. As if that was not enough disturbance to the birds during the height of the nesting season, shotguns were fired to provide scenic views of many birds flying up at once. Also, the guides were employed to capture individual egrets and release them in front of the cameras. Even turtles were wired to logs and at the proper moment turned loose to provide still more wildlife shots.

After so much disturbance, only a small fraction of the total number of birds returned to the rookery the next year. And with easy access to the rookery by way of the newly opened ditch, people went in to view the birds, and some even shot off firecrackers to make them fly. By 1959 the number of nests was down to two hundred, and by 1963 the rookery was completely deserted. The $5.3 million movie did not fare so well either. It was described as a three-hour bore and was poorly received.

With improved conditions in recent years, large wading birds are returning to Reelfoot Lake. The great blue heron, present the year round, is the most common species. Among other large waders are the green-backed heron, little blue heron, great egret, snowy egret, and black-crowned night heron. The anhinga is occasionally seen in summer, and an active nest was discovered in 1977. But the double-crested cormorant has yet to make a return as a breeding bird.

Many of the large wading birds seen at Reelfoot Lake in recent years are residents of a large rookery across the river in Missouri not far from Caruthersville. Among the nesters at that rookery are the only anhingas known to nest in Missouri. At the same time, there are one or more new rookeries at undisclosed locations at Reelfoot Lake. These rookeries are populated chiefly by great blue herons and great egrets.

Reelfoot Lake is even better known for its waterfowl. The national wildlife refuges support peak winter waterfowl populations of as many as 40,000 Canada geese and 250,000 ducks. The common winter ducks are the mallard, northern pintail, American wigeon, wood duck, and ring-necked duck. Often regarded as just another species of waterfowl, the American coot feeds along with the ducks and is present in good numbers the year round. The largest concentrations of geese and ducks are generally found in winter in fields set aside for waterfowl in the Kentucky portion of the national wildlife refuge. The wood duck and hooded merganser are common nesters, and the mallard occasionally nests.

One of the major attractions at Reelfoot Lake in winter is the large numbers of eagles that congregate here. Mid-December through mid-March is the season to see eagles in all their glory. For those who wish to take advantage of daily eagle tours, arrangements should be made with the Reelfoot Lake State Park, Route 1, Tiptonville, Tennessee 38079. The tours are by bus and leave at 9 A.M. for outings of as long as three hours. Participants can count upon seeing a fair share of the more than two hundred bald eagles that winter in the area and perhaps one or more golden eagles. The tours also provide a way of seeing wintering waterfowl.

Among the other ornithological treats of the lake are nesting ospreys, purple gallinules, and common moorhens. As at Blake's Reserve, the ospreys nest in dead or living cypress trees. The purple gallinule, resplendent in its purplish, bronzy green plumage, is often hard to find in among the water-lilies and American lotus. Much the same is true of its close relative the common moorhen. The warblers, at peak numbers during spring and fall migrations, also attract bird watchers to the lake. No fewer than thirty-five species have been recorded over the years. The prothonotary warbler, a common nesting species, is the most exciting warbler from the standpoint of color, and the Swainson's from that of rarity.

The blackbirds, cowbirds, grackles, and starlings that roost in the marshes at Reelfoot Lake during fall and winter provide an ornithological treat of another kind. The no less than six thousand acres of giant cutgrass (*Zizaniopsis miliacea*) that grows on newly formed land at the lake's edge supplies a roost at night for these birds. The evening and morning flights, in which millions of birds take part, are regarded as among the nation's most impressive wildlife spectacles.

The fish population is composed of species typical of the Mississippi River and its backwaters. Thus, the lake is well stocked with members of the sucker, catfish, and sunfish families. Fish in those families are able to tolerate the warm water temperatures in the summer and are reasonably well adapted to the muddy bottom and rank plant growth. Nevertheless, in parts of the lake covered by duckweed and other floating plants, sunlight cannot reach more beneficial underwater plants. They die, using up the oxygen, and large-scale fish kills are the result. Visiting Reelfoot Lake with Steve Maslowski in September, 1983, I found long windrows of dead fish lining the shores. Low water, owing to drought conditions, coupled with mats of floating vegetation, had led to an oxygen shortage that left thousands of fish dead. Fish kills are a recurring problem at the lake, and a solution is being sought through a number of proposed measures. One would be to raise the water level of the lake as a way of offsetting the siltation taking place. But a rise of even one foot would submerge many of the some three dozen Indian mounds that exist in the area. Of great archaeological value, they represent some of the best remaining mounds in the lower Mississippi Valley. Would anything in those mounds offer a clue about the authenticity of the Reelfoot and Laughing Eyes legend?

In spite of water and siltation problems of the kinds mentioned, Reelfoot supports incredibly dense populations of fishes and other freshwater organisms. Instead of the tea-colored, acidic water found in so many swamps, Reelfoot has relatively clear water with a pH on the alkaline side. Large underwater beds of hornwort (*Ceratophyllum demersum*) and pondweed, together with common emergent plants, such as American lotus, spatterdock, and giant cutgrass, testify to good growing conditions. So long as the oxygen supply does not become severely depleted, the lake will continue to offer some of the best fishing in the interior of the continent.

Of special interest to the sports fisherman is the lake's sizable population of well-known game fish. At the top of the list is the largemouth bass, normally present in good numbers but unpredictable about taking live bait or artificial lures. The lake offers such other game fish as the white crappie, black crappie, bluegill, warmouth bass, striped bass, and white bass.

More of a curiosity than a game fish is a strange relict of a past geological age—the paddlefish. A specimen over six feet long and weighing 173 pounds was once caught at Reelfoot. Another primitive fish, the bowfin, is common at Reelfoot and reaches a length of two to three feet. Far down the list in the esteem of fishermen, this well-known fish of swamps, small lakes, and sluggish streams puts up a tremendous fight if caught on a hook and line. The catfishes, much more highly rated, offer both sport and good eating. One of the largest fish of the lake, the flathead catfish, reaches as much as five feet in length and a weight of up to seventy pounds. It is known locally by such names as *morgan cat, mud cat,* and *leatherhead.* Formerly, many of the catfish were taken from hollow submerged stumps at night with the aid of gas lanterns. Today the lake's most important catfish is the channel cat. In much demand among both sports and commercial fishermen, it weighs up to fifty pounds and is a table delicacy. Buffalo fishes, represented by three species, and carp are of little interest to the angler but are taken in large numbers in the lake by commercial fishermen using nets.

The lake also has its very small fishes. The banded pygmy sunfish, only one to two inches in length, is one of the smallest. But it is eclipsed in smallness by the cypress darter, a one-inch or slightly longer inhabitant of bayous, swamps, and backwaters from southern Illinois to the Gulf Coast. Two other darters found at Reelfoot are also small and live up to their names by darting quickly from place to place.

The reptiles and amphibians at Reelfoot have benefited from the same conditions that have favored a large and varied fish population. I know of few swamps or lakes where snakes and turtles are more obvious or more abundant. Every pool, backwater, or ditch has its quota of turtles and water snakes. On warm, sunny days partially submerged logs and snags are lined with turtles large and small. If the visitor approaches one of these sunning spots, the turtles quickly splash into the water one by one. There was good reason for the frustrated cameramen of *Raintree County* to pay to have turtles wired to logs!

Whether snakes, turtles, or amphibians, the species found at Reelfoot are predominantly southern, and many are approximately at their northern range limits. The common turtles of the lake are the red-eared turtle, southern painted turtle, Mississippi mud turtle, and smooth and spiny softshell turtles. Of eighteen species of snakes recorded at the lake or nearby, eight are either at their northern range limits or are found no farther north than southern Illinois and southwestern Indiana.

The snakes, only a few of which ever show themselves, include the western mud snake, broad-banded water snake, green water snake, Mississippi ring-necked snake, midwest worm snake, canebrake rattlesnake, southern copperhead, and western cottonmouth. I always encounter a few of the latter when I visit Reelfoot. One October when I visited the lake, cottonmouths were moving eastward into the hills above the lake, where they would hole up for the winter. Gary Williamson, who was with me, counted ten dead ones that had been hit by cars on the highway. We also saw several live ones.

To find smaller, secretive species, such as the ring-neck, worm, and brown snakes, takes considerable searching under fallen logs and in the rubble of abandoned buildings. The northern brown snake is one of the most common of these recluses. Thanks to their ability to stay out of sight, the smaller snakes are relatively safe from the man who kills every snake he sees. Even within the supposedly safe limits of national wildlife refuges, one sees the wanton killing of snakes.

The three-toed amphiuma, one of the giant salamanders, is at home in the waters of Reelfoot Lake and reaches a large size, having been known to reach a length of about three and a half feet. Aside from this odd one, the salamanders found in and around the lake conform more to the image of what a salamander should look like. A search under rotting logs usually leads to the discovery of the handsome marbled salamander.

As might be expected in any shoal-water area, Reelfoot has an abundance of toads and frogs. The bullfrog, green frog, and pickerel frog are common in or near water, and the American toad and Fowler's toad can be found almost anywhere. Often heard but seldom seen, the western bird-voiced tree frog is particularly common. Much the same is true of the green tree frog, whose range coincides closely with that of the bald cypress. A final group, the lizards, are represented in swamplands adjoining the lake by the broad-headed skink. Three other lizards, the northern fence lizard, the five-lined skink, and the ground skink, are found on higher ground near the lake.

Reelfoot, with less than one-third of the land and water area of the Great Dismal Swamp, has almost as many reptiles and amphibians—about fifty-five species. The Great Dismal has slightly over sixty. In terms of visibility, I would say that the fauna is much more in evidence at Reelfoot. Every log seems to have its quota of sunning turtles, and every pond and ditch its water snakes. The only explanation I can think of is that Reelfoot, with its semialkaline water, has a greater population density of aquatic forms than the Great Dismal, with its acidic water.

On a recent visit to Reelfoot Lake, I stopped at the state park's visitors' center, located two miles east of Tiptonville and at the south end of the lake. After looking at the exhibits, I strolled out on a boardwalk that skirted the cypress-fringed borders of the lake. The trees, with their light green foliage, and the blue expanse of the lake so enthralled me that I sat on a bench for a while to drink it all in. On my way back I spoke to several fishermen who said they were catching a few crappies but that was all. Seldom do fishermen admit to having good luck. Following State Highway 22 north, I passed the usual motels and lakeside cottages and also sections of the state park. After driving for ten miles I came to the junction of State Routes 22 and 157. Turning left on Route 157, I came almost at once to the headquarters of the Reelfoot Lake and Lake Isom national wildlife refuges. There I visited a brand-new visitors' center with nice exhibits depicting the lake and its wildlife. After picking up maps and leaflets, I continued north for another mile on Route 157 and then took a dirt road to the left that led to the small community of Walnut Log and nearby Bayou du Chien, where, during the Night Riders' War, one of the land developers was killed and the other narrowly escaped by plunging into the water.

Soon I was inside the refuge and had the option of either driving or walking for two miles on a wildlife drive that followed the edge of the bayou. I decided to walk, thinking that I would see more wildlife. I was not disappointed. It was a quiet day, and no one was abroad to disturb the small mammals that I immediately saw. A pair of swamp rabbits in the road were so busy conducting their affairs that they failed to notice me. One of them, bounding off in my direction, came within inches of where I was standing. Walking a short way, I came close to a fox squirrel sitting on its haunches in the road. Soon another appeared, and waiting until the last moment, they scampered off at my approach. Fresh gnawing on saplings at the water's edge told of the work of beavers. Common once again after a long period of scarcity, beavers find a congenial home in the lily pad–dotted waterways of the wildlife refuge. But that day, like the bobcats and the mink, which have also recovered in numbers, the beavers did

not show themselves. The same was true of the river otter, which is making a comeback but a very slow one.

There are no longer elk or black bears in the region; therefore, the crashing I once heard in nearby underbrush was probably made by a white-tailed deer or a whole herd of them. Within the last ten years the coyote has put in an appearance, which is a not unexpected development, since this small version of the wolf has been steadily moving eastward from the Great Plains.

Continuing my walk, I saw signs that wild turkeys had been scratching below trees and feasting upon fallen acorns. The oak trees were being visited by red-bellied and red-headed woodpeckers—both of which are avid acorn eaters. I could see little of the water from the drive. But every so often I was aware of a flock of ducks or a heron flying up and disappearing over the treetops.

For the most part the plant life along the drive was the same as in eastern swamps. But an unfamiliar oak turned out to be bur oak (*Quercus macrocarpa*), and an unfamiliar dogwood was roughleaf dogwood (*Cornus drummondii*). Also, I was not used to pecan trees growing in a swamp. In the East, where it is introduced, the pecan is an upland species. But here, within its native range, it is a common tree of the river bottoms. Still another tree that I had to get accustomed to in this setting was the Kentucky coffee tree (*Gymnocladus dioica*). Although not at all common, the few trees I saw seemed as much at home in the swamp as sweet gums or bald cypresses were.

Less impressive than Reelfoot Lake, and scarcely heard of, is Murphy's Pond in western Kentucky. Only about twenty-five acres in size—or somewhat larger or smaller, depending upon the rainfall—Murphy's Pond is not shown on most maps. Its claim to fame is that it is an earthquake lake formed at the same time as Reelfoot Lake thirty miles to the southwest. For many years the pond slumbered. It was known only to local residents, who for the most part avoided it because of its large population of cottonmouths. According to one tale, some fishermen, using a lantern while fishing at night, suddenly saw hundreds of snakes in the water all around their boat. Thinking that the snakes were trying to get in the boat, they fled as quickly as possible.

In the 1960s a few naturalists began visiting the lake for the same reason that the local people stayed away. The naturalists were curious about the large numbers of reptiles and amphibians found in the pond and nearby cypress swamp. Writing in a 1965 state wildlife publication, Roger W. Barbour of the University of Kentucky stated that he was convinced that "at no place else on earth does the cottonmouth population approach that of Murphy's Pond." Although estimates of as many as three hundred cottonmouths per acre are probably much too high, there can be little doubt that this small wilderness area near the northern range limits of the cottonmouth is a rich area for them.

Barbour was also impressed by the fish, turtle, amphibian,

and bird populations of Murphy's Pond. "Bowfins flop and splash in the shallows," he wrote, "and turtles bask on the logs." He noted a large variety of amphibians—among them the crawfish frog, bird-voiced tree frog, green tree frog, central newt, three-toed amphiuma, and lesser siren. Higher up on the scale were nesting great egrets and a long list of mammals, including the muskrat, mink, raccoon, bobcat, fox squirrel, and swamp rabbit.

One more scary feature of Murphy's Pond is that it is among the few swampy areas I know of that can claim the presence of quicksand. A large spring that feeds the pond throughout the year is said to be surrounded by a broad belt of quicksand.

In 1966 the Nature Conservancy bought the pond and adjacent swampland to form a preserve of 235 acres. The preserve is presently held by the state of Kentucky and administered by Murray State University. Three miles south of Beulah, Kentucky, the preserve is not readily accessible by road.

Besides creating Reelfoot Lake and Murphy's Pond, the New Madrid earthquake disturbed a large swampy area in Arkansas fifty miles to the southwest of New Madrid and opened up new lakes all along the Mississippi within a radius of approximately a hundred miles. The swamp area in Arkansas that felt the effects of the earthquake had been shaken by another earthquake about a thousand years earlier. The original earthquake, by blocking the drainage system of the region, had created what was known as the Great Swamp. It was a swamp filled with cypress trees that stretched for a hundred miles along what is now the boundary between Arkansas and Missouri. We know little or nothing of the plants and wildlife that existed here. It is safe to say, however, that the swamp was bursting with life and that it was the home of a number of forms that today are either extinct or nearly so. But the swamp was cut almost before it was marked on maps or explored. Needing ties, railroad builders, as they pushed rail lines westward across the plains toward the end of the last century, were willing to pay good prices for cypress logs. What could be handier for the railroads than a cypress forest standing at the very gateway to the Great Plains?

In a period of only ten years most of the trees were cut and converted into ties and building materials. Then the land was drained and converted into cotton fields. By 1913 little was left of the Great Swamp except for a fringe of cypress swamp surrounding a body of water known as Big Lake. The lake, whose existence has been traced to two earthquakes, was once at the heart of the swamp. Wishing to save this last remnant, local citizens banded together to do what they could. Their message reached Washington. In 1915, Woodrow Wilson, by executive order, created the Big Lake National Wildlife Refuge.

Today within the 11,038-acre refuge there are extensive bodies of water and two stands of bald cypress that cover 2,600 acres. The trees are moderately large and are said to date back to the time of the New Madrid earthquakes. Still more cypress is found in a state wildlife management area that borders the refuge on its east side and that is approximately the same size as the refuge. Ducks, about 90 percent of them mallards, throng to these wetlands in fall and winter. They are joined by large numbers of geese and a few bald and golden eagles.

Returning to the east side of the Mississippi River, one finds still more earthquake lakes some fifty miles south of Reelfoot Lake and Lake Isom. These lakes, dating back to the New Madrid earthquakes, somehow survived the fate of being drained and are now within lands belonging to either the state of Tennessee, the Nature Conservancy, or the federal government—the custodian of nearby Chickasaw National Wildlife Refuge. Open Lake, the largest of these earthquake lakes, adjoins the Chickasaw National Wildlife Refuge and lies less than a mile from the Mississippi River. Sunk Lake, to the southwest—actually a series of small earthquake lakes—is within a 1,334-acre preserve established by the Nature Conservancy.

Both the Chickasaw National Wildlife Refuge, with 8,650 acres, and the Sunk Lake preserve offer critically needed habitat for the Mississippi kite, a bird listed as endangered by the state of Tennessee. Like Reelfoot Lake, these more southern earthquake lakes and nearby bottomlands offer ideal wintering grounds for geese, ducks, and eagles, which so often congregate at waterfowl refuges. In summer the great blue heron is the dominant large wading bird nesting at the more inland sites, whereas the cattle egret is the common nesting bird at rookeries overlooking the Mississippi River. Great egrets occupy both inland and riverside rookeries.

References

Maslowski, Karl. "Notes on the Birdlife of an Earthquake Lake." *Migrant,* VIII (1937), 58–60.

Nelson, Wilbur A. "Reelfoot: An Earthquake Lake." *National Geographic,* XLV (1924), 95–114.

Van Dresser, C. "Reelfoot: A Dying Lake." *Nature Magazine,* XLVIII (February, 1955), 90–93.

18 / Atchafalaya Swamp and the Red River

Nowhere else can one get a better feel for the vast swamps that once existed in the bayou region of southern Louisiana than along the Atchafalaya River. There, amid a labyrinth of waterways, is Louisiana's largest remaining swamp and also the largest of all southern swamps. Once covering 1.5 million acres, the Atchafalaya Swamp today is a smaller quiltwork made up of rivers, lakes, canals, levees, woodland, and agricultural lands. Scattered small towns and villages cling to edges of canals or lie behind levees near riverbanks. The works of man have only a tenuous hold in this domain in which water is ever on the brink of sweeping everything else away. To the east the Mississippi River waits to reclaim its old channel. It once flowed to the Gulf of Mexico by way of the Atchafalaya Basin.

The Atchafalaya River, besides being bordered by the largest southern swamp, has the distinction of being part of two river systems. It is a distributary of the Mississippi, and at the same time, it also receives most of the flow of the Red River. Somehow the Red, with its headwaters in Texas and Oklahoma, seems to lose its way as it approaches the Mississippi. Vacillating between the Mississippi and the Atchafalaya, it takes turns sending lesser and larger amounts of its flow into each of the two rivers. Early in the nineteenth century, it was the Mississippi that received most of the flow. A portion of the Atchafalaya was blocked by an immense logjam known as a raft. But after the raft was cleared away in 1855 by crews of men working with pullboats, both the Red and the Mississippi poured more of their waters into the Atchafalaya Basin.

The French-speaking Cajuns, who had been farming in the Atchafalaya Basin, now found their lands flooded by the higher water. Resourceful people that they were, they turned to fishing, trapping, and small-scale logging. Later, gathering Spanish moss for use in upholstering became an important industry. The swamp furnished them with virtually everything they needed.

Until about 1880, land clearing and logging had scarcely dented the vast hardwood and cypress forests that filled the Atchafalaya Basin. But having cut off the white pine in the Great Lakes region, lumber barons from the North began buying up the swamp in accord with the process that over-took so many of the other southern swamps. They would buy the land, cut the timber, and leave behind a forest of stumps.

A difference between the Atchafalaya Swamp and swamps treated in earlier chapters is that it held more timber and therefore took longer to cut. D. Gail Abbey, in a book on the swamp, described the harsh conditions under which the loggers operated: "The swamper, the man of these overflowed forests, who lives and works in these wilds, in some instances hundreds of miles from any civilization . . . must endure the companionship of snakes, alligators, and reptiles of all descriptions." Living in his floating hut, "the swamper was eternally feasted upon by mosquitoes and sand fleas . . . and with never a piece of dry clothing upon their weary shoulders be it hot or cold the swampers worked from early until late."

In January, 1988, with Gary Williamson and Charles Overholser, a relative of mine, I visited the site of Donner, a town that supported the largest lumber mill and logging operation in the history of the Atchafalaya Swamp. Near Gibson, in the southeastern corner of the Atchafalaya Swamp, Donner was a thriving community as long as there were still good-sized cypress trees to cut. But after the supply was exhausted in the 1930s, the inhabitants, taking what they could with them, left, never to return. A few started a new community some miles away, which they named Donner, after the old logging town.

With our guide, Jon Faslun, we went by boat through a maze of waterways that led deep into the swamp. Higher ground, in the form of an old levee, marked the site of the town. The only structures in evidence were the ruins of the sawmill and some distance away, surrounded by water, a large brick edifice that we were told had been the curing shed for green cypress. Steam, piped from a wood and coal furnace at the sawmill, was used for the curing process. The sawmill, once a huge structure, was now only a pile of bricks, concrete slabs, and well-preserved cypress beams.

Leaving Gary to comb the ruins of the mill for anything of herpetological interest, the rest of us set off to see if we could find anything left of the old town. Aside from broken bottles, scraps of tin, and a few bricks, we found nothing at all. The entire community had been swallowed up by the swamp.

Slowly sinking into the mud, almost anything the inhabitants had not taken with them had disappeared below the surface. Where there were once streets and houses, there was now a swamp little different from the surrounding swamp. Armadillos, nutria, mink, and otter were now the principal inhabitants.

By the time we met Gary back at the ruins of the mill, it was beginning to get dark. He, like us, had been shadowed by a barred owl that, curiously watching from a distance, seemed to be keeping us intruders under surveillance. Before departing, we took note of one other sign of man's former presence. Here and there we saw almost tree-sized shrubs with glossy green leaves. Survivors from the time of the old town, the plants were glossy privets (*Ligustrum lucidum*). They seemed as much at home on the old levees where they grew as the water oaks, sweet gums, cottonwoods, red maples, and sycamores all around them.

Jon Faslun reminded us that Donner had once had a population of 3,500. The town's existence from 1902 until 1936 had spanned the peak period of lumbering in the Atchafalaya Swamp. It seemed hard to believe as we left the scene of desolation.

The end of the logging era came during the 1930s, when loggers cutting timber on the east side met those cutting on the west side. They left behind stumps and broken trees. But regeneration is rapid in the Atchafalaya Swamp. On our trip to the former site of Donner we saw, on each side of the waterway, swamp forest that looked as untouched as if the trees had been growing for a hundred years. Yet the whole area had once been reduced to stumps. A far more serious threat to the Atchafalaya Basin has been the building of levees and channelization. Today the swamp is largely confined to a floodway from fifteen to seventeen miles wide and ninety miles long. On both sides of the swamp are levees built by the U.S. Army Corps of Engineers. The levees hold back floodwaters and sediment from areas outside the floodway. As a result, much of the basin that had been swampland is now dry land given over to agriculture.

The future fate of the Atchafalaya Swamp was sealed by a tremendous flood in 1927 that saw the Mississippi on one of its most disastrous rampages. To prevent another such flood from inundating towns, cities, and cropland along the lower Mississippi, the Corps of Engineers initiated their present levee-building program. They determined that if nothing were done to control the amount of water flowing from the Mississippi into the Atchafalaya River, by 1975 the Mississippi would change its course and send its entire flow through the Atchafalaya Basin. This would be a disaster to shipping and industrial interests centered in Baton Rouge and New Orleans. Within the past nine thousand years the Mississippi has changed its course to the Gulf no fewer than seven times. The river seemed on the point of doing it again.

As part of their plan to head off such an event, the Corps of Engineers, as authorized by Congress in 1954, erected what is known as the Old River Control Structure. A dike and spillway on the Mississippi about fifty miles above Baton Rouge, the control structure restricts the amount of water entering the Atchafalaya Basin. The amount is limited to 30 percent of the combined flow of the Red and Mississippi Rivers.

It is difficult to know what impact these changes are having upon the fauna of the swamp. But within the approximately fifteen-mile-wide floodway, the high water and sediment of colder months and the low water of summer and fall make for a spawning ground of incredible richness. But thousands of acres outside the floodway that was once swampland is turning into dry land and being converted into fields for growing soybeans and other crops.

One gains a rough picture of the Atchafalaya Swamp, as it was and as it is today, by driving between Baton Rouge and Lafayette on Interstate 10. Driving westward, the flat, open countryside becomes somewhat forested as one approaches the Atchafalaya crossing. Reaching the floodway, one drives for seventeen miles on an elevated highway that affords a good view of seemingly endless swamp broken only by lakes and rivers. When making the crossing, it is a good plan, if one wants to see more of the swamp, to take one of the exits that lead to roads running parallel to levees. The roads in turn lead to small towns and oil wells. High ground behind levees supports a somewhat different plant community than is found in the swamp proper, and a number of different bird species.

For the bird watcher, the diverse mixture of habitats along the side roads makes the area highly rewarding. When, in early May, Gary Williamson and I left the I-10 crossing at the Whiskey Bay and Butte La Rose exit, we almost immediately saw Mississippi kites overhead and we soon discovered two active nest sites. Stops alongside drier woodlands yielded such nontypical swamp birds as the painted bunting, loggerhead shrike, orchard oriole, and yellow-breasted chat. Waterbirds were almost constantly in view. Cattle egrets fed with cattle on the slopes of grassy levees. At the water's edge or flying overhead were large waders such as great egrets, snowy egrets, great blue herons, and little blue herons. The latter was the most common heron that we saw here and elsewhere in the swamp. At the end of two hours, we had seen sixty species—a larger number than we normally sight in the same time period in other swamps.

Another point of entry to the swamp is by way of Houma, a large town situated southwest of New Orleans and at the edge of three great ecosystems—agricultural lands planted largely in sugar cane to the east, marshlands and swamp to the south, and the Atchafalaya Swamp to the northwest. To get into a swamp any way but by boat from this southern terminal is almost impossible; thus, there is good reason to take advantage of the boat tour services with headquarters in the Houma area.

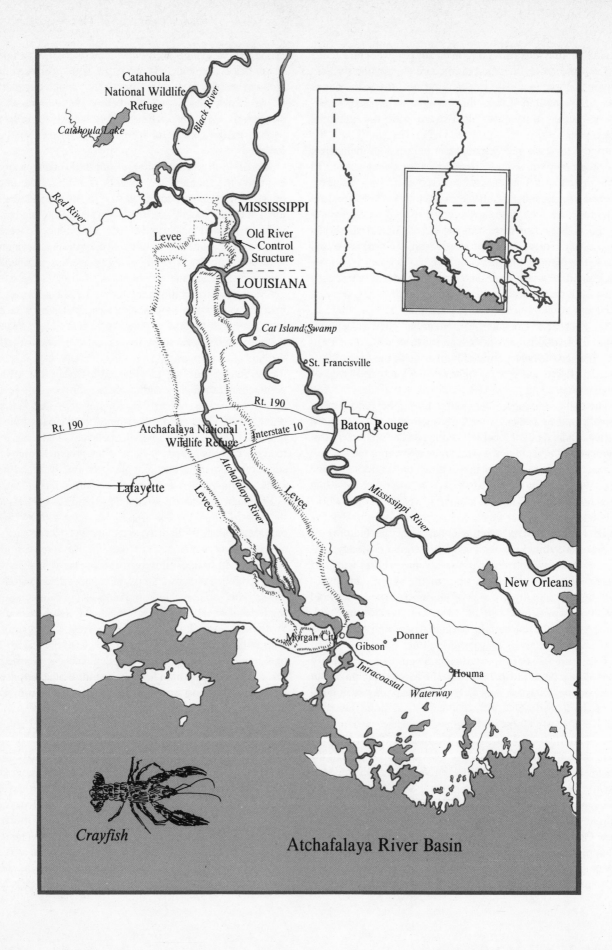

Catahoula
National Wildlife
Refuge

Catahoula Lake

Black River

Red River

Levee

MISSISSIPPI

Old River
Control
Structure

LOUISIANA

Cat Island Swamp

St. Francisville

Rt. 190

Rt. 190

Atchafalaya National
Wildlife Refuge

Interstate 10

Baton Rouge

Lafayette

Levee

Atchafalaya River

Levee

Levee

Mississippi River

New Orleans

Morgan City

Donner

Gibson

Houma

Intracoastal

Waterway

Crayfish

Atchafalaya River Basin

On the same January trip that we visited the deserted site of the sawmill town of Donner, we took Munson's Cypress Bayou Swamp Tour. The area covered was a maze of bayous and canals south of Houma that at one time supported magnificent stands of bald cypress. But the combined effects of logging and saltwater intrusion had all but destroyed the forests. Salt water had entered by way of canals and waterways dug by man and also, we were told, as a result of oil-drilling operations. In spite of man's impact upon the area, wildlife was abundant. Although alligators were in their dens at this season, we saw dozens of nutria—rather large musk-ratlike mammals introduced from South America. The nutria are now the most abundant fur-bearers of the Louisiana marshes. Our guide tossed doughnuts to any he saw on the banks or in the water of the bayou we were traveling through. The nutria responded eagerly to this fare.

Had we timed our visit to warmer months, beginning in April, we might have taken one of Annie Miller's tours and seen all the alligators we could have wished for. Nevertheless, we did meet Annie Miller, or "Alligator Annie," as she is called. No one could have guessed from her cultivated, soft-spoken manner that she and her husband Eddie have for years roughed it in the swamp, sometimes not knowing where their next meal would come from. For eighteen years they made their living collecting snakes for zoos. She told us that she had been bitten hundreds of times. Now her specialty is alligators. On her boat tours, she calls to her "pet" alligators by name, and they swim out to receive handouts in the form of tasty pieces of chicken.

Lewis A. Bannon, a licensed pilot, gave Gary and I a bird's-eye view of the swamp. Our flight in mid-March took place on a partly cloudy day with relatively poor visibility. Nevertheless, we could make out the main features of the panorama below us. There were the irregular outlines of lakes and bayous, straight lines of canals, rivers winding toward the Gulf, lonely cabins lost in the immensity of the swamp, and, in a few places, rows of small dwellings behind levees.

Had we followed the Atchafalaya River to its mouth, we would have seen the outlines of its newly forming delta that began to take shape during three consecutive flood years in 1973, 1974, and 1975. But we avoided the marshlands near the Gulf and spent our time cruising over the forested portions of the Atchafalaya Basin. We were able to make out three reasonably distinct belts of tree growth. There was a large northern belt that consisted chiefly of bottomland hardwoods. As we had already learned on the ground, that belt would be composed mostly of red maple, water oak, Nuttall oak, green ash, water hickory, box elder, sweet gum, and sugarberry. A middle belt composed chiefly of cottonwood, willow, and sycamore was the smallest of the three forest types. We had previously viewed that belt from the I-10 crossing. Finally, a large belt consisting chiefly of bald

cypress and water tupelo occupied the southernmost forested portion. Even on a cloudy day cypress trees can readily be recognized from the air.

During portions of our two-hour flight, we passed over large tracts of swamp without seeing a sign of man. Now and then we did see small boats or a line of barges being pulled by a tugboat. Some of the water traffic seemed connected with the many oil-drilling platforms scattered through the swamp. In many cases reachable only by canals dug by the oil companies, the platforms and their derricks stood out like skeletons of huge trees.

Because of poor visibility, about the only birds we could see from the plane were large white ones. They included white ibis, immature little blue herons, and great and snowy egrets. A flock of about five hundred white ibis passed below us on my side of the plane while Gary, looking out the opposite side, was counting the many great egrets he could see in flight or perched in trees. We decided that the Atchafalaya Swamp is the best we have ever visited for large wading birds.

The birds are only one manifestation of the swamp's faunal richness. The floodwaters, which bring silt and nutrients from the midcontinent, nourish a prolific fauna that begins with microscopic organisms and climbs to higher forms—fishes, amphibians, reptiles, birds, and mammals. In Chapter 6, I referred to C. C. Lockwood's report of billions of crayfish in the swamp and enormous fish hauls. Lockwood went on to say that about 135 million tons of silt are dropped in the Atchafalaya Basin each year. He saw no harm in that to the wildlife other than the fact that the silt deposits raise the level of the land, making it easier to use for agriculture.

The fate of this great swamp hangs in precarious balance. On the one hand, the Mississippi River threatens to inundate it with ever greater amounts of water and silt; on the other, man, with his roads, levees, oil wells, and agriculture, threatens to harness and tame the swamp to an even greater degree than he has already. In the meantime, the bottomlands, oblivious to those threats, yearly produce myriads of crayfish, and these, in turn, serve as food for fishes, wading birds, small mammals, and man, who considers them to be a great delicacy.

Although man and nature in the Atchafalaya Basin have been at odds with each other ever since early days of settlement, a turning point has been reached. Steps are presently being taken to safeguard the 600,000 acres of swamp and water that lie within the floodway. I am indebted to David M. Soileau of the United States Fish and Wildlife Service for providing me with the latest information concerning this preservation effort. He tells me that 200,000 acres are either in public ownership or soon will be. Of this total, 75,000 acres consists of bodies of fresh water that have always been under the jurisdiction of the state of Louisiana. The remaining public acreage is divided between Louisiana, the Corps of Engineers, and the Fish and Wildlife Service. The newly created Atchafalaya National Wildlife Refuge and a state wildlife management area are in the northern part of the floodway. Another state wildlife management area is in the southwestern part of the floodway.

The most novel feature of this program, and one that deserves to be emulated elsewhere, is a system of easements designed to allow private landowners to keep their holdings forested and undeveloped. Under the system landowners are paid for their cooperation. It may be too soon to predict that all of the present acreage within the floodway will remain essentially in the same condition as it is today. But the outlook gives cause for hope.

The story of the Atchafalaya Swamp, with its teeming wildlife and its changes in fortune, is mirrored elsewhere in Louisiana, in particular along the Red River, which, as noted above, is the name given to the Atchafalaya River above its junction with the Mississippi. Both portions of the river—the Atchafalaya and the Red—have had long histories of floods and blockage by rafts.

For a large part of its early history the Red River was blocked for many miles by a mass of logs and uprooted trees known as the Great Raft. Fresh material for the raft arrived whenever floodwaters eroded away forested banks of the Red and its tributaries. Thus, for a distance of about 160 miles from below present-day Natchitoches to well above Shreveport, the river was blocked by a floating island of logs, which, as it slowly disintegrated, provided enough humus to support a rank growth of shrubs, small trees, and herbaceous plants. The raft was a floating island that rose and fell with the water level.

In 1831 the federal government found just the man to remove the raft—Captain Henry M. Shreve, a designer and builder of steamboats, who, early in the nineteenth century, began operating a fleet of steamboats on the Ohio and Mississippi rivers. Using steam-operated "snag boats" of his own design and crews of men, he had cleared away most of the raft by 1836. However, new rafts kept appearing in the river, and they, too, had to be cleared away.

The rafts of the Red River, though an obstacle to navigation, did serve to create a complex system of lakes and swamps in northwestern Louisiana. Those swamplands became filled with cypress and other water-loving trees and were a haven for wildlife. But with the reopening of the Red River, the swamps drained back into the river. One after another, the lakes and their swamps ceased to exist, with man, as usual, aiding the process. But Caddo Lake and its surrounding swamplands provide an exception. Lying on the boundary between Texas and Louisiana, Caddo Lake, during the days of the Great Raft, was a main artery for steamboat traffic. In order to bypass the Great Raft, as many as two hundred steamboats a year followed a circuitous route

through bayous and Caddo Lake to reach the freer portions of the Red River that lay upstream. In 1873, after the last of the rafts was finally cleared away, commercial traffic by way of Caddo Lake all but came to an end.

Caddo Lake, like so many other lakes formed by the Great Raft, might have gradually dwindled away to almost nothing if it were not for a dam built in 1914 and later replaced by another dam. The dams have saved the lake and a surrounding cypress swamp, which together cover about forty thousand acres. A state park in Texas and a parish park in Louisiana provide protection for sections of the lake's irregular shoreline. When visiting Caddo Lake State Park in Texas one April, I encountered much the same flora and fauna that I found at Reelfoot Lake and in the Atchafalaya Swamp.

I learned, with the help of exhibits at the visitors' center, that the lake contains largemouth bass, white bass, bluegill, chain pickerel, channel catfish, bowfin, and alligator gar. Anyone who has tried their luck in the bayous and rivers of more eastern parts of Louisiana would feel at home here. Much the same is true for the herpetologist. Common turtles include the red-eared turtle, spiny softshell, Mississippi mud turtle, and river cotter. Common snakes include the western cottonmouth and the yellow-bellied water snake, a race of the more eastern red-bellied water snake.

The water birds, including ducks, American coot, common moorhen, pied-billed grebe, anhinga, herons, and egrets, are well represented. The red-shouldered hawk, turkey vulture, barred owl, and pileated woodpecker are members of other bird families found at the lake. The presence of such birds, as well as familiar fishes, reptiles, and amphibians, was to me just another expression of the relative uniformity of swamp fauna from the northernmost limits of the bald cypress's range in the Chesapeake Bay region southward and westward to this northwestern corner of Louisiana and to southwestern Oklahoma and the Big Thicket in Texas.

Downstream along the Red River is a second lake that does not fit any of the other lakes discussed so far. Catahoula Lake, about twenty miles east of Alexandria, baffled me every time I visited it. Its oblong shape does not conform to that of an oxbow lake, and it is downstream from the region affected by the Great Raft. And I could find no hint in literature on earthquakes that it was an earthquake lake. Finally, thanks to Hiram F. Gregory of Northwestern State University in Natchitoches, I learned that Catahoula Lake, a thirty-thousand-acre body of water in winter and dry in summer, was a rift, or graben, lake. Something new to my vocabulary, a *rift*, or *graben*, I learned, is a downthrust lying between two faults. The depression within the downthrust holding Catahoula Lake fills with water during the wet season in late fall and winter and becomes empty during the dry season in summer and early fall. The lake receives its water from rainfall and overflow from the Red River and also, at times, from the Black and Mississippi rivers to the east. The lake discharges water into those same rivers in early summer. As the lake subsides, huge mud flats appear, and with further drying, grasses and sedges spring up on the former lake bottom. One of the most common plants of the lake bottom is chufa (*Cyperus esculentus*), a sedge whose seeds and tubers are a favorite food of many waterfowl and the wild turkey. The largest chufa bed in North America is said to be the one at Lake Catahoula.

In earlier times the arrival of the dry period was the signal for the lake bed to be invaded by deer and probably also bison. Grazing animals were accompanied by cranes and wild turkeys. Such tempting prey was not overlooked by predators such as the Florida cougar and red wolf. As the lake began to fill in late fall, those types of wildlife departed and were replaced by thousands of ducks and geese. Feeding upon chufa, as well as on the seeds of grasses and millet, the waterfowl stayed until it was time for them to return north in the spring.

An excellent hunting ground, the lake attracted the American Indian for untold centuries, and then the white hunter. A hunting season for waterfowl is allowed on a 26,000-acre state wildlife management area, but not at the 5,308-acre Catahoula National Wildlife Refuge at the eastern end of Catahoula Lake. Hard-pressed ducks and geese flock to the national refuge when the hunting season gets under way. Numbers of waterfowl visiting the lake vary from 150,000 to 450,000—figures that show that Catahoula Lake is one of the most important wintering grounds for waterfowl in Louisiana.

Only a few species of woody plants can withstand the exacting conditions that exist at the perimeter of the lake. As might be expected, bald cypress is present and able to endure the drastic changes in water level. The Catahoula Lake cypress trees have enormously swollen bases and very tall knees. However, as Hiram Gregory informed me, the knees are disappearing, as people cut them to make lamp bases. He also told me that until the 1960s, the Catahoula Swamp extended east to the Black River, a distance of fifteen miles. But the swamp has been cleared to provide more land for the cultivation of soybeans and grain. As much as 88,000 acres have been cleared within the last several years.

Found along with the cypresses at Catahoula Lake are several other woody plants that can withstand the same difficult conditions. Among them are water elm, swamp privet, water locust, and buttonbush. Although water control structures have been built, the hydrology of the lake is still not drastically different from what it was in times past. The lake stays filled in winter and all but empty in summer. Hogs now share the chufa with birds and other forms of wildlife.

References

Abbey, D. Gail. *Life in the Atchafalaya Swamp*. Lafayette, La., 1979.

Comeaux, Malcolm L. *Atchafalaya Swamp Life: Settlement and Folk Occupations*. Geoscience and Man, II. Baton Rouge, 1972.

Hearn-O'Pry, Maude. *Chronicles of Shreveport*. Shreveport, 1928.

Lockwood, C. C. *Atchafalaya: America's Largest River Basin Swamp*. Baton Rouge, 1981.

McCall, Edith. *Conquering the Rivers: Henry Miller Shreve and the Navigation of America's Inland Waterways*. Baton Rouge, 1984.

19 / Vanished Species of the Big Thicket

The Big Thicket is a diverse region of rivers, swamps, and pinewoods in eastern Texas. Long regarded as a wilderness, the Big Thicket lies just west of the Louisiana line and resembles backwoods districts of that state. As in south Florida, several rare species lingered on in the Big Thicket much later than they did elsewhere. Even today there is hope that a few of the great rarities of the Big Thicket will continue to survive with the help of newly created parks and greater respect for game laws.

Besides being a haven for rare species, the Big Thicket is a last outpost for many of the more common species of the southern swamps. I use the word *last* because the Big Thicket is the last swamp, as one travels westward, that has much the same flora and fauna as the other swamps discussed in previous chapters. Although bald cypress reaches south-central Texas, its other close associates drop out along the way.

A warm climate, and as much as sixty inches of rainfall a year, make the Big Thicket a hothouse where plants flourish. The temperature exceeds 90°F on approximately 110 days a year. In a final burst of vigor before drier conditions set in, plants in the Big Thicket grow more rapidly, reach larger sizes, and exhibit more genetic differences than in any other area of equal size that I know of. And along with eastern species of both plants and animals are western ones that intrude along the Thicket's western borders.

Lying in a basin, with the Neches River on the east and the Trinity River on the west, the Big Thicket may once have covered several million acres. Today, a wilderness only in out-of-the-way corners, it covers about three hundred thousand acres.

Early explorers and pioneers, on reaching the Big Thicket region, were awed by the lush, almost impenetrable growth, and generally they chose to detour to the north or south in order to avoid the difficult going. The fact that the Thicket remained little visited and sparsely settled for many years made it a haven for wildlife. Until almost the end of the nineteenth century many rare species that had disappeared elsewhere were still holding on in its remote interior. But gradually the Big Thicket was opened up. Roads, lumbering operations, and increased settlement, as well as widespread hunting, made the future of animals such as the black bear and cougar ever more tenuous.

The black bear remained common until about 1885. To be sure, it had been hunted all along, first by the Indians and then by the early settlers. As in the Okefenokee Swamp, the black bear was killed on sight because of the inroads it made upon the hog population and because of its destruction of beehives. However, toward the end of the century, its existence was further threatened by zealous bear hunters whose main goal in life was to see how many bears they could kill. The names of Ben Hooks and Benjamin J. Lilly, among others, figure importantly in the last great bear hunts that took place in the Thicket. When Lilly had killed all the bears he could find in Texas, he moved to the Rockies to continue his hunting in more productive territory. According to J. C. Truett and D. W. Lay, the last bears in the Thicket, three in the first instance and one in the last, were killed in 1919 and 1928, respectively.

The cougar, another hard-pressed mammal that requires large tracts of wilderness for survival, also made a last stand in the Big Thicket. Relatively common in the early part of the nineteenth century, the cougar was hunted with the same determination as the black bear was. There were so few left toward the end of the century that Ben Lilly, also an ardent cougar hunter, could not find any to bag when he arrived on the scene. As for the present century, little is known for certain about the cougar in the Big Thicket and swamps throughout the South. Rumors of its presence persist, but positive proof is seldom forthcoming.

Still another member of the cat family, the jaguar, reaches or did reach the northeastern limits of its range in the Big Thicket region. This large spotted cat, about the same size of a cougar, is primarily tropical in distribution and probably was never common as far north as the Big Thicket. It seems that few were killed, and the last recorded shooting of a jaguar in the Thicket took place in 1902. Dangerous when cornered, the jaguar was not an animal to be trifled with.

The red wolf, another nearly vanished species, hung on for a longer period of time in the Big Thicket than did the bear, cougar, or jaguar. Indeed, the red wolf, whose range lay chiefly in eastern Texas and nearby Louisiana, might still be in the Big Thicket today but for its hybridizing with its relative the coyote. By the 1970s, there were few pure red wolves left in the wild. The coyote was increasing in numbers while the red wolf was on a downward path. The more successful species swamped the less successful one. For once, man is not to blame for the drastic reduction of an animal population.

I became familiar with the red wolf in 1951, when I was serving as a warden at a roseate spoonbill and large wading bird rookery in Galveston Bay belonging to the National Audubon Society. As much at home in the coastal marshes, where I was, as in the heavily timbered Big Thicket, the red wolf was making its last stand there. One day a cowboy rode down a red wolf, shot it, and brought it back to the small hamlet where I had my quarters. I asked him if I could have the carcass. He consented. I dug a deep hole, placed the remains in it, and covered them over. When I exhumed the remains several months later, the odor that they emitted was so overpowering that I wondered if I could still do science a service by preserving the bones. I had planned to present them to my zoology professor at the University of Florida, where I had recently been a student. Finally, I cleaned the bones as best I could and took them to the university. The best hope for the red wolf seems to lie in plans mentioned earlier to build up the captive population and release animals in suitable wild habitat where they will not come in contact with coyotes.

Larger, more showy birds, like the large mammals, also found sanctuary in the Big Thicket and later lost out as hunters penetrated its every recess. Hunting not only in the Big Thicket but everywhere else apparently was the reason for the decline and eventual extinction of the passenger pigeon and Carolina parakeet.

Flocks containing thousands of passenger pigeons appeared in the Big Thicket in fall and winter until about 1880. Observers said that the immense flocks blackened the sky. The birds fed greedily upon acorns and beechnuts and then returned north for the nesting season. In the Big Thicket, more than elsewhere, the passenger pigeon seems to have frequented southern river swamps. M. B. Hickman (quoted by Truett and Lay) told of flocks foraging daily for acorns and beechnuts along the Neches River during the winter of 1868. I know from my explorations that oaks and beeches are common in the Neches bottomlands. Oaks flourish on swampy ground, while the beech-tree, at the southwestern extremity of its range, grows on the higher ground of old levees. Beech is also commonly found with loblolly pine and southern magnolia in the uplands.

The last report of the passenger pigeon in Texas seems to have been in 1898. Only a few years later the passenger pigeon disappeared forever. The last one, a bird named Martha, died in the Cincinnati Zoo in 1914.

The Carolina parakeet disappeared from the Big Thicket sooner than the passenger pigeon. For the parakeet the Thicket was at the southwestern limit of its breeding range. One can visualize the birds nesting in large cypress trees along the Neches and Trinity rivers and traveling from one part of the Thicket to another in swift-flying flocks. But as we have seen, this colorful member of the parrot family held out longer in the Southeast than it did in more western portions of its range. According to Truett and Lay, the Carolina parakeet was plentiful in east Texas until about the time of the Civil War. A few birds were seen until 1875, but none thereafter.

The woodpeckers are well represented in the Big Thicket. One can hardly walk a hundred yards in well-wooded sections without encountering several species. But even in this largely successful family, there are species that have not done so well. On my first visit to the Big Thicket, I was impressed by the numbers of red-cockaded woodpeckers I saw. That was in 1960, before the mania for clear-cutting and planting endless rows of pine trees had become popular in that part of the country. To avoid the thorns and dense understory of the wooded tract I was exploring, I followed the cleared right-of-way along a power line. I had not gone far before I heard the harsh call notes of the red-cockaded woodpecker. I was surprised to find a flock in the dense pines and hardwoods that flanked the power line. I was used to finding this woodpecker in open, parklike pinewoods. However, the main requirement of the red-cockaded woodpecker, besides food, is mature pine trees. In the habit of drilling its roosting and nesting holes in older pine trees infected with red heart disease, it somehow is incapable of changing over to younger, healthy trees. In 1960 the Big Thicket still had plenty of mature, or, as the lumbermen call them, overage, pine trees. The red-cockaded was still plentiful.

Part of the red-cockaded's strategy is to drill numerous small holes below, and all around the entrance to, its cavity in a pine tree. Streams of sticky resin exude from these holes and coat the tree trunk. The resin makes an effective shield against predators. The fresher and stickier the resin is, the more it repels. But even a hardened coating is slippery enough to help deter predators, as I discovered one day when I saw a rat snake climbing up the trunk of a pine tree to reach a cavity that had once belonged to a red-cockaded woodpecker. The cavity's occupant was now a flying squirrel that, from all the evidence, had a litter of young at the bottom of the cavity. While the mother flying squirrel peered out of the entrance hole, as if mesmerized, the rat snake climbed ever higher. But just before reaching the entrance hole, the snake lost its grip and fell to the ground. In a second attempt the snake made its way up the other side of the trunk, where there was less resin, lunged toward the opening, made it, and disappeared into the cavity. The mother squirrel dropped back into the interior at the moment the snake made its lunge.

When I returned to the Big Thicket toward the end of 1966 to commence my search for the ivory-billed woodpecker, the leveling of forests to plant pine trees had become commonplace. Ironically, the greater the acreage in pine plantations, the less chance there would be for the survival of the red-cockaded woodpecker. The planted trees would be cut and used for pulpwood long before they were old enough to

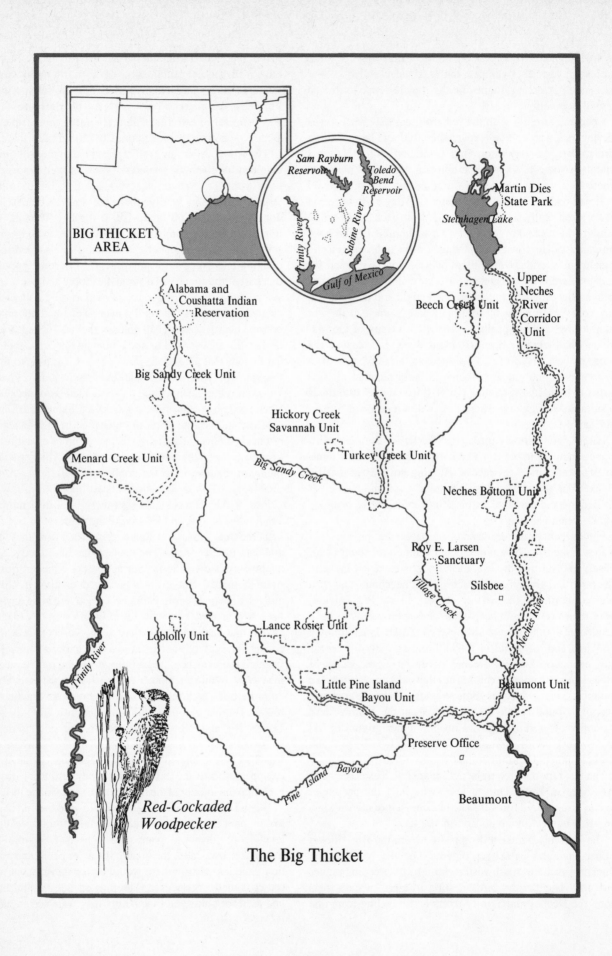

BIG THICKET
AREA

Sam Rayburn
Reservoir

Toledo
Bend
Reservoir

Trinity River

Sabine River

Gulf of Mexico

Martin Dies
State Park

Steinhagen Lake

Alabama and
Coushatta Indian
Reservation

Beech Creek Unit

Upper
Neches
River
Corridor
Unit

Big Sandy Creek Unit

Hickory Creek
Savannah Unit

Menard Creek Unit

Big Sandy Creek

Turkey Creek Unit

Neches Bottom Unit

Roy E. Larsen
Sanctuary

Village Creek

Silsbee

Neches River

Trinity River

Lance Rosier Unit

Loblolly Unit

Little Pine Island
Bayou Unit

Beaumont Unit

Preserve Office

Red-Cockaded
Woodpecker

Pine Island Bayou

Beaumont

The Big Thicket

meet the special requirements of this small, pine-loving woodpecker.

When tired out from a long day of often fruitless searching for the ivorybill, I would sometimes visit a stand of longleaf pines. There I would always find red-cockaded woodpeckers busily searching for food or, an endless occupation with them, tapping the resin wells they had drilled, in order to keep them open and flowing. Trees with roosting or nesting holes could be spotted from a long distance because the resin, on hardening, would turn white, making the tree trunk stand out like a beacon in a dimly lighted forest. Industrious and, in some ways, comical birds, the red-cockadeds were fascinating to watch and always buoyed my spirits.

I am afraid that there are few red-cockaded woodpeckers left in the Big Thicket today. Throughout its range, the red-cockaded is losing out because of the ever decreasing number of mature pine trees. The pulpwood industry is not entirely to blame. Older pine trees are vulnerable to attacks by the pine bark beetle and, like the giant cypress trees, to damage and destruction from lightning strikes. An endangered species, the red-cockaded woodpecker is receiving assistance and protection from federal and state agencies. It will certainly hold out longer than the ivory-billed woodpecker, but how much longer is an open question.

On my return to the Big Thicket in 1966, I discovered that there were still sizable segments of wilderness. But sooner or later one encountered an oil well, a barbed-wire fence, or someone with a chain saw. It seemed as though man was determined to tame the Big Thicket, first exploiting its riches and then turning what was left into cow pastures or homesites. Bitter fights were being waged at that time between developers and conservationists, hunters and foes of unbridled hunting. No one who set foot in the Big Thicket could hope to stay aloof from the disputes. Although the Big Thicket is inhabited by some of the kindest and most hospitable people in the world, there are deep factional differences, many of them going back for generations. The outsider should listen, but it is best not to take sides.

In the minds of the Big Thicket people, there was no doubt about the ivorybill. The bird was a part of their tradition, and there were many who professed to have seen it. But in many cases it was impossible to tell if a description was of a bird actually seen or if it came from the pages of a bird guide. Sometimes a Texan's pride is hurt if he has not also seen something as big or as rare as you have! I am told that it is equally difficult to obtain accurate information about the cougar. Local people are only too ready to say that they have seen or heard one. Thus, it is certain that both the ivorybill and the cougar still exist in the minds and imaginations of the people. Whether either still exists out in the external world, we do not know.

At some stage in the exploitation of a wilderness area, first local people, and then people far and wide around the country decide that the process must slow down, that something must be saved for future generations. The turning point for the Big Thicket came in 1974, when Congress established a Big Thicket National Preserve. The preserve comprises twelve units, some of them detached from other parts of the preserve and some joined to other units. These units, sometimes called "a chain of pearls," contain the best that the Thicket still has to offer in scenery, botany, and wildlife. The total number of acres in the preserve is 84,550.

A unique feature of the preserve is the corridors that follow many of the rivers and streams that traverse the Big Thicket. A part of the preserve, the corridors are narrow strips of green when viewed on the map. Yet they contain most of the Big Thicket's cypress and other bottomland timber. My search for the ivorybill was concentrated in these wooded bottomlands. However, my original sighting area was above Steinhagen Lake, a reservoir on the Neches River and outside the preserve. One of the wildest parts of the Big Thicket, this region of partially flooded bottomland timber is now a state wildlife area.

Each unit has something special to offer. The Lance Rosier Unit near Saratoga, for example, contains dwarf palmettos that are as much as fifteen to twenty feet tall—an extraordinary height, since in most of the Southeast the dwarf palmetto is recumbent, with its trunk lying on the ground and half buried. But here at the western limits of its range, the tree is no longer a dwarf but has an upright trunk. At the Turkey Creek Unit one finds the greatest variety of plants in the preserve. Mature longleaf pine, an important habitat for the red-cockaded woodpecker, is best represented in the Hickory Creek Savannah Unit. The Loblolly Unit is a small area that contains the best of the loblolly pine.

It takes days to explore the many units in the preserve. A boat or canoe is needed for the Neches River and smaller streams. Information about the preserve, where to go and what to see, can be obtained by writing or calling the Big Thicket National Preserve, P.O. Box 7408, Beaumont, Texas 77706. The phone number is (409) 839-2689.

A second important step in saving the best of the Big Thicket came in 1977 with the dedication of the Roy E. Larsen Sandyland Sanctuary. This preserve of 2,138 acres is on Village Creek, a tributary of the Neches River, and thanks to its dry sandy soil, it supports many plants typical of more arid parts of Texas. As described in the *Nature Conservancy News* for May–June, 1978, the preserve, one of seven ecosystems that make up the Big Thicket, "is one of the few places on the face of the globe where you can stand in one spot, and just by turning your body a bit, see a swamp that might remind you of the Everglades, a 'desert' bristling with cactus and Spanish-dagger yucca, and open-floor forest typical of the Appalachian mountains, and seepy southern pinelands." Among the many kinds of plants on the preserve is the national champion gallberry holly (*Ilex coriacea*).

Although the Big Thicket has lost some of its larger and more spectacular forms of animal life, much that is unique and priceless has been saved. In large part this has been achieved by linking important plant communities through a system of corridors based upon watercourses. The corridors permit mingling and contact between species that otherwise would be isolated. Even birds, though they can fly, often become isolated, and their populations dwindle if they are confined to a habitat of their choice that is not linked to other similar habitat. The red-cockaded woodpecker and wild turkey are examples.

Corridors are also essential for the reproduction and well-being of some game species such as the white-tailed deer and black bear. These species make seasonal movements or even migrate from one part of their range to another. Although we can no longer provide these mammals with large unpopulated blocks of land, we can link smaller blocks together, as has been done so judiciously in the Big Thicket. There the corridors are both interconnecting links and a place where the southern swamp at its westernmost extremity can hold its own. The corridors are also where the bald cypress makes a final stand in humid river valleys before it braves the plains and heights of south Texas and the Edwards Plateau.

The wisdom that went into the interconnecting units of the Big Thicket National Preserve could well be duplicated elsewhere. Using stream valleys as corridors, plant communities and whole ecosystems could be joined together in such a way as to permit movement by wildlife and also by people. What better way to explore parkland or wilderness areas than by hiking trails or boat or canoe trails?

The cypress tree has been my guiding star. Although it is a tree whose importance cannot be exaggerated, I have tried not to become blinded by its massive bulk. Beyond it are other priceless parts of our natural heritage that also need protection. The plan and the vision of the Big Thicket's corridors came too late to save some species, but they are saving many others.

Sizable portions of rivers and creeks in several southern states are now being protected by nature preserves, parks, and wildlife refuges. Outstanding examples are the Nassawango and the Pocomoke in Maryland, the Roanoke in North Carolina, the Four Holes and the Congaree in South Carolina, the Suwannee, the Apalachicola, and the Escambia in Florida, the Pascagoula in Mississippi, the Pearl and the Atchafalaya in Louisiana, and the Cache and the White in Arkansas. A good beginning has been made, but many more acres need to be set aside on many more creeks and rivers before the realm of the cypress tree can be called secure.

Reference

Truett, Joe C., and Daniel W. Lay. *Land of Bears and Honey: A Natural History of East Texas*. Austin, 1984.

Appendix I
Typical Woody Plants of Southern Swamps

Loblolly pine (*Pinus taeda*)

Spruce pine (*Pinus glabra*)

Bald cypress (*Taxodium distichum*)

Pond cypress (*Taxodium distichum* var. *nutans*)

Atlantic white cedar (*Chamaecyparis thyoides*)

Cane (*Arundinaria gigantea*)

Dwarf palmetto (*Sabal minor*)

Laurel greenbrier (*Smilax laurifolia*)

Coral greenbrier (*Smilax walteri*)

Black willow (*Salix nigra*)

Swamp willow (*Salix caroliniana*)

Swamp cottonwood (*Populus heterophylla*)

Wax myrtle (*Myrica cerifera*)

Bitternut hickory (*Carya cordiformis*)

Water hickory (*Carya aquatica*)

Smooth alder (*Alnus serrulata*)

River birch (*Betula nigra*)

Ironwood (*Carpinus caroliniana*)

Overcup oak (*Quercus lyrata*)

Swamp chestnut oak (*Quercus michauxii*)

Shumard oak (*Quercus shumardii*)

Southern red oak (*Quercus falcata*)

Cherrybark oak (*Quercus falcata* var. *pagodaefolia*)

Water oak (*Quercus nigra*)

Willow oak (*Quercus phellos*)

Laurel oak (*Quercus laurifolia*)

American elm (*Ulmus americana*)

Water elm (*Planera aquatica*)

Sugarberry (*Celtis laevigata*)

Red mulberry (*Morus rubra*)

Mistletoe (*Phoradendron serotinum*)

Tulip tree (*Liriodendron tulipifera*)

Sweet bay (*Magnolia virginiana*)

Southern magnolia (*Magnolia grandiflora*)

Pawpaw (*Asimina triloba*)

Red bay (*Persea borbonia*)

Spicebush (*Lindera benzoin*)

Virginia willow (*Itea virginica*)

Climbing hydrangea (*Decumaria barbara*)

Sweet gum (*Liquidambar styraciflua*)

Witch hazel (*Hamamelis virginiana*)

Sycamore (*Platanus occidentalis*)

Blackberry (*Rubus betulifolius*)

Swamp rose (*Rosa palustris*)

Red chokeberry (*Sorbus arbutifolia*)

Green hawthorn (*Crataegus viridis*)

Parsley hawthorn (*Crataegus marshallii*)

Black cherry (*Prunus serotina*)

Water locust (*Gleditsia aquatica*)

Sebastian bush (*Sebastiana ligustrina*)

Poison ivy (*Rhus radicans*)

Titi (*Cyrilla racemiflora*)

American holly (*Ilex opaca*)

Dahoon holly (*Ilex cassine*)

Possum haw (*Ilex decidua*)

Winterberry (*Ilex verticillata*)

Strawberry bush (*Euonymus americanus*)

Box elder (*Acer negundo*)

Red maple (*Acer rubrum*)

Red buckeye (*Aesculus pavia*)

Supplejack (*Berchemia scandens*)

Virginia creeper (*Parthenocissus quinquefolia*)

Muscadine grape (*Vitis rotundifolia*)

Summer grape (*Vitis aestivalis*)

Peppervine (*Amphelopsis arborea*)

Loblolly bay (*Gordonia lasianthus*)

St. John's-wort (*Hypericum* spp.)

Waterwillow (*Decodon verticillatus*)

Devil's-walking-stick (*Aralia spinosa*)

Black gum (*Nyssa sylvatica*)

Swamp tupelo (*Nyssa sylvatica biflora*)

Water tupelo (*Nyssa aquatica*)

Flowering dogwood (*Cornus florida*)

Swamp dogwood (*Cornus foemina*)

Sweet pepperbush (*Clethra alnifolia*)

Azalea (*Rhododendron* spp.)

Fetterbush (*Lyonia lucida*)

Swamp leucothoe (*Leucothoe racemosa*)

Sparkleberry (*Vaccinium* spp.)

Persimmon (*Diospyros virginiana*)

Sweetleaf (*Symplocus tinctoria*)

Silverbell (*Halesia* spp.)

American snowbell (*Styrax americanum*)

Water ash (*Fraxinus caroliniana*)

White ash (*Fraxinus americana*)

Pumpkin ash (*Fraxinus tomentosa*)

Swamp privet (*Forestiera acuminata*)

Crossvine (*Anisostichus capreolata*)

Trumpet creeper (*Campsis radicans*)

Buttonbush (*Cephalanthus occidentalis*)

Southern witherod (*Viburnum nudum*)

Southern arrowwood (*Viburnum dentatum*)

Elderberry (*Sambucus canadensis*)

NOTE: The plants are listed in taxonomic order.

Appendix II
Typical Birds of Southern Swamps

Pied-billed grebe
Double-crested cormorant
Anhinga
Great blue heron
Green-backed heron
Little blue heron
Cattle egret
Great egret
Yellow-crowned night heron
White ibis
Mallard
American black duck
Hooded merganser
Wood duck
Turkey vulture
Black vulture
Swallow-tailed kite
Mississippi kite
Sharp-shinned hawk
Red-tailed hawk
Red-shouldered hawk
Bald eagle
Osprey
American kestrel
Wild turkey
Purple gallinule
Common moorhen
American coot
Spotted sandpiper
American woodcock
Mourning dove
Yellow-billed cuckoo
Eastern screech owl
Great horned owl
Barred owl

Chimney swift
Belted kingfisher
Northern flicker
Pileated woodpecker
Red-bellied woodpecker
Red-headed woodpecker
Yellow-bellied sapsucker
Hairy woodpecker
Downy woodpecker
Eastern kingbird
Great-crested flycatcher
Eastern phoebe
Acadian flycatcher
Eastern wood pewee
Tree swallow
Barn swallow
Blue jay
American crow
Fish crow
Carolina chickadee
Tufted titmouse
White-breasted nuthatch
Brown creeper
Winter wren
Carolina wren
Northern mockingbird
Gray catbird
Brown thrasher
American robin
Wood thrush
Hermit thrush
Eastern bluebird
Blue-gray gnatcatcher
Golden-crowned kinglet
Ruby-crowned kinglet

Cedar waxwing
White-eyed vireo
Yellow-throated vireo
Solitary vireo
Red-eyed vireo
Black-and-white warbler
Prothonotary warbler
Swainson's warbler
Orange-crowned warbler
Northern parula warbler
Magnolia warbler
Black-throated blue warbler
Yellow-rumped warbler
Black-throated green warbler
Yellow-throated warbler
Pine warbler
Ovenbird
Louisiana waterthrush
Kentucky warbler
Common yellowthroat
Hooded warbler
American redstart
Red-winged blackbird
Rusty blackbird
Common grackle
Brown-headed cowbird
Scarlet tanager
Summer tanager
Northern cardinal
Indigo bunting
American goldfinch
Rufous-sided towhee
White-throated sparrow
Swamp sparrow

NOTE: The birds are listed in taxonomic order. Many of the species are seasonal visitors; others, including the titmice and most woodpeckers, are year-round residents; a few, including the purple gallinule, are rare or local in distribution.

Index